The
Least
You
Should
Know
about
English
Writing
Skills

FORM B
Fifth Edition

The Least You Should Know about English Writing Skills

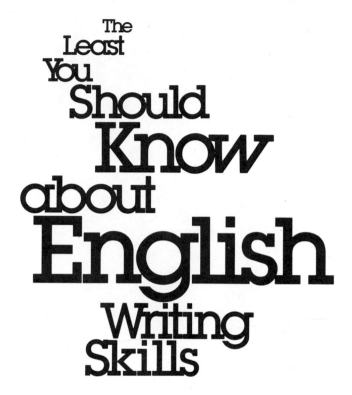

TERESA FERSTER GLAZIER

Harcourt Brace College Publishers

Fort Worth   Philadelphia   San Diego   New York   Orlando   Austin   San Antonio
Toronto   Montreal   London   Sydney   Tokyo

Publisher	Ted Buchholz
Acquisitions Editor	Michael Rosenberg
Senior Project Editor	Steve Welch
Production Manager	J. Montgomery Shaw
Senior Art Director	Diana Jean Parks

Requests for permission to make copies of any part of the work should be mailed to: Permissions Department, Harcourt Brace & Company, 8th Floor, Orlando, Florida 32887.

Address for Editorial Correspondence: Harcourt Brace College Publishers, 301 Commerce Street, Suite 3700, Fort Worth, TX 76102.

Address for Orders: Harcourt Brace & Company, 6277 Sea Harbor Drive, Orlando, FL 32887. 1-800-782-4479, or 1-800-433-0001 (in Florida).

Printed in the United States of America

Library of Congress Catalog Card Number: 93–77652

ISBN: 0-03-079097-2

9 0 1 2   066   9

To the Instructor

This book is for students who need to review the rules of English composition and who may profit from a simplified approach. The main features of the book are these:

1. It is truly basic. Only the indisputable essentials of spelling, grammar, sentence structure, and punctuation are included because research has shown that putting too much emphasis on mechanics is not the way to help students learn to write.
2. It stresses writing. A writing section, EIGHT STEPS TO BETTER WRITING (pp. 210–50), provides writing assignments to be used along with the exercises. The section has been kept brief because **students learn to write by *writing* rather than by reading pages and pages *about* writing.** Even though the section is only 40 pages (compared to 208 for the first part of the text), students will no doubt spend more time on it than on all the rest of the book. (Instructors who prefer to begin with the paragraph may use pages 223–29 first and then return to the beginning of the writing section on page 210.)
3. It stresses thinking. As students write logically organized papers, they learn that *writing* problems are really *thinking* problems.
4. It uses little linguistic terminology. A conjunction is a connecting word; gerunds and present participles are *ing* words; a parenthetical constituent is an interrupter. Students work with words they know instead of learning a vocabulary they'll never use again.
5. It has abundant practice sentences and paragraphs—enough so that students learn to use the rules automatically and thus *carry their new skills over into their writing.*
6. It includes groups of thematically related informative sentences on such subjects as the history of ice cream, underground cities, the longest national paved road in the world, a corn palace, the great magician Houdini, the world's largest shopping mall, changes the presidents have made in the White House, Wisconsin's rustic roads, the Calgary Stampede, helping toads to cross roads, sled-dog racing, the history of the Olympic Games, the annual great bicycle ride across Iowa, the art of juggling . . . thus making the task of doing the exercises interesting.

7. It provides answers at the back of the book so that students can correct their own work, thus teaching themselves as they go.
8. It includes at the end of the Writing Section five essays to read and summarize. Students improve their reading by learning to spot main ideas and their writing by learning to write concise summaries.
9. It can be used as a self-tutoring text. The simple explanations, abundant exercises, and answers at the back of the book provide students with a writing lab in their own rooms.

A packet of ready-to-photocopy tests covering all parts of the text (four for each section) is available to instructors. Also available is a disk of tests that will allow the instructor to send a class to a computer lab for testing. These aids are free upon adoption of the text and may be obtained from the local HB representative or from the English Editor, Harcourt Brace College Publishers, 301 Commerce Street, Suite 3700, Fort Worth, Texas 76102.

Students who have previously been overwhelmed by the complexities of English should, through mastering simple rules and through writing and rewriting simple papers, gain enough competence to succeed in further composition courses.

TFG

Contents

To the instructor   v

WHAT IS THE LEAST YOU SHOULD KNOW?

1. SPELLING

Your own list of misspelled words   6
Words often confused   7
More words often confused   17
   Proofreading exercise   26
Contractions   27
Possessives   33
   Review of contractions and possessives   41
   Proofreading exercise   42
Words that can be broken into parts   43
Rule for doubling a final consonant   44
   Progress test   46
A list of frequently misspelled words   47
Using your dictionary   49

2. SENTENCE STRUCTURE

Finding subjects and verbs   59
   Proofreading exercise   64
Subjects not in prepositional phrases   65
More about verbs and subjects   70
Correcting run-together sentences   76
   Proofreading exercise   84
Correcting fragments   85
More about fragments   93
   Review of run-together sentences and fragments   97
   Proofreading exercise   100
Using standard English verbs   101
Using helping verbs and irregular verbs   107
Avoiding dialect expressions   114
   Proofreading exercise   116
   Progress test   117
Making subjects, verbs, and pronouns agree   118
Choosing the right pronoun   124

Making the pronoun refer to the right word   127
Correcting misplaced or dangling modifiers   131
   Proofreading exercise   135
Using parallel construction   136
Correcting shift in time   143
Correcting shift in person   149
Correcting wordiness   155
Avoiding clichés   160
   Review of sentence structure   162
   Proofreading exercise   164

3. PUNCTUATION AND CAPITAL LETTERS

Period, question mark, exclamation mark, semicolon, colon, dash   166
Commas (Rules 1, 2, and 3)   173
Commas (Rules 4, 5, and 6)   179
   Review of the comma   186
Quotation marks   187
Capital letters   194
   Review of punctuation and capital letters   199
   Proofreading exercises   202
   Comprehensive test on entire text   206

4. WRITING

EIGHT STEPS TO BETTER WRITING

I.   Do some free writing   211
II.   Limit your topic   212
     ASSIGNMENT   1 A Moment I'd Like to Relive 213
     ASSIGNMENT   2 A Place I Like to Remember 215
III. Write a thesis statement   217
IV. Support your thesis with reasons or points   218
     ASSIGNMENT   3 Two Thesis Statements with Supporting   219
     Points
V.   Organize your paper from your thesis   221
VI. Organize each paragraph   223
     ASSIGNMENT   4 Writing a Paragraph   224
     ASSIGNMENT   5 A Decision I Have Made   226
VII. Write and rewrite   228
VIII. Proofread ALOUD   230
     ASSIGNMENT   6 Someone Who Has Influenced Me   230
     ASSIGNMENT   7 In Praise of Something   230
     ASSIGNMENT   8 Something I Can Do   230
     ASSIGNMENT   9 A Letter to Myself   231
     ASSIGNMENT 10 A Recent Accomplishment   231
     ASSIGNMENT 11 A Place I'd Like to Live   231

ASSIGNMENT 12 Advice That Hits Home   231
ASSIGNMENT 13 My Opinion on a Current Problem   231
Writing a summary
ASSIGNMENT 14 A 100-Word Summary   233
   "The Jeaning of America—and the World"
ASSIGNMENT 15 A 100-Word Summary   238
   "Iceman"
ASSIGNMENT 16 A 100-Word Summary   240
   "Turning Highway Rights into Wrongs"
ASSIGNMENT 17 A 100-Word Summary   242
   "The Best Idea America Ever Had"
ASSIGNMENT 18 A 100-Word Summary   245
   "A Few Thoughts on Penguins and Tourists"
Writing an application
ASSIGNMENT 19 A Letter of Application   247
Writing an evaluation
ASSIGNMENT 20 An Evaluation of My Performance   250

ANSWERS   252

INDEX   307

What Is the Least You Should Know?

What <u>Is</u> the Least You Should Know?

Most English textbooks try to teach you as much as they can. This one will teach you the least it can—and still help you learn to write acceptably. You won't have to bother with predicate nouns and subordinating conjunctions and participial phrases and demonstrative pronouns and all those terms you've been hearing about for years. You can get along without them if you'll learn thoroughly a few basic rules. You *do* have to know how to spell common words; you *do* have to recognize subjects and verbs to avoid writing fragments and run-together sentences; you *do* have to know a few rules of punctuation—but rules will be kept to a minimum.

Unless you know these few rules, though, you'll have difficulty communicating in writing. Take this sentence for example:

Let's eat grandfather before we go.

We assume the writer isn't a cannibal but merely failed to capitalize and put commas around the name of a person spoken to. If the sentence had read

Let's eat, Grandfather, before we go.

then no one would misunderstand. Or take this sentence:

The instructor flunked Mac and Chris and Ken passed.

Did Chris flunk or pass? There's no way of knowing unless the writer puts a comma either after *Mac* or after *Chris*. If the sentence reads

The instructor flunked Mac and Chris, and Ken passed.

we know Chris flunked, but if the sentence reads

The instructor flunked Mac, and Chris and Ken passed.

then we know Chris passed. Punctuation makes all the difference. What you'll learn from this book is simply to make your writing so clear that no one will misunderstand it.

The English you'll learn to write is called standard English, and it may differ slightly from the English spoken in your community. All over the country, various dialects of English are spoken. In northern New England, for example, people leave the *r* off certain words and put an *r* on others. President Kennedy said *dollah* for *dollar*, *idear* for *idea*, and *Cubar* for *Cuba*. In black communities many people leave the *s* off some verbs and put an *s* on others, saying *he walk* and *they walks* instead of *he walks* and *they walk*.

But no matter what English dialect people *speak*, they all must *write* the same dialect—standard English. You can say, "Whacha doin? Cmon," and everybody will understand, but you can't *write* that way. If you want your readers to understand what you write, you'll have to write the way English-speaking people all over the world write—in standard English. Being able to write standard English is essential in college, and it probably will be an asset in your career.

It's important to master every rule as you come to it because many rules depend on the ones before. For example, unless you learn to pick out subjects and verbs, you'll have trouble with run-together sentences, with fragments, with subject-verb agreement, and with punctuation. The rules are brief and clear, and it won't be difficult to master all of them . . . *if you want to*. But you do have to want to!

Here's the way to master the least you should know:

1. Study the explanation of each rule carefully.
2. Do the first exercise (ten sentences). Correct your answers by those in the Answer Section at the back of the book. If you miss even one answer, study the explanation again to find out why.
3. Do the second exercise and correct it. If you miss a single answer, go back once more and study the explanation. You must have missed something. Be tough on yourself. Don't just think, "Maybe I'll hit it right next time." Go back and master the rules, and *then* try the next exercise. It's important to correct each group of ten sentences before going on so that you'll discover your mistakes while you still have sentences to practice on.
4. You may be tempted to quit when you get several exercises perfect. Don't! Make yourself finish every exercise. It's not enough to *understand* a rule. You have to *practice* it. Just as understanding

the strokes in swimming won't help unless you actually get into the pool and swim, so understanding a rule about writing isn't going to help unless you practice using it.

If you're positive, however, after doing five exercises, that you've mastered the rules, take Exercise 6 as a test. If you miss even one answer, you must do all the rest of the exercises. But if you get Exercise 6 perfect, then spend your time helping one of your friends. Teaching is one of the best ways of learning.

5. But rules and exercises are not the most important part of this book. The most important part begins on page 210—when you begin to write. The Writing Assignments, grouped together in the back of the book for convenience, are to be used along with the exercises. At the end of most chapters in the front part of the book, you'll be referred to the Writing Assignments in the back. Also you'll sometimes be asked to do another kind of writing—Journal Writing, which calls for just a few sentences in your daily journal using the rules you've learned that day.

Mastering these essentials will take time. Generally, college students are expected to spend two hours outside of class for each hour in class. You may need more. Undoubtedly, the more time you spend, the more your writing will improve.

Spelling

1

1 Spelling

Anyone can learn to spell. You can get rid of most of your spelling errors by the time you finish this book if you want to. It's just a matter of deciding you're going to do it. If you really intend to learn to spell, master the first seven parts of this section. They are

YOUR OWN LIST OF MISSPELLED WORDS
WORDS OFTEN CONFUSED
CONTRACTIONS
POSSESSIVES
WORDS THAT CAN BE BROKEN INTO PARTS
RULE FOR DOUBLING A FINAL CONSONANT
A LIST OF FREQUENTLY MISSPELLED WORDS

Master these seven parts, and you'll be a good speller.

YOUR OWN LIST OF MISSPELLED WORDS

On the inside back cover of this book, write correctly all the misspelled words in the papers handed back to you. Review them until you're sure of them. That will take care of most of your errors.

WORDS OFTEN CONFUSED

By mastering the spelling of these often-confused words, you'll take care of many of your spelling problems. Study the words carefully, with their examples, before trying the exercises.

a, an	Use *an* before a word that begins with a vowel sound (*a, e, i,* and *o,* plus *u* when it sounds like *uh*). Note that it's not the letter but the *sound* of the letter that matters.

          an actor, an echo, an idol, an oven
          an heirloom, an honor (silent *h*)
          an upheaval, an umpire (the *u*'s sound like *uh*)
Use *a* before a word that begins with a consonant sound (all the sounds except the vowels, plus *u* or *eu* when they sound like *you*).
          a prize, a haircut, a harmonica
          a union, a uniform, a unit (the *u*'s sound like *you*)
          a eulogy, a European trip (*eu* sounds like *you*)

accept, except

Accept is a verb and means "to receive willingly."
      I *accept* an apology or an invitation.
Except means "excluding" or "but."
      I answered all *except* the last question. (all but . . .)

advice, advise

Advise is a verb (pronounce the *s* like *z*).
      I *advise* you to go.
Use *advice* when it's not a verb.
      I need some *advice*.

affect, effect

Affect is a verb and means "to influence."
      Her opinion will *affect* my decision.
Effect means "result." If *a, an,* or *the* is in front of the word, then you'll know it isn't a verb and will use *effect*.
      Her words had an *effect* on my decision.
      His warning had no *effect* on the team.

all ready, already   If you can leave out the *all* and the sentence still makes sense, then *all ready* is the form to use. (In that form, *all* is a separate word and could be left out.)

    I'm *all ready* to go. (*I'm ready to go* makes sense.)
    Dinner is *all ready*. (*Dinner is ready* makes sense.)
But if you can't leave out the *all* and still have the sentence make sense, then use *already* (the form in which the *al* has to stay in the word).

    I'm *already* late. (*I'm ready late* doesn't make sense.)

are, or, our

Are is a verb.
    We *are* working hard.
Or is used between two possibilities, as "tea *or* coffee."
    Take it *or* leave it.
Our shows we possess something.
    Our class meets at eight.

brake, break

Brake means "to slow or stop motion." It's also the name of the device that slows or stops motion.
    You *brake* to avoid an accident.
    You slam on your *brakes*.
Break means "to shatter" or "to split." It's also the name of an interruption, as "a coffee break."
    You *break* a dish or an engagement or a record.
    You enjoy your Thanksgiving *break*.

choose, chose

I will *choose* my course of study right now.
I *chose* my course of study yesterday.

clothes, cloths

She makes her own *clothes*.
We used soft *cloths* to polish the car.

coarse, course

Coarse describes texture, as *coarse* cloth.
    The sofa was upholstered in *coarse* cloth.
Course is used for all other meanings.
    Of *course* I enjoyed that *course*.

complement, compliment

The one spelled with an *e* completes something or brings it to perfection.
    A 30° angle is the *complement* of a 60° angle.
    His blue tie *complements* his gray suit.
The one spelled with an *i* has to do with praise. Remember "*I* like compliments," and you'll remember to use the *i* spelling when you mean praise.
    She gave him a *compliment*.
    He *complimented* her on her well-written paper.

conscious, conscience

Conscious means "aware."

I was not *conscious* that it was raining.

The extra *n* in *conscience* should remind you of NO, which is what your conscience often says to you.

My *conscience* told me not to cut class.

dessert, desert

Dessert is the sweet one, the one you like two helpings of. So give it two helpings of *s*.

We had chocolate cake for *dessert*.

The other one, *desert*, is used for all other meanings.

Don't *desert* me.

The camel moved slowly across the *desert*.

do, due

You *do* something.

I *do* the best I can.

But a payment or an assignment is *due*; it is scheduled for a certain time.

My paper is *due* tomorrow.

does, dose

Does is a verb.

He *does* his work well.

A *dose* is an amount of medicine.

That was a bitter *dose* to swallow.

feel, fill

Feel describes your feelings.

I *feel* ill.

I *feel* happy about that B.

Fill is what you do to a cup.

Will you *fill* my cup again?

fourth, forth

The number *fourth* has four in it. (But note that *forty* does not. Remember the word *forty-fourth*.)

This is our *fourth* game.

That was our *forty-fourth* point.

If you don't mean a number, use *forth*.

She walked back and *forth*.

have, of

Have is a verb. When you say *could have*, the *have* may sound like *of*, but it must not be written that way. Always write *could have, would have, should have, might have*.

I should *have* finished my work sooner.

Then I could *have* gone home.

Use *of* only in a prepositional phrase (see p. 65).

I often think *of* him.

hear, here

The last three letters of *hear* spell "ear." You *hear* with your ear.

I can't *hear* you.

The other spelling *here* tells "where." Note that the three words indicating a place or pointing out something all have *here* in them: *here, there, where.*

Where are you? I'm right *here.*

it's, its

It's is a contraction and means "it is" or "it has."

It's too late now. (It is too late now.)

It's been a long time. (It has been a long time.)

Its is a possessive. (Possessives such as *its, yours, hers, ours, theirs, whose* are already possessive and never take an apostrophe. See p. 34.)

The committee gave *its* report.

knew, new

Knew has to do with knowledge (both start with *k*).

New means "not old."

I *knew* I wanted a *new* job.

know, no

Know has to do with knowledge (both start with *k*).

I *know* what I'm doing.

No means "not any" or the opposite of "yes."

I have *no* money. *No,* I can't go.

EXERCISES

Underline the correct word. Don't guess! If you aren't sure, turn back to the explanatory pages. When you've finished ten sentences, compare your answers with those at the back of the book. Correct each group of ten sentences before continuing so you'll catch your mistakes while you still have sentences to practice on.

☑EXERCISE 1

1. My brother Mark and I (<u>are</u> our) great winter sports fans, and we regret that we didn't get to the Winter Olympics in Calgary in 1988.
2. Since we missed them, we decided last summer to ride (are <u>our</u>) (knew <u>new</u>) Hondas to Canada and at least see the setting where the Olympics were held.
3. We were gone about a month, and we (<u>do</u> due) (<u>feel</u> fill) that it was one of the best trips we have ever taken.

4. We hadn't been (conscience <u>conscious</u>) of the vast preparations that were made for the Olympics.

5. Of all the (knew <u>new</u>) structures that were built, we were most impressed with the Olympic Oval, which is the first fully enclosed speed skating track in North America.

6. (<u>It's</u> Its) the length of two football fields, seats four thousand spectators, and cost $39.9 million.

7. Now speed skaters (<u>are</u> our) able to train regardless of the outdoor weather.

8. I (<u>hear</u> here) that speed skaters at the Olympic Oval reach speeds of more than 48 km (a <u>an</u>) hour.

9. Since the Olympic Oval is now used as a recreational facility for the city, of (coarse <u>course</u>) Mark and I skated on it.

10. I (<u>know</u> no) we (choose <u>chose</u>) a good way to spend (are <u>our</u>) vacation, and we (all ready <u>already</u>) would like to go back.

☑EXERCISE 2

1. I (<u>hear</u> here) there's talk of getting rid of the penny.

2. (<u>It's</u> Its) (a <u>an</u>) unusual day when I don't have dozens of pennies in my pocket.

3. When something costs 97 cents, I of (coarse <u>course</u>) hand over a dollar bill and (<u>accept</u> except) still more pennies.

4. I keep looking for those jars that (<u>are</u> our) placed on counters for charitable contributions.

5. But I never can find one when I'm (conscience <u>conscious</u>) of my bulging pocket.

6. When I (<u>do</u> due) find one, I of (coarse <u>course</u>) give it a fistful.

7. I (<u>know</u> no) that (are <u>our</u>) country once even had a half-cent piece but got rid of it in 1857.

8. Now I (<u>hear</u> here) talk of getting rid of the penny and marking everything up or down to the nearest nickel.

9. But then (<u>it's</u> its) likely they'd want to get rid of nickels.

10. Since the penny has Abraham Lincoln's head on it, my (<u>conscience</u> conscious) tells me I shouldn't treat it with such disdain.

☑EXERCISE 3

1. (<u>It's</u> Its) not unusual to find a moose in (you're <u>your</u>) backyard if you live in Anchorage, Alaska.

2. Anchorage has over 200,000 people, but within the city limits 2,000 wild moose live and roam.

3. The city limits include tracts of undeveloped land (were <u>where</u>) the moose find plenty of fodder.

4. But they also like the leaves and small branches of trees in the yards, and they (<u>are</u> our) not easily shooed away.
5. Of (coarse <u>course</u>) they also make meals of the cabbage, broccoli, and other vegetables in the people's gardens.
6. In one incident a moose stepped into a busy downtown intersection and (choose <u>chose</u>) not to budge.
7. A police officer inched his car toward the moose, hoping to nudge it aside.
8. The moose reared, kicked the hood of the car into a crumple, and ambled away.
9. Traffic accidents kill about a hundred moose a year, but a still greater hazard is on the cleared railroad tracks (were <u>where</u>) the moose like to walk in the winter.
10. The people of Anchorage, however, (<u>are</u> our) glad to have the moose share (<u>their</u> there) city.

☑EXERCISE 4

1. For my history paper, I've been reading (a <u>an</u>) article about Demosthenes, an Athenian statesman who has been called the greatest orator of all time.
2. As a boy, he was clumsy and (conscience <u>conscious</u>) of a speech impediment.
3. He (<u>knew</u> new) that people couldn't understand him and that they laughed at him.
4. But he had a strong will and (choose <u>chose</u>) to (<u>do</u> due) something about his problem.
5. He went to the seashore where no one could (<u>hear</u> here) him and practiced speaking with pebbles in his mouth.
6. The (affect <u>effect</u>) was amazing; he began to speak more distinctly.
7. Then with his (knew <u>new</u>) voice he shouted until he could (<u>hear</u> here) himself above the roar of the waves.
8. Years later his forceful speeches giving (<u>advice</u> advise) to his countrymen to resist King Philip of Macedon were called "philippics."
9. Even today (a <u>an</u>) especially bitter speech is called a "philippic."
10. (<u>It's</u> Its) amazing that such (a <u>an</u>) unpromising youngster could (<u>have</u> of) become such a great orator.

☑EXERCISE 5

1. Tomorrow I must (<u>choose</u> chose) my extracurricular activity.
2. I (all ready <u>already</u>) (<u>know</u> no) the two activities I enjoy most, but (it's its) hard to (<u>choose</u> chose) between them.
3. Both activities (<u>are</u> our) important to me.
4. In fact I've (all ready <u>already</u>) had experience in each.

5. In high school I had a part in several plays, and I (<u>do</u> due) love acting.
6. But I also played my xylophone in the school orchestra and got (complements <u>compliments</u>) on my playing.
7. I'm (conscience <u>conscious</u>) that I should (<u>have</u> of) given the question more thought before now.
8. Tomorrow night I must either try out for the first dramatic production (are <u>or</u>) else go to the first orchestra rehearsal.
9. I (<u>know</u> no) my choice will have (a <u>an</u>) (affect <u>effect</u>) on my future.
10. I wonder which I'll (<u>choose</u> chose).

☑EXERCISE 6

1. I've been reading (a <u>an</u>) article that asks—and answers—some interesting questions. (Hear <u>Here</u>) (<u>are</u> our) a few of them.
2. Do you (<u>know</u> no) which is the longest river in the world?
3. (Its <u>It's</u>) the Nile, which flows from Lake Victoria in Uganda north through Egypt to the Mediterranean.
4. And do you (<u>know</u> no) what is the longest railway in the world?
5. (Its <u>It's</u>) the great Trans-Siberian Railroad, which is over 4,000 miles long.
6. Do you (<u>know</u> no) what is the longest paved road in a single country?
7. Of (coarse <u>course</u>) (its <u>it's</u>) the Trans-Canada Highway, which goes from the Atlantic to the Pacific and is 4,860 miles long.
8. I never (<u>knew</u> new) before that the General Sherman, a redwood in Sequoia National Park in California, is the most massive living thing.
9. Nor did I (<u>know</u> no) that the oldest living thing in the world today is a bristlecone pine in Great Basin National Park in Nevada.
10. (Its <u>It's</u>) nicknamed Methuselah, and scientists have determined from (<u>its</u> it's) rings that (its <u>it's</u>) 4,600 years old.

☐EXERCISE 7

1. I've just read (a <u>an</u>) article stating that at death the average American has spent a total of seven years watching television.
2. Most people are not (conscience <u>conscious</u>) of how much they watch.
3. They don't really (<u>choose</u> chose) to watch TV; they simply snap the set on without thinking because they (are <u>our</u>) uncomfortable without it.
4. Instead of a freely chosen diversion, television has become (a <u>an</u>) addiction requiring a nightly fix, and many people suffer withdrawal symptoms if the set must be sent out for repair.
5. The article has had (a <u>an</u>) amazing (affect <u>effect</u>) on my thinking.
6. Of (coarse <u>course</u>) I (all ready <u>already</u>) (<u>knew</u> new) I was spending too much time watching TV, but I didn't (<u>know</u> no) it would eventually add up to seven years of my life.

7. Seven years (does dose) seem like a lot of time to spend watching other people live. I think (it's its) time to (brake break) my TV habit.
8. I should (accept except) the (advice advise) of my (conscience conscious) to snap the set off and (do due) my own living.
9. I could be seeing friends, pursuing a hobby, (are or) doing any number of other interesting things.
10. In the end, I don't want to have spent seven years of my life watching others live when I could (have of) been living myself.

Source: Jeffrey Schrank, Snap, Crackle, and Popular Taste.
New York: Dell Publishing Co. 1977

☐EXERCISE 8

1. You can't (choose chose) what happens to you, but you can (choose chose) how you react.
2. I (know no) I didn't react as I should (have of) when I failed my math test.
3. I should simply (have of) given a (complement compliment) to my friend who passed.
4. My (conscience conscious) bothers me now as I look back.
5. Of (coarse course) I had put (forth fourth) great effort in that (coarse course).
6. Therefore it was hard to (accept except) failure.
7. The hardest problem on the test concerned the (complement compliment) of an angle.
8. Now I (know no) how to (do due) the problem, but of (coarse course) (it's its) too late.
9. I (hear here), however, that the test won't have a great (affect effect) on (are our) grades.
10. I've (all ready already) decided to make (a an) exceptional effort to pass the next test.

☐EXERCISE 9

1. I never (knew new) anything about Nobel prizes (accept except) their name.
2. But last week I read (a an) article about them.
3. Alfred Nobel, the Swedish inventor of dynamite, left a fund to provide prizes for persons that Swedish educational institutes (choose chose).
4. The prizes go to those who the judges (feel fill) have conferred the greatest benefit on humanity.
5. The prizes are given in the fields of physics, chemistry, physiology (are or) medicine, literature, and peace.
6. They were first awarded in 1901 and have been given annually ever since (accept except) during the two world wars.

7. In 1968 (a an) economics prize was added by the central bank of Sweden.
8. (It's Its) often been the custom to divide a prize among two (are or) three winners.
9. Of (coarse course) sometimes a winner refuses to (accept except) a prize, as when Hitler forbade Germans to (accept except) prizes because the peace prize had been given to one of his enemies.
10. A Nobel prize, which in 1991 amounted to a diploma, a gold medal, and $969,000, is the greatest (complement compliment) anyone could receive.

☐EXERCISE 10

1. I should (have of) registered for this (coarse course) earlier.
2. (It's Its) bound to have (a an) (affect effect) on my writing.
3. Most of the material is (knew new) to me, but I'm (all ready already) to work hard.
4. (Are Our) instructor has given me some (advice advise) that I intend to (accept except).
5. I'm going to (do due) all the exercises and of (coarse course) write all the papers.
6. I (know no) (it's its) going to be work, but I (accept except) the challenge.
7. I (hear here) this (coarse course) is basic for all other composition (coarses courses).
8. I'm glad I (choose chose) to take this one first, (are or) I might (have of) had trouble.
9. My (conscience conscious) tells me I'd better put (forth fourth) considerable effort.
10. I've (all ready already) received a (complement compliment) on one of my papers.

JOURNAL WRITING

The surest way to learn these Words Often Confused is to use them immediately in your own writing. Therefore begin to keep a journal, writing each day at least three sentences making use of some words or rules you've learned that day. If you write about things that interest you, then you'll be inclined to reread your journal occasionally and thus review what you've learned.

WRITING ASSIGNMENT

The writing assignments, grouped together for convenience at the back of the book, are to be used along with the exercises. Turn to page 211 for your first writing assignment, or follow your instructor's directions concerning the assignments.

BEWARE

Don't assume that because the Writing Section is at the back of the book and has only 40 pages, it's not important. IT'S THE MOST IMPORTANT PART OF THE BOOK, and you should spend more time on it than on all the rest of the book. It has been kept brief because *you learn to write by writing*, not by reading pages and pages *about* writing.

MORE WORDS OFTEN CONFUSED

Study these words carefully, with their examples, before attempting the exercises. When you've mastered all forty word groups in these two sections, you'll have taken care of many of your spelling problems.

lead, led

The past form of the verb is *led*.
> She *led* the parade yesterday.

If you don't mean past time, use *lead*, which rhymes with *bead*. (Don't confuse it with the metal *lead*, which rhymes with *dead*.)
> She will *lead* the parade today.

loose, lose

Loose means "not tight." Note how l o o s e that word is. It has plenty of room for two *o*'s.
> My shoestring is *loose*.

The other one, *lose*, has room for only one *o*.
> They are going to *lose* that game.

moral, morale

Pronounce these two words correctly, and you won't confuse them—*móral, moréle*.
Moral has to do with right and wrong.
> It was a *moral* question.

Morale is "the spirit of a group or an individual."
> The *morale* of the team was excellent.

passed, past

Passed is a verb.
> He *passed* the house.

Use *past* when it's not a verb.
> He walked *past* the house. (It's the same as *He walked by the house,* so you know it isn't a verb.)
> He's coasting on his *past* reputation.
> In the *past* he had always *passed* his exams.

personal, personnel

Pronounce these two correctly, and you won't confuse them—*pérsonal, personnél*.
> That was his *personal* opinion.

Personnel means "a group of employees."
> She was in charge of *personnel* at the factory.

piece, peace

Remember "piece of pie." The one meaning "a *piece* of something" always begins with *pie*.
> I gave him a *piece* of my mind.

The other one, *peace*, is the opposite of war.
> They signed the *peace* treaty.

principal,
principle

Principal means "main." Both words have *a* in them:

principa**l**

m**a**in

The *principal* of the school spoke. (main teacher)

The *principal* problem is financial. (main problem)

She lost both *principal* and interest. (main amount of money)

A *principle* is a "rule." Both words end in *le*:

principl**e**

ru**le**

She had high moral *principles*. (rules)

That's against my *principles*. (rules)

quiet, quite

Pronounce these two correctly, and you won't misspell them. *Quiet* rhymes with *diet*.

Be *quiet*.

Quite rhymes with *bite*.

I'm *quite* sure of it.

right, write

Right means "correct" or "proper."

I got ten answers *right*.

Write is what you do with a pen.

I'll *write* you a long letter soon.

than, then

Than compares two things.

I'd rather have this *than* that.

Then tells when (*then* and *when* rhyme, and both have *e* in them).

She finished shopping; *then* she went home.

their, there,
they're

Their is a possessive (see p. 34).

Their 1965 car is now a classic.

There points out something. (Remember that the three words indicating a place or pointing out something all have *here* in them: *here*, *there*, *where*.)

There is where I left it.

There were clouds in the sky.

They're is a contraction (see p. 27) and means "they are."

They're happy now. (They are happy now.)

threw, through

Threw means "to throw something" in past time.

He *threw* the ball. I *threw* away my chance.

If you don't mean "to throw something," use *through*.

I walked *through* the door.

She's *through* with her work.

two, too, to

Two is a number.
I made *two* B's last semester.
Too means "more than enough" or "also."
The lesson was *too* difficult and *too* long. (more than enough)
I found it boring *too*. (also)
Use *to* for all other meanings.
He likes *to* snorkel. He's going *to* the beach.

weather, whether

Weather refers to atmospheric conditions.
I don't like cold *weather*.
Whether means "if."
I don't know *whether* I'll go.
Whether I'll go depends on the *weather*.

were, where

Were is a verb.
We *were* miles from home.
Where refers to a place. (Remember that the three words indicating a place or pointing out something all have *here* in them: *here, there, where*.)
Where is he? There he is.
Where are you? Here I am.

who's, whose

Who's is a contraction and always means "who is" or "who has."
Who's there? (Who is there?)
Who's been eating my pie? (Who has been ...?)
Whose is a possessive. (Possessives such as *whose, its, yours, hers, ours, theirs* are already possessive and never take an apostrophe. See p. 34.)
Whose coat is this?

woman, women

Remember that the word is just *man* or *men* with *wo* in front of it.
wo man ... *woman* ... one woman
wo men ... *women* ... two women
That *woman* is my aunt.
Those *women* are helping with the canvass.

you're, your

You're is a contraction and always means "you are."
You're welcome. (You are welcome.)
Your is a possessive.
Your bike is in the driveway.

EXERCISES

Underline the correct word. When you've finished 10 sentences, compare your answers with those at the back of the book. WATCH OUT! Don't do more than 10 sentences at a time, or you won't be teaching yourself while you still have sentences to practice on.

☐EXERCISE 1

1. I had never tried to ski before, but I (knew new) it would be (quiet quite) easy.
2. I decided to (accept except) (a an) invitation from friends to go skiing on Whistler Mountain.
3. I rented skis, boots, and poles, and of (coarse course) I (choose chose) warm (clothes cloths).
4. The (weather whether) was perfect as we started (are our) trip.
5. My friends promised to teach me on (a an) easy slope as they (lead led) me to the chair lift.
6. I walked in my skis (threw through) the snow and let a chair sweep me up from behind.
7. As the chair carried me to the mountain, I (all ready already) felt exhilarated, for I (knew new) it was going to be a great day.
8. At the top, however, I was supposed to ski off the moving chair as it got close to the ground, but of (coarse course) I tripped on my skis and fell in the snow, much to the amusement of everyone watching.
9. But (than then) I got some helpful (advice advise), and by the end of the day I was skiing the beginners' slope pretty well.
10. It was really a great day—(accept except) for that chair lift.

☐EXERCISE 2

1. I've been reading about (a an) interesting (knew new) project in the tropical rain forests of Ecuador.
2. (Its It's) the project of Conservation International, which is based in Washington, D.C.
3. (There Their) plan is to show the people of Ecuador that rain forests (are our) more valuable if left standing.
4. To (do due) this they are making buttons from tagua nuts, which grow on palm trees in the rain forests.
5. The tagua nuts (are our) ivory-like nuts of golf ball size.
6. Conservation International has had five million buttons made from tagua nuts.
7. And now I (hear here) that U.S. clothing manufacturers have agreed to buy the tagua buttons.
8. (Their There) (are our) going to be three valuable results from the project.

9. First it will encourage Ecuador to (choose chose) conservation for the tagua nut tree.
10. Second it will reduce soil erosion by keeping the trees standing.

☐EXERCISE 3

1. Third, it will replace the ivory for which so many elephants have (all ready already) been slaughtered.
2. Of (coarse course) using the tagua nuts is only one of the plans of Conservation International.
3. They intend to use some (too two) thousand other rain forest products in making furniture, baskets, and medications.
4. All (their there) efforts are going to have (a an) (affect effect) in keeping the rain forest green.
5. Also, people everywhere will (hear here) about the project.
6. Thus they will come to see that (its it's) better to leave the forests standing.
7. Products made from trees in other countries may be found valuable (to too).
8. Maybe the Forest Service in the U.S. will even discover ways to use all of (are our) trees for something besides lumber.
9. (Than Then) the forests that (are our) now being clear cut may remain standing.
10. And (its it's) all because of those tagua nuts.

☐EXERCISE 4

1. Last summer I visited (a an) interesting aquarium.
2. (It's Its) the Monterey Bay Aquarium in California, and (it's its) the largest indoor aquarium on the West Coast.
3. (A An) unusual aspect of the Aquarium is (it's its) regional focus.
4. The exhibits of more (than then) 300 species of plants and animals show what is under the water along the central California coast.
5. Most spectacular is a giant kelp forest, which is like a magnificent cathedral when looked at (threw through) the glass walls.
6. If (you're your) a nondiver, you can now see for the first time what a forest of giant kelp is really like.
7. (It's Its) (quiet quite) (a an) amazing view (threw through) this tallest aquarium tank in the country.
8. Of (coarse course) I stroked a starfish in the hands-on tide pool and also looked (threw through) a free telescope at some pelicans.
9. (Than Then) I walked (passed past) the tank (were where) little sea otters were diving and playing.
10. I was (quiet quite) surprised to learn that the annual food bill for one sea otter is $10,000.

☐EXERCISE 5

1. I never (knew new) much before about the origin of the Olympic Games.
2. Now I (know no) (there they're) named for athletic contests held in ancient Greece (threw through) many centuries.
3. (It's Its) probable that they began in 776 B.C. in the valley of Olympia.
4. After that, they were held every four years, and that (lead led) to measuring time by the four-year interval between the games— (a an) Olympiad.
5. At first the only event was a race the length of the stadium, but later (a an) additional event was the pentathlon, which consisted of running, wrestling, leaping, throwing the discus, and hurling the javelin.
6. As the years (passed past), boxing and chariot racing were added.
7. (Than Then) the games lasted for five days.
8. (Their There) was no greater honor for any Greek (than then) to (accept except) the simple branch of wild olive given to a winner.
9. The winners were praised in poetry and song, and (their there) strength and beauty were preserved in statues.
10. In A.D. 394 the games were abolished, but in 1896 the first modern Olympic Games (were where) held in a (knew new) marble stadium constructed in Athens for the purpose.

☐EXERCISE 6

1. I was (quiet quite) surprised to learn that the U.S. sent (a an) Olympic team to the first modern Olympic Games in Athens in 1896.
2. The games had not been held for the (passed past) 1,500 years.
3. The 10 U.S. contestants met in New York but found that (their there) boat fare was going to be higher (than then) they had expected.
4. Finally they got enough money and set (forth fourth) on a German steamship for the 10-day trip to Naples.
5. Of (coarse course) (there they're) was (know no) room on deck to practice (their there) broad jumps or pole vaults or 100-meter dashes.
6. From Naples (their there) was a train ride to Brindisi, (were where) they took a steamer to Patras in Greece.
7. (Than Then) they had a 10-hour train ride across Greece to Athens.
8. When they arrived, they (were where) glad they had 12 days to get in shape.
9. They hadn't been given the (right write) date, however, and had to perform the next morning.
10. They didn't (know no) (who's whose) fault the misunderstanding was, but even so they won 9 of the 12 track events.

☐EXERCISE 7

1. Not since I was a little kid had I flown a kite, and even (than then) it was just (a an) ordinary kite.
2. Now I have a high performance kite, which is (quiet quite) different.
3. It has (two too) separate strings that I hold with each of my hands.
4. When I go out in nice windy (weather whether), I can pull on either string and make the kite turn whichever way I (choose chose).
5. (It's Its) really (quiet quite) a responsive kite.
6. I (do due) spins with it and make it go wherever I want it to.
7. When the wind is strong enough, the fabric flutters and makes a noise like that of a little plane. The (affect effect) is striking.
8. On a windy day of (coarse course) several colorful kites like mine (are our) flying in the park and dancing around in the sky.
9. People walking by always stop to watch and are (quiet quite) impressed.
10. I (do due) have a lot of fun soaring my kite.

☐EXERCISE 8

1. In the (passed past) few weeks I've been low on cash.
2. I decided, therefore, to (accept except) the (advice advise) of my best friend and get a part-time job.
3. I finally found a job cleaning the parking lot for a (knew new) downtown office building.
4. (It's Its) not the kind of job I wanted.
5. I don't enjoy cleaning up after people, but I (know no) someone has to (do due) it.
6. Also the job (does dose) pay well, and of (coarse course) that's important.
7. I sweep up empty pop bottles and fast-food containers, and (their there) (are or) always lots of apple cores and prune pits.
8. I've even found mounds of cigarette butts (were where) somebody dumped a car ashtray.
9. (Do Due) people not realize that someone will have to clean up after them?
10. If everybody had to clean up a parking lot just once, (than then) maybe they'd think twice before dumping (their there) garbage.

☐EXERCISE 9

1. Have you been (conscience conscious) of the number of birds that have the color red in (their there) names?
2. When you think of birds, (it's its) likely that you think of blue or gray or black.

3. But (quiet quite) a few birds have some red feathers.
4. Of (coarse course) there is the redheaded woodpecker and the rose-breasted grosbeak.
5. (Than Then) there is the cardinal.
6. My grandmother always called cardinals redbirds. She would say, "Come see the (too two) redbirds in (are our) cherry tree."
7. Next I thought of the scarlet tanager and the ruby-throated hummingbird.
8. I got so interested in bird names that I turned to *Birds of North America*.
9. (Their There) I saw the American redstart, the common redpoll, and the roseate spoonbill.
10. I (know no) there must be more if I had time to look (farther further).

☐EXERCISE 10

1. In only one continent is (their there) (peace piece) among all nations.
2. (It's Its) Antarctica, which is about the size of the United States and Mexico combined and which is the highest continent because (it's its) ice cap is three miles deep.
3. (It's Its) become a model of international cooperation, hosting scientists from 18 nations.
4. The scientists have signed a treaty stating that Antarctica will be devoted to peaceful research and that (their there) will be (know no) military units, territorial claims, (are or) nuclear testing.
5. The scientists study the earth's magnetic fields, the "hole" in the ozone layer of the upper atmosphere, fossil bones of 231 million years ago, and meteorites more ancient (than then) those found elsewhere in the (passed past).
6. Research is being carried on (their there) that can be done nowhere else.
7. Nations work together. For example, a French-Russian group is drilling a deep hole (threw through) the ice cap.
8. And (hear here) is the only place in the world (were where) Russia and the United States have submitted to unrestricted mutual inspections.
9. Also, Germany has built a (knew new) ship for Antarctic research, and a dozen U.S. research programs (are our) taking place aboard that ship.
10. For 30 years the (moral morale) among the scientists has been good. (Their There) experience suggests that the Antarctic treaty might be a model for nations around the world.

JOURNAL WRITING

In your journal write several sentences using any words you may formerly have had trouble with.

Journal writing is a good idea not only because it will help you remember these words often confused but also because it will be a storehouse for ideas you can later use in writing papers. Here are some ideas you might consider writing your sentences about:

— your goals
— your thoughts about a class discussion
— a new idea you've gained from a course
— your reaction to a movie or play
— an experience that has made you think
— what you've learned from a friendship
— how you're working through a problem
— how your values are changing

WRITING ASSIGNMENT

From now on, along with doing the exercises, you will be expected to follow your instructor's directions concerning the writing assignments which begin on page 211.

Proofreading Exercise

See if you can correct all six errors in this student paper before checking with the answers at the back of the book.

I LEARNED TO PAINT

Yesterday I learned to paint. Oh, I had painted before, and I thought I ~~new~~ *knew* how. But that was before yesterday.

Yesterday a friend ~~whose~~ *whose* a professional painter helped me paint my apartment. First of all, we spent hours filling all the cracks and removing all the hooks and nails and outlet covers. We washed the kitchen walls to get off any grease, and we lightly sanded one wall that was rough. Of ~~coarse~~ *course* we had ~~all ready~~ *already* moved all the furniture away from the walls. We didn't even open the paint cans until the day was half over. ~~Than~~ *THEN* we used paint-brushes to paint all the corners and edges that a roller wouldn't get to. Finally, in the very last hour of ~~are~~ *our* long day, we used the rollers to paint the walls. That part of the job went quickly, and the whole place looked great when we had finished.

I learned a lot yesterday. I learned that when you want to paint a room, you don't simply start painting.

CONTRACTIONS

Two words condensed into one are called a contraction.

is not	isn't	you have	you've

The letter or letters that are left out are replaced with an apostrophe. For example, if the two words *do not* are condensed into one, an apostrophe is put where the *o* is left out.

do not	don't

Note how the apostrophe goes in the exact place where the letter or letters are left out in these contractions:

I am	I'm
I have	I've
I shall, I will	I'll
I would	I'd
you are	you're
you have	you've
you will	you'll
she is, she has	she's
he is, he has	he's
it is, it has	it's
we are	we're
we have	we've
we will, we shall	we'll
they are	they're
they have	they've
are not	aren't
cannot	can't
do not	don't
does not	doesn't
have not	haven't
let us	let's
who is, who has	who's
where is	where's

One contraction does not follow this rule: *will not* becomes *won't*.

In all other contractions that you're likely to use, the apostrophe goes exactly where the letter or letters are left out. Note especially *it's, they're, who's,* and *you're*. Use them when you mean two words. (See p. 34 for the possessive forms—*its, their, whose,* and *your*—which don't take an apostrophe.)

EXERCISES

Put an apostrophe in each contraction. Then compare your answers with those at the back of the book. Be sure to correct each group of 10 sentences before going on so that you'll catch your errors while you still have sentences to practice on.

☐EXERCISE 1

1. Were studying contractions, and Im finally getting the hang of them.
2. Well, that shouldnt be hard.
3. It isnt if I just remember to put the apostrophe where the letter or letters have been left out.
4. Thats the idea.
5. Im now sure of the difference between its and it's.
6. Yes, thats important.
7. In our class everybodys trying to pass all the daily tests.
8. It would have been good if youd learned these rules long ago.
9. Were all aware of that, but its not too late yet.
10. Thats right. Its never too late.

☐EXERCISE 2

1. Ive always wanted to see some of the museums in Chicago.
2. And one day I decided Id make the trip.
3. Its only about a hundred miles from our campus to Chicago, and a railroad line runs directly there.
4. I decided Id jump a freight car.
5. Id often seen it done in old movies.
6. So early one morning I went out to the railroad tracks to wait for a train.
7. I must have waited about three hours, but finally a freight train came roaring by.
8. The only trouble was it wasnt going my way.
9. Also it was going so fast that Id never have been able to jump on.
10. I decided then that Id better forget about those old movies.

☐EXERCISE 3

1. Ive heard that laughing out loud is an indication of mental health.
2. Wont smiling do, or doesnt that count?
3. No, its laughing aloud thats the indicator.
4. Well, my dad must be in good mental health; hes always chuckling.
5. Its supposed to be good for your physical health too.
6. Thats reasonable; a good belly laugh is relaxing.
7. Ive been thinking that Ive never heard our history prof laugh.

8. Thats right. I havent either.
9. Lets make a project of seeing whether we can make him laugh.
10. Ill bet we cant, but Im willing to try.

☐EXERCISE 4

1. Theres something comfortable about clothes youve worn for years.
2. I have a coat thats been with me for a long time, and I wouldnt feel comfortable without it.
3. Its getting a little worn at the elbows, and some day itll have to go, but a new one wont be the same.
4. Its a part of me, and Im afraid my friends wouldnt recognize me in any other coat.
5. Its too bad its wearing out, but maybe with a couple of elbow patches itll last one more year.
6. Ive been so busy decorating our house that I havent had time even to think of getting a new coat.
7. Ive given the living room a first coat of paint, and now its ready for the second.
8. Ive never done any painting before, and Im enjoying it.
9. Its satisfying to see the house look its best for a change.
10. Whether Ive saved much money is anybody's guess.

☐EXERCISE 5

1. Ive been reading an article about travel today compared with travel in 1840.
2. Im amazed at the difference.
3. I knew, of course, that travel today is lots faster, but I didnt know how much faster.
4. Today if youre traveling with someone wholl share the driving, youll probably cover about 600 miles a day.
5. If youre starting from Omaha on Interstate 80, youll probably reach Sacramento in three days—easy.
6. Back in 1840 youd start out in your ox-drawn homemade canvas-and-wood wagon, nudging it onto the westbound lane of the Great Platte River Road.
7. Even if your companion shared the driving, youd not make more than 15 miles a day.
8. If the weather was good, youd possibly reach California's gold-mining area in four and a half months—hard.
9. Its difficult to realize the great difference.
10. At least Im no longer inclined to yearn for the good old days.

Source: *Audubon,* May 1989

☐EXERCISE 6

1. Why dont evergreen trees lose their needles the way deciduous trees lose their leaves?
2. Actually they do lose them; they just dont lose them all at once.
3. When they lose their needles, theyre constantly replacing them with new ones.
4. Its true, though, that evergreen needles do last a long time.
5. Ive just learned that bristlecone pine needles last about 30 years before theyre ready to fall.
6. Evergreen needles are tough and lasting whereas other leaves arent.
7. Ive learned something else thats interesting about leaves.
8. A tree may lose its leaves in the autumn in one climate and be ever-green in another climate.
9. Thats true of the red maple.
10. A red maple in New England loses all its leaves in the autumn, but a red maple in Florida doesnt lose them all at once.

☐EXERCISE 7

1. Weve had icy streets ever since weve been back from our vacation.
2. Its no fun to walk in this weather. Im staying inside.
3. But Im going skiing this weekend if weve had snow by then.
4. Youre welcome to come too if youd like to.
5. But I suppose youll be working on your term paper.
6. Youll have yours finished before Ive written my first sentence.
7. Im writing a paper about children and TV.
8. Its not only watching violence thats harmful to children.
9. Its the fact that when theyre watching TV, theyre doing nothing else.
10. Theyre missing a chance to play a game, to draw a picture, or to hit a baseball instead of watching someone else do it.

☐EXERCISE 8

1. It wasnt anything but a name to me, but I decided Id explore Death Valley National Monument on my way west.
2. Ive learned since that the Valley is a sunken chunk of the earth's crust.
3. Its encircled by mountains that keep in its heat and keep out any breezes.
4. Its the driest and hottest desert in North America.
5. As I started down the 17-mile road that drops 4,000 feet into the valley, I wasnt prepared for the sudden increase in temperature.
6. When I reached the 200-square-mile salt pan, I wasnt surprised to learn that its temperature has gone as high as 134° in the shade.

7. The salt pan is a residue of a salt lake that existed more than 20,000 years ago, and its 8,000 feet thick.
8. Many pioneers narrowly escaped death trying to cross this pan. One of them looked back and said, "Good-bye, Death Valley," and thats how it got its name.
9. From such a desolate place, I couldnt believe it when I saw palm trees in the distance.
10. But there they were at Furnace Creek, one of the few places where theres enough water for a small community. I decided Id stop there a while.

☐EXERCISE 9

1. Id always thought a dictionary was the supreme authority.
2. When Id find the pronunciation or meaning of a word in the dictionary, I knew that was it.
3. Now Ive learned that dictionary makers dont pretend to be authorities.
4. They dont decide whats correct and what isnt.
5. They merely record pronunciations and meanings that are most common.
6. Dictionary makers read vast amounts of literature and then record whats the most common meaning of a word.
7. Likewise they get many reports concerning the pronunciation of a word and then record whats most common.
8. Also Im realizing that meanings change over the years.
9. For example, in 1919 "broadcast" meant "to scatter seed," but by 1921 its more common meaning had become "to transmit a program by radio."
10. Five hundred years ago "hood" was what a monk wore; today its the cover over a car engine.

☐EXERCISE 10

1. Im trying to decide on a major.
2. Its a decision thats going to affect my entire life.
3. I dont want to get into a field that just brings in money.
4. If Im going to work, Ive got to like the job Im doing.
5. Its got to be fun, or I dont want it.
6. I dont think theres much difference between work and play.
7. If youve found the right job, its as much fun as play.
8. Ive known people who say their jobs are fun.
9. Thats what Im looking for.
10. And thats why its so important that I choose the right major.

JOURNAL WRITING

Doing exercises helps you learn a rule, but even more helpful is using the rule in writing. In your journal write some sentences using contractions. You might write about your reaction to the week's news. Or choose your own subject.

WRITING ASSIGNMENT

Turn to the writing section at the back of the book for your writing assignment.

POSSESSIVES

The trick in writing possessives is to ask yourself the question, "Who (or what) does it belong to?" (Modern usage has made *who* acceptable when it comes first in a sentence, but some people still say, "*Whom* does it belong to?" or even "*To whom* does it belong?") If the answer to your question ends in *s*, simply add an apostrophe. If it doesn't end in *s*, then add an apostrophe and *s*.

one boys bike	Who does it belong to?	boy	Add *'s*	boy's bike
two boys bikes	Who do they belong to?	boys	Add *'*	boys' bikes
the mans hat	Who does it belong to?	man	Add *'s*	man's hat
the mens hats	Who do they belong to?	men	Add *'s*	men's hats
childrens game	Who does it belong to?	children	Add *'s*	children's game
a days work	What does it belong to?	day	Add *'s*	day's work

This trick will always work, but you must ask the question every time. Remember that the key word is *belong*. Who (or what) does it belong to? If you ask the question another way, you may get an answer that won't help you. Also, if you just look at a word without asking the question, you may think the name of the owner ends in *s* when it really doesn't.

TO MAKE A POSSESSIVE

Ask "Who (or what) does it belong to?"
If the answer ends in *s*, just add an apostrophe.
If it doesn't end in *s*, add an apostrophe and *s*.

Cover the right-hand column and see if you can write the following possessives correctly. Ask the question each time.

that mans jacket	_____	man's
the mens team	_____	men's
Donnas apartment	_____	Donna's
James apartment	_____	James'
the Smiths house	_____	the Smiths'
Mrs. Smiths house	_____	Mrs. Smith's

(Sometimes you may see a variation of this rule. *James' book* may be written *James's book*. That is correct too, but the best way is to stick to the simple rule. You can't be wrong if you follow it.)

A word of warning! Don't assume that because a word ends in *s* it is necessarily a possessive. Make sure the word actually possesses something before you add an apostrophe.

A few words are already possessive and don't need an apostrophe added to them. Memorize this list:

my, mine	its
your, yours	our, ours
his	their, theirs
her, hers	whose

Note particularly *its, their, whose,* and *your.* They are already possessive and don't take an apostrophe. (They sound just like the contractions *it's, they're, who's,* and *you're,* which stand for two words and of course have to have an apostrophe.)

As a practice exercise, cover the right-hand column below with a sheet of paper, and on it write the correct form (contraction or possessive). If you miss any, go back and review the explanations.

(It) sunny today. _____	It's
(You) package has arrived. _____	Your
(Who) going with me? _____	Who's
(They) hoping to finish today. _____	They're
The puppy broke (it) leash. _____	its
(Who) book is this? _____	Whose
The storm lost (it) force. _____	its
(Who) keeping score? _____	Who's
(They) planning their vacation. _____	They're
(It) up to you now. _____	It's
(You) correct. _____	You're
(They) garden has a pool. _____	Their
(You) excused. _____	You're
(Who) car is in the driveway? _____	Whose
I like (you) new outfit. _____	your

Here's one more practice exercise. Cover the right-hand column with a sheet of paper, and on it write the possessives.

1. My sisters spent the summer at my grandparents home.

grandparents'. (You didn't add an apostrophe to *sisters*, did you? The sisters don't possess anything.)

2. Students grades depend on their term papers.

Students' (Who do the grades belong to?)

3. My friends spent an evening at Charles house.

Charles' (Who does the house belong to?)

4. Charles was invited to my mothers apartment.

mother's (Charles doesn't possess anything in this sentence.)

5. Sarahs job is less challenging than yours.

Sarah's (*Yours* is already possessive and doesn't take an apostrophe.)

6. Last nights game was exciting.

night's (The game belonged to last night.)

7. The Morgans apartment has been redecorated.

Morgans' (Who does the apartment belong to?)

8. The Morgans redecorated their apartment.

(No apostrophe in this sentence. *Their* is already possessive. The sentence merely tells what the Morgans did.)

9. The girls team beat the womens team.

girls', women's (Did you ask who each team belongs to?)

10. The girls enjoy playing on their team.

(No apostrophe. *Their* is already possessive, and the girls don't possess anything in this sentence.)

11. The two instructors gave the same test.

(No apostrophe. The sentence merely tells what the instructors did.)

12. The two instructors tests were the same.

instructors' (Who did the tests belong to?)

13. Lynn borrowed someone elses car.

someone else's (Who did the car belong to?)

14. My last semesters grades were an improvement.

semester's (The grades belonged to last semester.)

15. The sign above the gate said "The Hansons."

Hansons (meaning the Hansons live there) or Hansons' (meaning it's the Hansons' house).

EXERCISES

Put the apostrophe in each possessive. WATCH OUT! **First**, make sure the word really possesses something; not every word ending in *s* is a possessive. **Second,** remember that certain words are already possessive and don't take an apostrophe. **Third**, remember that even though a word seems to end in *s*, you can't tell where the apostrophe goes until you ask the question, "Who (or what) does it belong to?" In the first sentence, for example, "Who does the car belong to?" "Everybody." Therefore you'll write *everybody's*.

☐EXERCISE 1

1. Is everybodys car available this morning?
2. Jennifers car is parked across the street.
3. Whose car is in the driveway?
4. It's probably either Jeromes or Connies.
5. Andys motorbike is in the driveway too.
6. We're all planning a days trip to Turkey Run State Park.
7. Everybodys interest in the park is different.
8. Andys only aim is to ride on the bridle trail.
9. Ashleys plan is to take a guided nature tour.
10. Some peoples interest is mainly in the famous home-cooked dinner at the Lodge.

☐EXERCISE 2

1. I've just read an article about the bodys most amazing instrument—the human hand.
2. More than half of the bodys bones are in the hands and feet.
3. And the human hand is the bodys chief engineering marvel.
4. A persons hand has 25 joints that allow it to make 58 different motions.
5. A handshake, a gesture, a pat, a wave, a touch all communicate meaning just as words do.
6. Ones life would be very different without the motions of the hand.
7. Also amazing is a hands ability to perform unlike tasks such as threading a needle and laying a brick.
8. Across the land hundreds of surgeons specialize in reconstructing injured hands.
9. A surgeons skill is important for everyone but especially for musicians, artists, and typists.
10. Never take your hands actions lightly.

☐EXERCISE 3

1. Our instructor read everyone's paper aloud in class this morning.
2. One person's paper was on law enforcement; another person's was on making Scotch shortbread.
3. I like hearing other students' papers read.
4. I think Sue's confidence was boosted by hearing all the good remarks about her paper.
5. Everybody liked Nick's paper on Carl Sandburg's poetry.
6. It was better organized than Bevs paper on Dickens *Oliver Twist.*
7. I was really pleased with everyones comments about my paper.
8. Actually we profit as much from the students evaluations as from the instructors.
9. Now of course everybodys paper will be rewritten.
10. The instructors and the students comments have given us ideas that will help us rewrite.

☐EXERCISE 4

1. My youngest brothers only request for Christmas was a computer.
2. We agreed to get him one, but everybodys reason for doing so was different.
3. My moms idea was that it might help him with his math.
4. My sisters reason was that it would make him learn to type.
5. My dads idea was that it would keep him away from the video arcades.
6. I suppose my little brothers reason for wanting one was that he saw computers at all his friends houses.
7. When he unwrapped the computer Christmas morning, everybodys excitement was high.
8. With Dads help he got it hooked up and started to play a math game.
9. But before long my brothers interest began to wane.
10. Will he eventually make good use of the computer? It's anybodys guess.

☐EXERCISE 5

1. Ivans ability in juggling is quite a social asset.
2. He performed magic tricks for our daughters birthday party.
3. The childrens delight was obvious.
4. The success of the party was due mainly to Ivans skill.
5. The afternoons final excitement was a trip to the zoo.
6. We spent most of our time at the monkeys cages.
7. The monkeys seemed to enjoy watching us as much as we did them.
8. A bear stood on its hind legs.

9. And a bear cub was being nuzzled by its mother.
10. The most beautiful spot in the zoo is the aviary with its birds and trees and flowers.

☐EXERCISE 6

1. My sisters hobby is flower arranging.
2. She took a semesters course in Japanese flower arranging last spring.
3. And now she has even given a demonstration at the local Womens Club.
4. She finds the flowers for her arrangements in Dads garden.
5. Her best friends hobby is pottery making.
6. The two girls hobbies go nicely together.
7. My sisters Japanese arrangements are perfect for her friends low pottery vases.
8. Both girls spend hours on their hobbies.
9. Last month one of their arrangements took a prize at the county fair.
10. My sisters plan is to major in art in college.

☐EXERCISE 7

1. Last week a few of my friends and I went to see one of Ohios famous museums—the College Football Hall of Fame, not far from Cincinnati.
2. There we saw more than 500 photographs of famous players and coaches.
3. And the Time Tunnel text and pictures trace the evolution of football.
4. The Greeks game of *harpastum* is supposed to have been the beginning of football.
5. The ancient game included throwing, kicking, running with a ball, and even tackling.
6. Later, soccer and rugby were forerunners of todays game.
7. We saw Knute Rocknes statue and heard a recording of one of his famous speeches.
8. The next day we went to Ohios other football museum—the Pro Football Hall of Fame in Canton.
9. Among the prized exhibits is Joe Namaths football uniform.
10. Also we listened to a recorded account of Tom Dempseys record-breaking 63-yard field goal.

☐EXERCISE 8

1. My oldest brothers ambition is to be a mountain climber.
2. So he was delighted at our familys decision to drive to Grand Teton National Park.
3. His first days program there included a training class in the School of Mountaineering.

4. A beginners training includes learning safety precautions and proper climbing techniques.
5. My brothers excitement was unbounded as he made a practice climb on a small peak.
6. Meantime the rest of the familys enjoyment was mainly in following the self-guiding trails and taking photographs.
7. Some of my dads photographs were worth framing.
8. My sisters favorite trail was the Jenny Lake Nature Trail.
9. Our weeks stay was not long enough to see all we wanted to see.
10. But my brothers longing to climb a really tall peak was satisfied.

□EXERCISE 9

1. One of Japans oldest customs is now losing favor.
2. A Japanese childs ability to eat with chopsticks was once taken for granted.
3. Now almost half the elementary school children in Japan have failed to learn one of Japans most distinctive customs.
4. A child used to be taught to use chopsticks at home, but now the parents preference is often for knives and forks.
5. Many of the countrys artistic customs are disappearing.
6. Peoples dress has been westernized.
7. Both womens and mens clothes follow Western trends, and the kimono is less often seen.
8. Childrens clothes are almost always Western.
9. Womens taste in decorating their houses is straying from the artistic Japanese style.
10. Even Japans beautiful tea ceremony is no longer a daily occurrence.

□EXERCISE 10

1. I've been reading about the worlds coldest, hottest, and wettest places.
2. The worlds coldest recorded temperature was −128.6°F in Vostok, Antarctica, on July 3, 1983.
3. The record low in the U.S. was −80°F at Prospect Creek, Alaska, on January 23, 1971.
4. The worlds highest temperature was 136°F in el Azizia, Libya, in 1922.
5. Death Valley, California, had 43 consecutive days of 120° heat in 1917.
6. Our countrys greatest 24-hour snowfall was 76 inches in 1921 in Silver Lake, Colorado.
7. This countrys largest hailstone fell in Potter, Nebraska, in 1928, and measured 5.41 inches in diameter according to official records.
8. Mt. Waialeale in Kauai, Hawaii, boasts the worlds greatest annual precipitation with up to 350 rainy days a year.

9. In 1934 the worlds highest surface wind speed was 231 miles per hour on Mt. Washington, New Hampshire.
10. But no other countrys record will probably ever come up to that of Iquique, Chile, which had no rain for 14 years.

JOURNAL WRITING

In your journal write some sentences using the possessive forms of the names of the members of your family or the names of your friends.

WRITING ASSIGNMENT

As you continue with the exercises, continue also with the writing assignments in the latter part of the book.

Review of Contractions and Possessives

Add the necessary apostrophes. Try to get these exercises perfect. Don't excuse an error by saying, "Oh, that was just a careless mistake." A mistake is a mistake. Be tough on yourself!

☐EXERCISE 1

1. There'll be more snow tonight, I'm afraid.
2. Loren's car doesn't have snow tires, and he's going to need them.
3. He'd better buy some, or he'll be in trouble on those hills.
4. I'm glad we aren't going with him.
5. We're staying at home this weekend for a change.
6. Tonight we'll go to the program put on by the Women's Club.
7. Tomorrow we'll work on our hobbies, and the children will watch their favorite TV program.
8. It's "Mr. Rogers' Neighborhood," which is one of the best children's programs.
9. It's good especially for children who get too much criticism.
10. Its theme is that everyone is an important person.
11. Mr. Rogers' message is that each person is acceptable and unique.
12. It's a psychiatric theory thats good for adults too.

☐EXERCISE 2

There's a little lake with steep rocky sides and crystal clear water that you can see down into forever. Some say it's bottomless, but everyone agrees it's deep.

There's one spot where a big tree grows over the lake, and someone's tied a rope to one of its branches to swing on. It's a great sensation, I discovered, to swing out over the water and then let go. I think everyone gets an urge to yell as loud as possible to enhance an awkward dive. It's a great feeling to cast off from the high rocks holding onto the rope as it swings out over the water. Just before the farthest point of the rope's travel is the best place to let go and drop into the water. Those with initiative try flips and twists as they dive, but however it's done, it's a great sensation. Some say it's for kids, but I hope I never grow too old to have fun at it.

Proofreading Exercise

Can you correct the 12 errors? No answers are provided at the back of the book for this exercise.

THOSE WADDLING PENGUINS

I like watching penguins in zoos. They look a bit like humans as they waddle along on two feet. Ive always hoped Id someday get to a seashore and see a colony of them, but now I no thats unlikely because penguins live only in frigid regions in the Southern Hemisphere. But millions of them are there. On an island colony in the South Atlantic their are between 14 and 21 million penguins.

A penguins feathers are designed for life in cold water. They are small and stiff, almost like scales, overlapping tightly so they cant be ruffled by wind or wave. The feathers our more dense then those of any other bird, and an undercoat of woolly down about a inch thick traps body warmth.

Parents share parental duties. The female emperor penguin lays her one egg and shoves it across the ice to her mate for incubation while she heads out to sea to hunt food. The male balances the egg on top of his feet and keeps it warm with his belly fat. During the long dark winter the male penguins huddle together to stay warm in temperatures that can drop below −70 degrees F. Without food the males have to live on there fat reserves for two months until the eggs hatch and their mates return to feed the chicks. Only than can the males head out to sea for food.

Source: *International Wildlife,* Mar. Apr. 1991

WORDS THAT CAN BE BROKEN INTO PARTS

Breaking words into their parts will often help you spell them correctly. Each of the following words is made up of two shorter words. Note that the word then contains all the letters of the two shorter words.

book keeper	. . . bookkeeper	room mate	. . . roommate
over run	. . . overrun	tail light	. . . taillight
over rate	. . . overrate	with hold	. . . withhold

Becoming aware of prefixes such as *dis, inter, mis,* and *un* is also helpful. Then when you add a prefix to a word, the spelling will be correct.

dis appear	disappear	mis informed	misinformed
dis appoint	disappoint	mis spell	misspell
dis approve	disapprove	mis step	misstep
dis satisfied	dissatisfied	un aware	unaware
dis service	disservice	un natural	unnatural
inter act	interact	un necessary	unnecessary
inter racial	interracial	un nerve	unnerve
inter related	interrelated	un noticed	unnoticed

Note that no letters are dropped, either from the prefix or from the word.

Have someone dictate the above list for you to write and then mark any words you miss. Memorize the correct spellings by noting how each word is made up of a prefix and a word.

RULE FOR DOUBLING A FINAL CONSONANT

Most spelling rules have so many exceptions that they aren't much help. But here's one that has almost no exceptions and is really worth learning.

Double a final consonant when adding an ending that begins with a vowel (such as *ing, ed, er*) if all three of the following are true:

1. **the word ends in a single consonant,**
2. **which is preceded by a single vowel (the vowels are *a, e, i, o, u*),**
3. **and the accent is on the last syllable (or the word has only one syllable).**

We'll try the rule on the following words to which we'll add *ing, ed,* or *er*.

begin   1. It ends in a single consonant—*n*,
        2. preceded by a single vowel—*i*,
        3. and the accent is on the last syllable—*be gin'*.
        Therefore we double the final consonant and write *beginning, beginner*.

stop   1. It ends in a single consonant—*p*,
        2. preceded by a single vowel—*o*,
        3. and the accent is on the last syllable (there is only one).
        Therefore we double the final consonant and write *stopping, stopped, stopper*.

motor   1. It ends in a single consonant—*r*,
        2. preceded by a single vowel—*o*,
        3. but the accent isn't on the last syllable. It's on the first—*mo'tor*.
        Therefore we don't double the final consonant. We write *motoring, motored*.

sleep   1. It ends in a single consonant—*p*,
        2. but it isn't preceded by a single vowel. There are two *e*'s.
        Therefore we don't double the final consonant. We write *sleeping, sleeper*.

Note that *qu* is treated as a consonant because *q* is almost never written without *u*. Think of it as *kw*. In words like *equip* and *quit*, the *qu* acts as a consonant. Therefore *quit* does end in a single consonant preceded by a single vowel, and the final consonant is doubled—*quitting*.

Also note that *bus* may be written either *bussing* or *busing*. The latter, contrary to our rule, is more common.

EXERCISES

Add *ing* to these words. Correct each group of 10 before continuing so you'll catch any errors while you still have words to practice on.

☐EXERCISE 1

1. put
2. control
3. admit
4. mop
5. plan

6. hop
7. jump
8. knit
9. mark
10. creep

☐EXERCISE 2

1. return
2. swim
3. sing
4. benefit
5. loaf

6. nail
7. omit
8. occur
9. shop
10. interrupt

☐EXERCISE 3

1. begin
2. spell
3. prefer
4. interpret
5. hunt

6. excel
7. wrap
8. stop
9. wed
10. scream

☐EXERCISE 4

1. feel
2. murmur
3. turn
4. weed
5. subtract

6. stream
7. expel
8. miss
9. get
10. stab

☐EXERCISE 5

1. forget
2. misspell
3. fit
4. plant
5. pin

6. trust
7. sip
8. flop
9. reap
10. fight

Progress Test

This test covers everything you've studied so far. One sentence in each pair is correct. The other is incorrect. Read both sentences carefully before you decide. Then write the letter of the correct sentence in the blank.

_____ 1. A. It dosen't matter whether he phones me or not.
        B. His opinion won't have any effect on my decision.

_____ 2. A. I'm planning a week's vacation in the spring.
        B. The hostess past the piece of pie to me.

_____ 3. A. It's regretable that our team lost.
        B. The seal was flopping about in the water.

_____ 4. A. The Larson's apartment is too small for such a crowd.
        B. My father's job is his principal interest.

_____ 5. A. I omitted the fourth question on my test.
        B. Of coarse I know what you're intending to do.

_____ 6. A. His work sounds more interesting than yours.
        B. I'm quiet sure I'm right about that problem.

_____ 7. A. I've all ready learned quite a bit in this course.
        B. An honest opinion is all I'm asking for.

_____ 8. A. You should of seen all the new clothes she bought.
        B. Diana's conscience won't let her cheat.

_____ 9. A. It's quite an honor to be invited.
        B. I hear the womens' athletic club is looking for new members.

_____ 10. A. Its a good idea to cut out desserts if you want to lose weight.
        B. The Kellys have invited us over for the evening.

_____ 11. A. She's the most studious person I've ever known.
        B. My puppy flunked it's obedience test.

_____ 12. A. Your going to be quite cold in those clothes.
        B. This weather is too cold to suit me.

_____ 13. A. Who's car is that in the Jacobsons' driveway?
        B. Won't he be through with his new job soon?

_____ 14. A. I don't intend to lose my temper.
        B. Elizabeths' report was excellent.

_____ 15. A. When he was captain, he lead the team to victory.
        B. My instructor's advice was good.

A LIST OF FREQUENTLY MISSPELLED WORDS

Have someone dictate this list of commonly misspelled words to you and mark the ones you miss. Then memorize the correct spellings.

Pronounce these words correctly, and you won't misspell them: *athlete, athletics, nuclear*. And be sure to pronounce every syllable in these words: *environment, government, mathematics, probably, studying*. Also try to think up memory devices to help you remember correct spellings. For example, you *labor* in a *laboratory*; the two *l*'s in *parallel* are parallel; and the *r* separates the two *a*'s in *separate*.

1. absence	33. disastrous	65. humorous
2. across	34. discipline	66. immediately
3. actually	35. discussed	67. independent
4. a lot	36. disease	68. intelligence
5. amateur	37. divide	69. interest
6. among	38. dying	70. interfere
7. analyze	39. eighth	71. involved
8. appearance	40. eligible	72. knowledge
9. appreciate	41. eliminate	73. laboratory
10. argument	42. embarrassed	74. leisure
11. athlete	43. environment	75. length
12. athletics	44. especially	76. library
13. awkward	45. etc. (et cetera)	77. likely
14. becoming	46. exaggerate	78. lying
15. beginning	47. excellent	79. marriage
16. belief	48. exercise	80. mathematics
17. benefit	49. existence	81. meant
18. buried	50. experience	82. medicine
19. business	51. explanation	83. neither
20. certain	52. extremely	84. ninety
21. college	53. familiar	85. ninth
22. coming	54. February	86. nuclear
23. committee	55. finally	87. occasionally
24. competition	56. foreign	88. opinion
25. complete	57. government	89. opportunity
26. consider	58. grammar	90. parallel
27. criticism	59. grateful	91. particular
28. definitely	60. guarantee	92. persuade
29. dependent	61. guard	93. physically
30. develop	62. guidance	94. planned
31. development	63. height	95. pleasant
32. difference	64. hoping	96. possible

97. practical
98. preferred
99. prejudice
100. privilege
101. probably
102. professor
103. prove
104. psychology
105. pursue
106. receipt
107. receive
108. recommend
109. reference
110. relieve
111. religious
112. repetition
113. rhythm
114. ridiculous
115. sacrifice
116. safety
117. scene
118. schedule
119. secretary
120. senior
121. sense
122. separate
123. severely
124. shining
125. significant
126. similar
127. sincerely
128. sophomore
129. speech
130. straight
131. studying
132. succeed
133. success
134. suggest
135. surprise
136. thoroughly
137. though
138. tragedy
139. tried
140. tries
141. truly
142. unfortunately
143. unnecessary
144. until
145. unusual
146. using
147. usually
148. Wednesday
149. writing
150. written

USING YOUR DICTIONARY

By working through the following 13 exercises, you'll become familiar with what you can find in an up-to-date desk dictionary.

1. PRONUNCIATION

Look up the word *irreparable* and copy the pronunciation in this space.

Now under each letter with a pronunciation mark over it, write the key word having the same mark. You'll find the key words at the bottom of one of the two dictionary pages open before you. Note especially that the upside-down *e* (ə) always has the sound of *uh* like the *a* in *ago* or *about*. Remember that sound because it's found in many words.

Next, pronounce the key words you have written, and then slowly pronounce *irreparable*, giving each syllable the same sound as its key word.

Finally note which syllable has the heavy accent mark. (In most dictionaries the accent mark points to the stressed syllable, but in one dictionary it is in front of the stressed syllable.) The stressed syllable is *rep*. Now say the word, letting the full force of your voice fall on that syllable.

When more than one pronunciation is given, the first is more common. If the complete pronunciation of a word isn't given, look at the word above it to find the pronunciation.

Look up the pronunciation of these words, using the key words at the bottom of the dictionary page to help you pronounce each syllable. Then note which syllable has the heavy accent mark, and say the word aloud.

neophyte   indefatigable   indictment   cowardice

2. DEFINITIONS

The dictionary may give more than one meaning for a word. Read all the meanings for each italicized word and then write a definition appropriate to the sentence.

1. His book was published *posthumously*. _____

_____

2. He spent more time on his *avocation* than on his job. _____

_____

3. She had always felt an *antipathy* toward cats. _____

_____

4. You'd have to be pretty *credulous* to believe that story. _____

_____

5. The drizzle turned into a *veritable* downpour. _____

_____

3. SPELLING

By making yourself look up each word you aren't sure how to spell, you'll soon become a better speller. When two spellings are given in the dictionary, the first one (or the one with the definition) is the more common.

Underline the more common spelling of each of these words.

theater, theatre   travelog, travelogue
plough, plow   donut, doughnut

4. COMPOUND WORDS

If you want to find out whether two words are written separately, written with a hyphen between them, or written as one word, consult your dictionary. For example:

half sister	is written as two words
brother-in-law	is hyphenated
stepson	is written as one word

Write each of the following correctly.

teddy bear _____   counter clockwise _____

dining room _____   out moded _____

self conscious _____   non cooperative _____

5. CAPITALIZATION

If a word is capitalized in the dictionary, that means it should always be capitalized. If it isn't capitalized in the dictionary, then it may or may not be capitalized, depending on how it's used (see p. 194). For example:

Latino is always capitalized

college is capitalized or not, according to how it's used
　　　　She's attending college.
　　　　She's attending Pasadena City College.

Write these words as they are given in the dictionary (with or without a capital) to show whether they must *always* be capitalized or not.

Government _____   Mother _____

God _____   English _____

Dragonfly _____   Republican _____

6. USAGE

Just because a word is in the dictionary is no indication that it's in standard use. The following labels indicate whether a word is used today and, if so, where and by whom.

obsolete	now gone out of use
archaic	not now used in ordinary language but retained in some biblical, literary, and legal expressions
colloquial informal	used in informal conversation but not in formal writing
dialectal regional	used in some localities but not everywhere
slang	popular but nonstandard expression
nonstandard substandard	not used by educated people

Look up each italicized word and write the label indicating its usage. Dictionaries differ. One may list a word as slang whereas another will call it colloquial. Still another may give no designation, thus indicating that particular dictionary considers the word in standard use.

1. She brought home a *poke* of potatoes from the grocery store. _____

2. She'll *beef* about any plans we make. _____

3. I'm going *irregardless* of the cost. _____

4. He's a *whiz* at math. _____

5. She likes *boughten* dresses best. _____

6. I got the *brush-off* from the boss. _____

7. He's always *goofing off*. _____

8. She *hath* no faults who *hath* the art to hide them. _____

7. DERIVATIONS

The derivations or stories behind words will often help you remember the current meanings. For example, if you heard that a doctor had given a patient a placebo and you consulted your dictionary, you would find that *placebo* originally was a Latin word meaning "I shall please." Knowing the derivation is a help in remembering the present-day definition—"a harmless, unmedicated substance given merely to please the patient."

Look up the derivation of each of these words. You'll find it in square brackets either just before or just after the definition.

gymnasium _____

circus _____

dandelion _____

pandemic _____

July _____

8. SYNONYMS

Sometimes at the end of a definition, a group of synonyms is given. For example, at the end of the definition of *beautiful*, you'll find several synonyms. And if you look up *handsome* or *pretty*, you'll be referred to the synonyms under *beautiful*.

List the synonyms for the italicized words.

1. The *old* mansion is being turned into a boys' club. _____

_____

2. His actions *puzzle* me. _____

_____

3. Her *anger* was gradually building. _____

_____

9. ABBREVIATIONS

Find the meaning of the following abbreviations.

mm _____ e.g. _____

i.e. _____ RCMP _____

10. NAMES OF PEOPLE

The names of famous people will be found either in the main part of your dictionary or in a separate Biographical Names section at the back.

Identify the following.

Paul Gauguin _____

Kamehameha I _____

Jacob Grimm _____

Luther Burbank _____

11. NAMES OF PLACES

The names of places will be found either in the main part of your dictionary or in a separate Geographical Names section at the back.

Identify the following.

Mackinac Island _____

James Bay _____

Petrified Forest _____

Kilauea _____

12. FOREIGN WORDS AND PHRASES

Give the language and the meaning of the italicized expressions.

1. I got tired of his saying *Gesundheit* each time I sneezed. _____

   _____

2. We learned about the new ruling only after it was already a *fait accompli*.

   _____

3. I had a feeling of *déjà vu* when I read her poem. _____

4. They were acting *in loco parentis*. _____

13. MISCELLANEOUS INFORMATION

Find these miscellaneous bits of information in your dictionary.

1. How long is the Mississippi River? _____

2. How many pounds are in a kilogram? _____

3. What is the meaning of the British term *gaol*? _____

4. What is the plural of son-in-law? _____

5. What is the capital of Alaska? _____

6. When did Mahatma Gandhi die? _____

7. What is the population of Tacoma, Washington? _____

8. What is another name for Ursa Minor? _____

9. What are the names of the Great Lakes? _____

   _____

10. What is Parkinson's Law? _____

   _____

Sentence Structure

2

2 Sentence Structure

Among the most common errors in writing are fragments and run-together sentences. Here are some fragments:

Having given the best years of his life to his farm
Although we had food enough for only one day
The most that I possibly could do

They don't make complete statements. They leave the reader wanting something more.

Here are some run-together sentences:

The snow was packed the skiing was great.
We missed Kathy she was too busy to come.
We'll go again next Friday maybe she can come then.

Unlike fragments, they make complete statements, but the trouble is they make *two* complete statements, which shouldn't be run together into one sentence without correct punctuation. The reader has to go back to see where there should have been a pause.

Both fragments and run-together sentences bother the reader. Not until you get rid of them will your writing be clear and easy to read. Unfortunately there is no quick, easy way to learn to avoid them. You have to learn a little about sentence structure—mainly how to find the subject and the verb in a sentence so that you can tell whether it really is a sentence.

FINDING SUBJECTS AND VERBS

When you write a sentence, you write about *something* or *someone*. That's the subject. Then you write what the subject *does* or *is*. That's the verb.

<u>Birds</u> <u><u>fly</u></u>.

The word *Birds* is the something you are writing about. It's the subject, and we'll underline it once. *Fly* tells what the subject does. It shows the action in the sentence. It's the verb, and we'll underline it twice. Because the verb often shows action, it's easier to spot than the subject. Therefore always look for it first. For example, in the sentence

Paul drives to the campus every day.

which word shows the action? Drives. It's the verb. Underline it twice. Now ask yourself who or what drives. Paul. It's the subject. Underline it once.

Study the following sentences until you understand how to pick out subjects and verbs.

Last night hail dented the top of my car. (Which word shows the action? Dented. It's the verb. Underline it twice. Who or what dented? Hail. It's the subject. Underline it once.)

Yesterday Kent jogged five kilometers. (Which word shows the action? Jogged. Who or what jogged? Kent.)

This year my sister works at Hardee's. (Which word shows the action? Works. Who or what works? Sister.)

Often the verb doesn't show action but merely tells what the subject *is* or *was*. Learn to spot such verbs as *is, are, was, were, seems, appears*.

Joe is my friend. (First spot the verb <u><u>is</u></u>. Then ask who or what is. <u>Joe</u> <u><u>is</u></u>.)

That guy in the red shirt is our team captain. (First spot the verb <u>is</u>. Then ask who or what is. <u>Guy</u> <u><u>is</u></u>.)

Shannon seems happy these days. (First spot the verb <u><u>seems</u></u>. Then ask who or what seems. <u>Shannon</u> <u><u>seems</u></u>.)

He appears tired. (First spot the verb <u><u>appears</u></u>. Then ask who or what appears. <u>He</u> <u><u>appears</u></u>.)

Sometimes the subject comes after the verb.

In the middle of the street stood the lost puppy. (Who or what stood? <u>Puppy</u> <u>stood</u>.)

Where is the meeting? (Who or what is? <u>Meeting</u> <u>is</u>.)

There was a big crowd at the game. (Who or what was? <u>Crowd</u> <u><u>was</u></u>.)

There were not enough seats for everyone. (Who or what were? <u>Seats</u> <u>were</u>.)

Here are your skates. (Who or what are? <u>Skates</u> <u><u>are</u></u>.)

Note that *there* and *here* (as in the last three sentences) are never subjects. They simply point out something.

In commands, the subject often is not expressed. It is *you* (understood).

Keep calm. (<u>You</u> <u><u>keep</u></u> calm.)

Shut the door. (<u>You</u> <u><u>shut</u></u> the door.)

As you pick out subjects in the following exercises, you may wonder whether, for example, you should say the subject is *dunes* or *sand dunes*. It makes no difference so long as you get the main subject, *dunes*, right. In the answers at the back of the book, usually—but not always—the single word is used. Don't waste your time worrying about whether to include an extra word with the subject. Just make sure you get the main subject right.

EXERCISES

Underline the subject once and the verb twice. Find the verb first, and then ask **Who** or **What**. When you've finished 10 sentences, compare your answers carefully with those at the back of the book.

☐EXERCISE 1

1. During spring vacation I visited the Indiana Dunes State Park.
2. That trip was a great experience.

3. The sand dunes shift constantly.
4. Beyond the dunes is the lake.
5. I watched the white froths of foam on the slate and silver water.
6. I walked along the smooth beach for miles.
7. Far out I saw a boat with vacationers.
8. Their voices broke the silence.
9. At night the dunes are spectacular in the moonlight.
10. And the stars seem quite close.

☐EXERCISE 2

1. The invisible "black holes" in space were once huge stars.
2. A "black hole" is simply the remnant of a collapsed star.
3. The star's gravity crushed it to the size of a golf ball.
4. Then gravity crushed it further to "nothing."
5. Thus it "disappeared."
6. It became a "black hole."
7. Our sun is five billion (5,000,000,000) years old.
8. It is ten billion light-years to the farthest quasar.
9. There are one hundred billion galaxies in the universe.
10. Try to imagine such numbers.

☐EXERCISE 3

1. The names of the days of the week have interesting origins.
2. Monday is the moon's day.
3. Tuesday is the day of Tiu, the Anglo-Saxon god of war.
4. Wednesday is the day of Woden, chief god in Germanic mythology.
5. Thursday is the day of Thor, god of thunder in Scandinavian myths.
6. Friday is the day of Frigga, wife of Woden and goddess of love.
7. Saturn gave his name to Saturday.
8. The sun's day is Sunday.
9. Most people say these names without thinking of their origins.
10. Think sometimes of their early meanings.

☐EXERCISE 4

1. Last summer my brother and I went to the Calgary Stampede.
2. There is limited parking space at the Stampede grounds.
3. But buses from all over the city bring people there.
4. The chuck wagon races are the most exciting part of the Stampede.
5. Two outriders are necessary for each chuck wagon.
6. At the starting sign, the outriders toss the camp stove on the wagon.
7. Then they jump aboard.
8. And the wagon starts at a frightening speed.
9. Sometimes there are serious accidents.
10. It is a dangerous but exciting sport.

☐EXERCISE 5

1. Litter is everywhere.
2. Even the world's highest mountain has rubbish.
3. Mount Everest base camp at 17,000 feet is full of litter.
4. Climbers leave debris of all sorts.
5. They leave pots, plates, plastic bags, cooking gas, and oxygen bottles.
6. They even leave tents.
7. Now Nepal hopes to end the problem.
8. A new rule requires 10 extra porters on each expedition.
9. Their job is to haul away the litter.
10. Thus each expedition now plans to leave the world's highest mountain clean and beautiful.

☐EXERCISE 6

1. Scientists wanted to study the emperor penguin.
2. It is the largest of all penguins.
3. But Antarctica is a cold place to study it.
4. And the scientists wanted to study it for months.
5. So they brought some penguin eggs to San Diego.
6. They finally succeeded in hatching an emperor penguin chick.
7. A large stuffed Snoopy dog became the young chick's "mother."
8. In the wild, emperor penguin chicks nestle on the feet of their mother.
9. So the newly hatched chick nestled on the feet of the Snoopy dog.
10. Now scientists have an emperor penguin for long-term study.

☐EXERCISE 7

1. On summer evenings nighthawks swoop through the air.
2. They become active just before dark.
3. Watch for them.
4. The nighthawk emits a nasal "Peent" cry.
5. It has a large froglike mouth from ear to ear.
6. During flight the nighthawk opens its mouth.
7. It catches insects in its open mouth.
8. In cities the nighthawks nest on flat-topped buildings.
9. They sit lengthwise on limbs but diagonally on wires.
10. Listen for nighthawks sometime just before dusk.

☐EXERCISE 8

1. Dog sleds are no longer the principal means of transportation in the North.
2. But sled-dog racing is increasingly popular.
3. From New Hampshire to Alaska, sled-dog races are annual events.
4. Sled-dog racers call themselves "mushers."

5. Their Alaskan husky dogs, weighing 45 to 50 pounds, have astonishing power.
6. They love to run and to pull sleds over miles of snow.
7. Many dogs run 20 miles per hour.
8. At night they stay outdoors in temperatures of $-50°$ F.
9. Day by day the mushers prepare their dogs for the All-Alaska Sweepstakes.
10. It is a grueling 408-mile round-trip out of Nome.

☐EXERCISE 9

1. The U.S. presidential libraries contain valuable historical materials.
2. The exhibits include historic documents and possessions of the presidents.
3. The Carter Presidential Center in Atlanta and the Richard Nixon Library in Yorba Linda, California, are among the most recent.
4. Gerald Ford is the only president with two libraries.
5. One is on the University of Michigan campus at Ann Arbor.
6. The other is in Grand Rapids, Ford's hometown.
7. The latter offers a 20-minute film on Ford's life.
8. The John F. Kennedy Library overlooks the Boston Harbor.
9. It draws the biggest crowds of all the libraries.
10. In 1980 half a million people visited it.

☐EXERCISE 10

1. The Lyndon B. Johnson Library in Austin, Texas, has 36 million pages of documents.
2. The Harry S Truman Library in Independence, Missouri, contains Truman's White House piano.
3. The Dwight D. Eisenhower Center in Abilene, Kansas, illustrates Ike's military and political years.
4. Eisenhower's boyhood home is on the grounds of the center.
5. The Herbert Hoover Library in West Branch, Iowa, is the least visited of all the libraries.
6. The reason is its remoteness from major population centers.
7. The Franklin D. Roosevelt Library in Hyde Park, New York, celebrated the 100th anniversary of FDR's birth in 1982.
8. Five former presidents attended the opening of the Ronald Reagan Presidential Library in the hills near Los Angeles in November 1991.
9. It is the most recent of all the presidential libraries.
10. Visit one of these libraries sometime.

WRITING ASSIGNMENT

As you continue the exercises, you are expected to continue the writing assignments from the latter part of the book.

Proofreading Exercise

In this paragraph are errors from all the material you've studied. Can you correct the four errors before checking with the answers at the back of the book? The errors are in the first five lines.

SUGAR RAY LEONARD

People find it hard to believe that Sugar Ray Leonard, the boxing champion, grew up in poverty. They think that anyone who speaks as well as he does must of come from at least a middle-class home. But Leonards parents were poor. He was one of seven children and didnt go beyond high school. He was eager to succeed, however, and his ambition lead him to work on language skills. "I used to practice reading from a magazine before a mirror," he says, "so I could learn good grammar and enunciation and get out of the slang of the streets—from the *dis* and *dats* and *Wha's happenin, man*. I knew if I was going to be more than just a fighter, I'd have to learn the language."

SUBJECTS NOT IN PREPOSITIONAL PHRASES

A prepositional phrase is simply a preposition and the name of someone or something. (See the examples in the columns below.) We don't use many grammatical terms in this book, and the only reason we're mentioning prepositional phrases is to get them out of the way. They're a bother in analyzing sentences. For example, you might have difficulty finding the subject and verb in a long sentence like this:

> During the first week of his vacation, one of the fellows drove to the North Woods in his new car.

But if you cross out all the prepositional phrases like this:

> ~~During the first week of his vacation~~, one ~~of the fellows~~ drove ~~to the North Woods in his new car~~.

then you have only two words left—the subject and the verb. Even in short sentences like the following, you might pick the wrong word as the subject if you didn't cross out the prepositional phrases first.

> One ~~of my friends~~ lives ~~in Phoenix~~.
> Most ~~of the team~~ went ~~on the trip~~.

The subject is never in a prepositional phrase. Read this list several times to learn to recognize prepositional phrases.

about the desk	**beyond** the desk	**on** the desk
above the desk	**by** the desk	**outside** the desk
across the desk	**down** the street	**over** the desk
after vacation	**during** vacation	**past** the desk
against the desk	**except** the desk	**since** vacation
along the street	**for** the desk	**through** the desk
among the desks	**from** the desk	**to** the desk
around the desk	**in** the desk	**toward** the desk
at the desk	**inside** the desk	**under** the desk
before vacation	**into** the desk	**until** vacation
behind the desk	**like** the desk	**up** the street
below the desk	**near** the desk	**upon** the desk
beneath the desk	**of** the desk	**with** the desk
beside the desk	**off** the desk	**within** the desk

besides

NOTE: Don't mistake *to* and a verb for a prepositional phrase. For example, *to run* is not a prepositional phrase because *run* is not the name of something. It's a verb.

EXERCISES

Cross out the prepositional phrases. Then underline the subject once and the verb twice. Correct each group of 10 sentences before going on.

☐EXERCISE 1

1. One of the most interesting places on our trip was the Japanese garden in the East-West Center in Honolulu.
2. We followed a bamboo-shaded path through the garden.
3. Clumps of ferns bordered the path.
4. Near the path flowed a little stream.
5. In small pools beside the stream were orange and black and white tropical fish.
6. Here and there were Japanese stone lanterns.
7. At the top of the garden was a small waterfall.
8. Stone slab steps beside the waterfall led to a Japanese teahouse.
9. An atmosphere of peace enveloped the garden.
10. Some of the best things in life are still free.

☐EXERCISE 2

1. The living room in my apartment was dull and uninteresting.
2. It contained plenty of ordinary furniture but nothing exciting.
3. Not a single piece of furniture was worth a second look.
4. I had to do something about it.
5. I didn't have a lot of money to spend however.
6. Therefore from a nearby greenhouse I bought a large potted palm.
7. I set that palm carefully in one corner of the living room.
8. Then I walked across the room to see the effect.
9. Amazing! That one palm gave the entire room a tropical atmosphere.
10. And I've enjoyed my living room ever since.

☐EXERCISE 3

1. The largest island in the world is Greenland.
2. New Guinea in the Pacific is the second largest.
3. Both of these islands contain unexplored regions.
4. The interior of Greenland is under an ice cap.
5. In New Guinea a rugged interior discourages travel.
6. Some of the primitive people in New Guinea still use stone tools.
7. Their small thatched houses often stand on poles above the swampy ground.
8. Villages sometimes communicate by the beat of drums.
9. Many of the people have little knowledge of our civilization.
10. Some of the tribes never go outside their own valleys.

☐EXERCISE 4

1. One of the greatest magicians of all time was Houdini.
2. After his birth in Budapest in 1874, his family moved to New York City.
3. From the age of 14, he practiced magic tricks.
4. At 17 he became a professional magician.
5. One of his tricks was his Metamorphosis Trick.
6. The meaning of *metamorphosis* is "change."
7. In this trick he escaped, with his hands bound, from a locked trunk.
8. Then Houdini's brother, with hands also bound, appeared in the trunk.
9. On another occasion 40,000 people watched Houdini's daring hand-cuffed jump from a Pittsburgh bridge.
10. In about three minutes he freed himself under water.

☐EXERCISE 5

1. The 49th state is one of the most scenic places in the United States.
2. At the beginning of last summer I flew to Anchorage in Alaska.
3. From there I took a number of backpacking trips.
4. Alaska has 8,000 miles of scenic highways.
5. Within its vastness, everything is big.
6. For example, the Malaspina Glacier is 1,700 square miles in area.
7. One of the longest navigable rivers in the world is the Yukon.
8. The 20,320-foot Mount McKinley is the tallest peak in North America.
9. Mount McKinley is in Denali National Park.
10. Snow perpetually covers the upper two-thirds of the mountain.

☐EXERCISE 6

1. Tobogganing over hard-packed snow is an exciting sport.
2. The Indians were the first to use toboggans.
3. They probably transported things on them.
4. A modern toboggan carries as many as 12 people.
5. A steersman in the rear trails a foot in the snow to guide the toboggan.
6. In the Far North snowshoeing is popular.
7. Snowshoes for traveling in the woods are only two feet long.
8. But Alaskan snowshoes for racing are seven feet long.
9. The first to use snowshoes were the Indians.
10. They probably tied branches of a fir tree to their feet.

Underline the subject once and the verb twice. If you aren't sure, cross out the prepositional phrases first.

☐EXERCISE 7

1. The longest paved road in any single country in the world is the Trans-Canada Highway.
2. Canada completed the highway in 1962.
3. About 4,860 miles long, it goes from the Pacific to the Atlantic.
4. At its beginning in Victoria, British Columbia, is a monument.
5. Through vast forests, over rugged terrain, along lakes, across wide plains, and past capital cities, the highway spans the country.
6. With some 500 bridges and a few automobile ferries, the road crosses rivers and straits.
7. Along the highway about every 50 miles are parks for resting or picnicking.
8. About every 100 to 150 miles are parks for camping.
9. Near the highway are a number of national parks.
10. At the maritime city of St. John's in New Brunswick, the highway comes to its end.

☐EXERCISE 8

1. I just read an article about Alan Shepard, the first man to fly in space.
2. That day in 1961 the weather was bad.
3. Shepard waited more than three hours in his tiny Mercury capsule.
4. Then finally at 9:34 A.M. the weather improved.
5. And his Redstone rocket roared to life.
6. He hurtled skyward on the first leg of America's greatest adventure.
7. The enormous dangers in space flight bothered Shepard not at all.
8. He looked down at the Florida coast a hundred miles below.
9. Then he reached a top speed of over 5,000 miles an hour.
10. His 15-minute flight was the beginning of America's adventures into space.

☐EXERCISE 9

1. It's interesting to discover the origin of words.
2. For example your pet *terrier* got its name from the French word for earth [TERRE earth].
3. A terrier digs in the earth to find small animals in burrows.
4. *Companion* comes from the Latin roots [COM with + PANIS bread].
5. A companion shares bread with you.
6. *Preposterous* from the Latin roots [PRE before + POST after] means having the after part before as a horse with its tail in front.
7. Such a horse is preposterous or absurd.

8. In starting a new project we often use the expression "start from scratch."
9. During the early Olympic Games a leader always scratched a line in the sand for the runners to start from.
10. Thus they started from scratch.

□EXERCISE 10

1. An organization, "The Telephone Pioneers of America," includes telephone employees and retirees.
2. One of its purposes is to help physically disabled people.
3. The organization, for example, wants blind children to be able to play softball.
4. The members outfit softballs and bases with sound devices.
5. The sound devices enable blind children to make real home runs and to play a real game.
6. Also the organization invented the "Hot Tryke" for lame children.
7. The children use the strength in their arms to propel the Trykes forward.
8. Another organization, "The Paralyzed Veterans of America," helps people in wheelchairs to get jobs and to buy cars with special equipment for them.
9. It also co-sponsors the National Veterans Wheelchair Games.
10. Many disabled Americans, through the help of these organizations, find increased satisfaction and pleasure in their lives.

MORE ABOUT VERBS AND SUBJECTS

Sometimes the verb is more than one word. Here are a few of the many forms of the verb *drive*:

I drive	I will be driving	I may drive
I am driving	I will have been driving	I could drive
I have driven	I will have driven	I might drive
I have been driving	I am driven	I should drive
I drove	I was driven	I would drive
I was driving	I have been driven	I must drive
I had driven	I had been driven	I could have driven
I had been driving	I will be driven	I might have driven
I will drive	I can drive	I should have driven

Note that words like the following are never part of the verb even though they may be in the middle of the verb:

already	even	never	only
also	ever	not	really
always	finally	now	sometimes
before	just	often	usually

Heather had never driven a car before. She had always taken the bus.

Two verb forms—*driving* and *to drive*—look like verbs, but neither can ever be the verb of a sentence. No *ing* word by itself can ever be the verb of a sentence; it must have a helping verb in front of it.

Lester driving his new car (not a sentence because there is no proper verb)
Lester was driving his new car. (a sentence)

And no verb with *to* in front of it can ever be the verb of a sentence.

To drive mountain roads (not a sentence because there is no proper verb and no subject)
I like to drive mountain roads. (a sentence)

These two forms, *driving,* and *to drive,* may be used as subjects, or they may have other uses in the sentence.

<u>Driving</u> <u><u>is</u></u> expensive. <u>To drive</u> <u><u>is</u></u> expensive. <u>I</u> <u><u>like</u></u> to drive.

But neither of them can ever be the verb of a sentence.

Not only may a verb be composed of more than one word, but also there may be more than one verb in a sentence:

<u>Pablo</u> <u><u>read</u></u> the text and <u><u>did</u></u> the exercises.

Also there may be more than one subject.

<u>Pablo</u> and <u>Rita</u> <u><u>read</u></u> the text and <u><u>did</u></u> the exercises.

EXERCISES

Underline the subject once and the verb twice. Be sure to include all parts of the verb. Also watch for more than one subject and more than one verb. It's a good idea to cross out the prepositional phrases first.

☐EXERCISE 1

1. Yesterday I read an article about yew trees.
2. I had never even heard of yew trees before.
3. The yew tree is an evergreen tree with green needles.
4. It grows in forests along the Pacific coast from Alaska to California and also in Michigan.
5. Loggers always considered it a trash tree and threw away its bark and used its wood for fence posts.
6. Then in 1991 the medical community announced the discovery of taxol.
7. Taxol is made from the bark of hundred-year-old yew trees and cures several kinds of cancer.
8. But it takes the taxol from three of those yew trees for a single cancer cure.
9. Therefore yew trees are now in great demand.
10. And much more research about taxol is still necessary.

☐EXERCISE 2

1. Until recent years, most zoos were almost like prisons.
2. The animals were kept in wire or glass cages with nowhere to roam.

3. Today most zoos have at least some natural settings.
4. At the zoo in Phoenix, Arizona, for example, animals roam in a four-acre "African landscape."
5. The main reason for the change to more natural settings is the rapid extinction of animals in the wild.
6. Today one hundred species worldwide become extinct each year. The prospect is for one hundred species a day by the turn of the century.
7. By providing more natural surroundings, the zoos are promoting more social behavior including mating.
8. Zoos worldwide have also undertaken artificial breeding programs.
9. Eventually the number of animals in zoos should increase. Many of the animals will be turned back into the wild.
10. Visitors also enjoy the animals in their natural settings rather than in cages.

☐EXERCISE 3

1. Just for fun browse through the *Guinness Book of World Records* sometime.
2. There you will find some amazing facts.
3. The heaviest man alive in 1993 weighed 891 pounds.
4. So don't be discouraged about your weight.
5. The best-selling record of all time is "White Christmas" by Irving Berlin with sales of 170,884,207 copies by 1987.
6. The best-selling album is "Thriller" by Michael Jackson with a sale of over 47 million copies by 1993.
7. The first auto race was from Paris to Bordeaux and back in 1895 with an average speed of 15.01 miles per hour.
8. The highest speed reached for bicycle racing is 152.284 mph at Bonneville Flats, Utah.
9. The most translated poem is "If" by Rudyard Kipling.
10. It first appeared in 1910 and has since appeared in 27 languages.

☐EXERCISE 4

1. Seals spend most of their time in the water but are descended from land animals.
2. They have warm blood, breathe air, and bear living young on land.
3. A seal can close its eyes and ears in diving and can hold enough air in its lungs to stay underwater for several minutes.
4. It uses its flippers for swimming but also uses them like legs to pull itself along on the ground.
5. During the winter some seals, such as the northern fur seal, spend six or eight months in the water and never go ashore.
6. Some northern fur seals travel about 8,000 kilometers from the Bering Sea almost to Mexico and back.

7. No one knows the reason for their long winter trip.
8. In the summer seals gather in their breeding grounds or rookeries with as many as a million seals within a radius of 80 kilometers.
9. In the past seals were killed for their fur and for oil and food.
10. Now, however, conservationists have been successful in protecting them.

☐EXERCISE 5

1. Cities of the future may look different from those of today.
2. In some cities skyscrapers are going underground.
3. At the University of Minnesota, for example, the Engineering Building goes 110 feet beneath the campus with only 20 feet above ground.
4. Five floors for the labs and offices have been excavated from glacial rock and limestone.
5. Above ground is the equipment for lighting and heating.
6. One advantage of underground buildings is the conservation of energy.
7. Minnesota's climate varies during the year by about 130° F but remains about 50° F all year round below ground.
8. Most of the underground space is lighted by natural light.
9. Reflective lenses on the roof beam sunlight down to the lowest levels.
10. Occupants find the buildings light and airy.

☐EXERCISE 6

1. Lincoln was born in a crude log cabin near Hodgenville, Kentucky.
2. The cabin was chinked with clay and had only one room 18 by 16 feet with only one window and one door.
3. Today the cabin has been placed inside an impressive six-columned Grecian-style temple.
4. At 21, Lincoln moved to New Salem, Illinois, and spent six years there.
5. He worked as a rail-splitter, clerk, surveyor, and postmaster and studied law by candlelight.
6. From New Salem, Lincoln was first elected to the Illinois General Assembly.
7. Today New Salem has been reconstructed to portray that old town.
8. Visitors can ramble through homes, shops, a school, a gristmill, a sawmill, and the Rutledge Tavern.
9. The buildings have been reproduced and furnished like those of 1830.
10. Visitors can also take a trip on the Sangamon River in a steamship like the one of Lincoln's day.

☐EXERCISE 7

1. In my reading I have been learning a lot of miscellaneous facts.
2. For example, a giraffe's tongue may be as long as 1½ feet.
3. Badgers can run backward or forward equally fast.

4. In a pencil dot there are more atoms than the number of people on earth.
5. The estimated life span of Neanderthal man was 29 years.
6. The brightest star in the sky is Sirius in the constellation Canis Major.
7. There are at least 750,000 words in the English language.
8. The earliest form of perfume was incense.
9. Later the Egyptians extracted scent from flower petals and then rubbed the fragrant oil on their bodies.
10. A perfume jar in King Tutankhamen's tomb was still faintly fragrant after more than three thousand years.

☐EXERCISE 8

1. I have been reading about one of the greatest runners of all time.
2. He is Kip Keino from Kenya in Africa.
3. Kip did his practice running in the 6,000-foot elevations in the foothills of his homeland.
4. He burst into the top ranks of running in 1965 by setting 3,000- and 5,000-meter world records.
5. His thin-air training in his homeland prepared him for his first Olympic Games triumph in 1968 in Mexico City.
6. There at 7,200 feet above sea level he won the 1,500-meter gold and the 5,000-meter silver.
7. He returned to the Olympics in 1972 and won more gold in the 3,000-meter steeplechase and a silver medal in the 1,500-meter.
8. Today he still represents his nation well.
9. He and his wife have taken over one hundred children into their home.
10. For such efforts *Sports Illustrated* in 1987 called Kip Keino one of the Sportsmen of the Year.

☐EXERCISE 9

1. Shoes have had a long history.
2. In ancient times people covered their feet with bark, leaves, or animal skins and held the materials in place with thongs.
3. Sandals of papyrus leaves have been found in Egyptian tombs of 2000 B.C.
4. During the Renaissance, people of high rank wore shoes with long toes and sometimes tied the toes up to their knees with small chains.
5. The highest-ranking persons wore shoes with the longest toes.
6. Some shoes were two-and-a-half feet from heel to toe.
7. In 1324, Edward II originated shoe sizes, with a third of an inch between sizes.
8. Some Venetian ladies imitated Oriental styles and wore shoes with soles of blocks of wood.

9. Until the middle of the nineteenth century all shoes were made by hand.

10. Not until the time of the Civil War were shoes made differently for right and left feet.

☐EXERCISE 10

1. I have been reading about the origin of the names of some common products.

2. Many products, of course, were named after their producers.

3. Bird's Eye products, for example, were named for the frozen food pioneer, Clarence Birdseye.

4. But the names of some other products have interesting stories behind them.

5. The Chevrolet was named for the famed race driver of the early 1900s, Louis Chevrolet.

6. Maxwell House coffee was first served in the Maxwell House, a hotel in Nashville, Tennessee, and took its name from the hotel.

7. On a visit there, Teddy Roosevelt asked for a second cup and called the coffee "good to the last drop."

8. The buses between Duluth and Hibbing, Minnesota, were painted gray because of the dusty roads.

9. A hotel owner along the way likened them to running greyhound dogs.

10. From that remark the Greyhound buses of today got their name.

JOURNAL WRITING

From your most recent paper, copy three sentences, and underline the subject and verb in each.

WRITING ASSIGNMENT

Continue with your writing assignments. Have someone dictate to you your list of spelling words on the inside back cover. Can you spell them all correctly now?

CORRECTING RUN-TOGETHER SENTENCES

Any group of words having a subject and verb is a clause. The clause may be independent (able to stand alone) or dependent (unable to stand alone). Every sentence you have worked with so far has been an independent clause because it has been able to stand alone. It has made a complete statement.

If two independent clauses are written together with no punctuation or with merely a comma, they are called a run-together sentence. (Some textbooks call them a run-on sentence, a comma splice, or a comma fault.) Here are some examples.

> She mowed the lawn he prepared the lunch.
> She mowed the lawn, he prepared the lunch.
> I like camping therefore I enjoyed the trip.
> I like camping, therefore I enjoyed the trip.

Run-together sentences can be corrected in one of three ways:

1. Make the two independent clauses into two sentences.

> She mowed the lawn. He prepared the lunch.
> I like camping. Therefore I enjoyed the trip.

2. Connect the two independent clauses with a semicolon.

> She mowed the lawn; he prepared the lunch.
> I like camping; therefore I enjoyed the trip.
> I wrote a rough draft of my paper; then I revised it.
> I revised it once more; finally it was finished.

When a connecting word such as

also	however	otherwise
consequently	likewise	then
finally	moreover	therefore
furthermore	nevertheless	thus

is used between two independent clauses, it always has a semicolon before it, and it may have a comma after it, especially if there seems to be a pause between the word and the rest of the sentence.

> I like camping; however, I was too busy to go.
> I had work to do; furthermore, I was short of cash.
> She likes canvassing; also, she considers it a duty.
> The voter turnout was small; nevertheless, our candidate won.

The semicolon before the connecting word is required. The comma after it is a matter of choice.

3. Connect the two independent clauses with a comma and one of the following words: *and, but, for, or, nor, yet, so.*

> She mowed the lawn, and he prepared the lunch.
> I like camping, but I was too busy to go.
> I helped with the canvass, for it was my duty.
> We'd better hurry, or we'll never finish.
> I've never tried scuba diving, nor do I want to.

But be sure there are two independent clauses. The first sentence below has two independent clauses. The second sentence is merely one independent clause with two verbs, and therefore no comma should be used.

> She jogged two kilometers, and then she had breakfast.
> She jogged two kilometers and then had breakfast.

THE THREE WAYS TO PUNCTUATE INDEPENDENT CLAUSES

> He went to his room. He needed to study.
> He went to his room; he needed to study.
> He went to his room, for he needed to study.

Learn these three ways, and you'll avoid run-together sentences. (On page 89 you'll learn a fourth way.)

You may wonder when to use a period and capital letter and when to use a semicolon between two independent clauses. In general, use a period and capital letter. Only if the clauses are closely related in meaning should you use a semicolon.

EXERCISES

In each independent clause underline the subject once and the verb twice. Then be ready to give a reason for the punctuation.

☐EXERCISE 1

1. It takes weeks for a monarch butterfly to develop; its development is called metamorphosis.
2. Butterfly eggs are laid on milkweed leaves. From the eggs little caterpillars emerge.
3. The caterpillars eat milkweed leaves, but in turn the caterpillars may be eaten by birds.
4. A caterpillar sheds its skin several times during its growth; each time the new skin is slightly larger.
5. Finally the caterpillar is full grown, and it sheds its skin a final time.
6. Now it has turned into a beautiful chrysalis or sack. The chrysalis is jade green dotted with gold.
7. For several weeks the chrysalis is quiet. Changes are occurring within it.
8. Then finally it cracks open, and an adult monarch butterfly with soft limp wings emerges.
9. Soon the wings dry and harden. Then the monarch flies away.
10. It goes to find a mate and to start another generation.

Most—but not all—of the following sentences are run-together. If the sentence has two independent clauses, separate them with the correct punctuation—comma, semicolon, or period with a capital letter. In general, use the period with a capital letter rather than the semicolon. But either way is correct. Thus your answers may differ from those at the back of the book.

☐EXERCISE 2

1. I never liked math I always slept through class.
2. Then I suddenly woke up I had failed my midterm.
3. I went to see my professor and he confirmed my fears.
4. I had only one chance I had to do well on the final.
5. In other words, in four weeks I had to learn an entire semester's work I got busy.
6. I worked hours and hours and hours I hardly slept at all.
7. I walked into that final confident and began doing each problem in a frenzy.
8. It took a week to get the grades during that week I slept.

9. Then the report came and I opened it.
10. I had not only passed but got a good mark I must have aced that final.

☐EXERCISE 3

1. My high school adviser was close to me she was almost my best friend.
2. She was busy but she always made time for me.
3. Sometimes she would just listen occasionally she would give advice.
4. At first I wasn't interested in her suggestion about a career then I changed my mind.
5. It is going to take time but eventually I should get a good position.
6. I hope to finish college in three more years then I'll apply for a job.
7. According to my adviser, in education we need a balance between receiving and sending.
8. Reading is receiving writing is sending.
9. Writing is hard work but it's satisfying.
10. It's not much fun to write but it's fun to have written.

☐EXERCISE 4

1. The first man to reach the North Pole alone was Naomi Uemura he planted the Japanese flag at the Pole on May 1, 1978.
2. Uemura was then at the top of the world every direction was south.
3. His sledge had been pulled across the frozen Arctic by his 17 huskies it took 57 days to travel 477 miles.
4. Sometimes temperatures dropped as low as $-68°$ F and blizzards slowed him down.
5. He wore modern thermal underwear but the rest of his clothing was Eskimo gear.
6. One morning he was awakened by the barking of his dogs and he saw a giant white polar bear coming toward his tent.
7. Uemura was frightened and decided to play dead in his sleeping bag.
8. The bear destroyed the tent and ate the food supply then he poked the sleeping bag and turned it over.
9. Uemura lay still in the bag and finally the bear wandered off.
10. The next morning the bear returned and Uemura shot him at a range of 55 yards.

☐EXERCISE 5

1. In 1991 I attended the largest sports event in the world it was the International Special Olympics Games in Minneapolis/St. Paul.
2. Six thousand mentally disadvantaged athletes participated and they came from more than 90 countries.
3. Their 2,000 coaches came with them and 10,000 family and friends also came along.

4. Eventually about 30,000 cheering fans welcomed the athletes and later watched them in the 16 different sports.
5. At the opening ceremony dozens of the athletes in their national colors paraded past the applauding and waving crowd in the crowd were Hollywood stars, past Olympic heroes, and foreign dignitaries.
6. The most emotional moment of the two-hour-long procession of athletes came with the entrance of 100 Minnesota athletes, they were led by the Chairman of the Games, Irwin Jacobs, and his daughter Sheila.
7. Mr. Jacobs gave his retarded daughter Sheila credit for his success she had persuaded him to pledge 8 million dollars to back the Games.
8. Eunice Kennedy Shriver was the founder of the Special Olympics she said to the crowd: "On this day twenty-three years ago Special Olympics was born."
9. Then she continued: "Tonight we open the largest sports event in the world this year, your eighth International Special Olympics Games."
10. One of the directors then added: "This is a serious competition it is not just a recreation program."

☐EXERCISE 6

1. About seven million Americans or about 3 percent of the population have a mental disability the percentage is about the same worldwide.
2. Thus millions of families know the initial heartbreak of mental disability then comes the long process of learning self-sufficiency.
3. For many the Special Olympics competition has greatly enhanced the family's self-esteem their child can at last participate in sports.
4. One mother gave great praise to the Special Olympics her daughter had not been able to compete in school sports because of her disability.
5. "She now has found her own level of competition," the mother said.
6. Behind the joy of all the families lie years of struggle the games are the reward of patience.
7. In the 1960s mentally disadvantaged athletes were not allowed to participate in team sports but in 1991 the athletes took part in more than one thousand team events.
8. Each day tens of thousands of spectators came to watch the athletes in aquatics, basketball, cycling, table tennis, volleyball, and the rest of the 16 sports.
9. Tickets for all events were free and attendance was overwhelming.
10. The Special Olympics have been of value to the mentally disadvantaged and they have broadened the vision of many of the rest of us.

☐EXERCISE 7

1. In 1983 the frog and toad population in Eastern Europe began to decline the reason was that the little amphibians were killed as they crossed highways.

2. The mating urge drove hundreds of toads to their breeding ponds but to get to the ponds they had to cross a highway.
3. Signs were put up warning motorists about the toads but still about 20 tons of toads were killed each year.
4. Finally the Toads on Roads campaign was organized the volunteers scooped up live toads in plastic buckets.
5. The volunteers then carried the toads across the highway and deposited them by their breeding ponds.
6. Last year 8,000 Toads on Roads volunteers relocated about 200,000 toads and children were among the volunteers.
7. The children often dragged their parents out to help and the parents were surprised to find it a rewarding experience.
8. The volunteers have also built six toad tunnels, 11 inches in diameter, that allow the toads to hop under the highways.
9. The idea of toad patrols has spread to other countries and in Scandinavia, the Netherlands, Germany, and Switzerland toads are being carried across pavements during a three-week period each year.
10. The result is an increase in the amphibian population throughout Eastern Europe.

Source: *National Geographic,* March 1992

☐EXERCISE 8

1. Last week I visited a one-room country school I had never been in one before.
2. My grandfather had sometimes told me about attending one but it was all new to me.
3. In the front of the room was a huge coal-burning stove beside it was a coal bucket full of coal.
4. The teacher had to get to school at least an hour early she had to make the fire in the stove.
5. On the walls hung coal oil lamps with the coal oil still in them and their glass chimneys were clear and clean.
6. Most of the desks were double two students sat side by side.
7. In each desk was a small round hole for an ink bottle also there was a long groove in the desk for pencils.
8. On the front and side walls were the blackboards and chalk and erasers were in the narrow trays below them.
9. At recess the boys played baseball in the schoolyard and the girls skipped rope or played hide-and-seek.
10. At noon the lunch pails came out and the students traded pie and cake.

☐EXERCISE 9

1. I've been making a collection of quotations many of them have to do with work and success.

2. David Lloyd George said, "Don't be afraid to take a big step if one is indicated you can't cross a chasm in two small jumps."

3. A certain amount of tension is good for one unstring the guitar and the harmony is gone.

4. John Ruskin said that education does not mean teaching people to know what they do not know it means teaching them to behave as they do not behave.

5. According to Plato, we can easily forgive a child who is afraid of the dark the real tragedy of life is when adults are afraid of the light.

6. Henry Ford said, "Old men are always advising young men to save money that is bad advice don't save every nickel invest in yourself I never saved a dollar until I was forty years old."

7. George Bernard Shaw wrote four novels in the first nine years of his writing career none was accepted by a publisher.

8. A Chinese proverb says, "When the moon is fullest it begins to wane when it is darkest it begins to grow."

9. Always behave like a duck keep calm and unruffled on the surface but paddle like the devil underneath.

10. There are two ways to get to the top of an oak tree you can climb it or you can sit on an acorn.

Punctuate this paragraph so there will be no run-together sentences. No answers are provided at the back of the book.

☐EXERCISE 10

I never cared much about running but finally one morning two of my friends persuaded me to join them. I liked it and began running with them three mornings a week. Before long we were all running 10 kilometers at a pretty good pace. Then one of my friends had an idea the Vancouver Sun Fun Run was scheduled for the next week and he thought we should register. We did and the day of the race found us on our way downtown to join about 7,000 other runners. The streets were crowded we couldn't get any closer than a block from the starting line, and when we heard the starting pistol, we had to wait about two minutes before the runners in front of us got going. There is a sensation of excitement in a real race it made me run faster than I usually do. Still my friends pulled ahead of me and I lost track of them. There were runners in front of me as far as I could see but there were lots of runners behind me too. I thought I was passing more runners than were passing me. Finally when I came to the Burrard Bridge, I knew that the finish line was only a few blocks ahead. I tried to increase my speed for the home stretch. Then with only a block to go I recognized my friends right in front of me I had caught up to them. We all finished together and were happy with the time we had made. We all swore that we'd do it again next year.

JOURNAL WRITING

Write three sentences to illustrate the three ways of punctuating two independent clauses in a sentence. Master this section before you go on. It will take care of many of your punctuation errors.

Proofreading Exercise

Can you correct the six errors in this student paper? You'll find errors in words confused, contractions, and run-together sentences. Challenge your instructor to find all six on the first try. No answers are provided at the back of the book.

THOSE MODERN ANCIENT EGYPTIANS

Last summer I went to the Field Museum in Chicago and saw a exhibit entitled "Inside Ancient Egypt." Some of the customs of the ancient Egyptians amazed me.

The exhibit showed copies of the wall paintings in a tomb of about 2450 B.C. In one painting a man is getting a haircut and in the next a man is getting a shave. Behind the barber stands an apprentice barber ready to hand over a fresh razor. Conversations are written in hieroglyphs above each picture. Next a overseer of an estate is receiving a manicure and another scene shows a scribe seated and receiving a pedicure. The rest of the pictures are of the marketplace, and people are selling fish, bread, green onions, figs, bunches of grapes, vegetables, and linen.

Its amazing to me that manicures and pedicures were common more then 4,000 years ago.

CORRECTING FRAGMENTS

There are two kinds of clauses: independent (which we have just finished studying) and dependent. A dependent clause has a subject and a verb just like an independent clause, but it can't stand alone because it begins with a dependent word (or words) such as

after	since	whereas
although	so that	wherever
as	than	whether
as if	that	which
because	though	whichever
before	unless	while
even if	until	who
even though	what	whom
ever since	whatever	whose
how	when	why
if	whenever	
in order that	where	

Whenever a clause begins with one of the above dependent words (unless it's a question, which would never give you any trouble), it is dependent. If we take an independent clause such as

We finished the game.

and put one of the dependent words in front of it, it becomes dependent:

After we finished the game
Although we finished the game
As we finished the game
Before we finished the game
Since we finished the game
That we finished the game
While we finished the game

As you read the clause, you can hear that it doesn't make a complete statement. It leaves the reader expecting something more. Therefore it can no longer stand alone. It's a fragment and must not be punctuated as a sentence. To correct such a fragment, add an independent clause:

After we finished the game, we went to the clubhouse.
We went to the clubhouse after we finished the game.
We were happy that we finished the game early.
While we finished the game, the others waited.

In other words **EVERY SENTENCE MUST HAVE AT LEAST ONE INDEPENDENT CLAUSE.**

Note in the examples that when a dependent clause comes at the beginning of a sentence, it is followed by a comma. Often the comma prevents misreading, as in the following sentence:

When the instructor entered, the room became quiet.

Without a comma after *entered,* the reader would read *When the instructor entered the room* before realizing that that was not what the author meant. The comma prevents misreading. Sometimes if the dependent clause is short and there is no danger of misreading, the comma is omitted, but it's safer simply to follow the rule that a dependent clause at the beginning of a sentence is followed by a comma.

You'll learn more about the punctuation of dependent clauses on page 174, but right now just remember the above rule.

Note that sometimes the dependent word is the subject of the dependent clause:

I finished the cookies <u>that</u> <u>were</u> left.

Sometimes the dependent clause is in the middle of the independent clause:

The cookies that were left didn't last long.

And sometimes the dependent clause is the subject of the entire sentence:

<u>What I was doing</u> <u>was</u> important.

Also note that sometimes the *that* of a dependent clause is omitted:

This is the house that Jack built.
This is the house Jack built.
I thought that you liked math.
I thought you liked math.

And finally the word *that* doesn't always introduce a dependent clause. It may be a pronoun (That is my book) or a describing word (I like that book).

EXERCISES

Underline the subject once and the verb twice in both the independent and the dependent clauses. Then put a broken line under the dependent clause.

☐EXERCISE 1

1. You have to practice until using the rules of writing becomes automatic.

2. When you know a few rules, writing becomes easier.

3. The only difference between an independent and a dependent clause is that the dependent clause begins with a dependent word.

4. If you know the dependent words, you'll have no trouble.

5. If you don't, you may not punctuate your sentences correctly.

6. A comma is required when a dependent clause comes first in a sentence.

7. When a dependent clause comes first in a sentence, a comma often prevents misreading.

8. When you have done a few sentences, the rule becomes easy.

9. It will help you when you are punctuating your papers.

10. When you punctuate correctly, your reader can read with ease.

Underline each dependent clause with a broken line.

☐EXERCISE 2

1. There's a cleanup crew out there that is working day and night.
2. It is cleaning the forest floor of debris, which amounts to about 3,000 pounds of dead plants and animals per acre every year.
3. First the debris is attacked by microorganisms, which may number 10 billion in just 60 cubic inches of forest soil.
4. Then fungi and mushrooms soften the debris still more until it can be eaten by earthworms and insects.
5. As these creatures pass the debris through their digestive systems, the digested material returns vital minerals to the soil.

6. In a single acre in one year, earthworms can digest some 10 tons of debris and soil, which then nourish new plants and animals.
7. Charles Darwin said that without earthworms all vegetation would perish.
8. This recycling process, which involves billions of organisms, is relatively rapid.
9. Although pine needles may take three or four years to be turned into soil, red and yellow autumn leaves take only two.
10. Without this cleanup crew that recycles the forest floor, soil would not be replenished, and plants would cease to grow.

Source: *National Wildlife,* April–May 1983

☐EXERCISE 3

1. In my reading this week I've learned some facts that I never knew before.
2. In Boettcher Hall in Denver, which is the first "surround" music hall in the country, the orchestra performs in the center of the hall, and the audience is seated all around it.
3. Whereas most seats are within 65 feet of the stage, no seat is farther than 85 feet away.
4. The hall, which opened in 1978 to raves from the public and from music and architecture critics, will do much for the Denver Symphony.
5. Other cities that have "surround" music halls are Mexico City and Berlin.
6. Another fact is that the city with the most telephones per capita is Washington, D.C.
7. It has 158.6 phones per 100 persons whereas the national average is 77 phones per 100 persons.
8. Finally I've learned some facts about our universe that amaze me.
9. I've learned that the light from one galaxy started to come to us 100 million years ago when dinosaurs were on earth, but it is reaching us only now.
10. And some matter in the universe is so dense that one teaspoonful of it would weigh as much as 200 million elephants.

If the clause is independent and therefore a sentence, put a period after it. If the clause is dependent and therefore a fragment, add an independent clause either before or after it to make it into a sentence. Remember that if the dependent clause comes first, it should have a comma after it.

□EXERCISE 4

1. Where we camped last year

2. While she sat in the shade and drank lemonade

3. Don't try to stop me

4. Because I know she will understand

5. After I came home and took a long shower

6. Because most of my nervousness is caused by drinking too much coffee

7. As I become more and more sure of myself

8. I enjoy hang gliding

9. Before I took this course and learned a few rules

10. The cost of living in an apartment isn't really so great

On pages 76–77 you learned three ways of correcting run-together sentences. Now that you are aware of dependent clauses, you may use a fourth way. In the following run-together sentence

We had driven 479 miles we stopped for the night.

you can make one of the two independent clauses into a dependent clause by putting a dependent word in front of it, as in the following examples:

Since we had driven 479 miles, we stopped for the night.
We stopped for the night after we had driven 479 miles.
When we stopped for the night, we had driven 479 miles.

Correct the following run-together sentences by making one of the clauses dependent. In some sentences you will want to put the dependent clause first; in others you may want to put it last or in the middle of the sentence. Since various words can be used to start a dependent clause, your answers may differ from those suggested at the back of the book.

□EXERCISE 5

1. Yesterday we went to the zoo I hadn't been there for ages.

2. We went first to the sea lion tank I wanted to feed the sea lions.

3. They ignored the fish that we threw to them they had been fed too many fish.

4. Long ago they were named sea lions someone thought they roared like lions.

5. They are really a type of seal and are related to fur seals they lack the valuable coats of the fur seals.

6. In another part of the zoo small whales performed tricks they can be trained just like seals.

7. Next we saw a sable antelope she had a one-day-old baby.

8. She prodded the baby with her knee she wanted to make it walk.

9. She was persistent finally she made it take a couple of steps.

10. I always learn a lot at the zoo I should go more often.

□EXERCISE 6

1. I've often said "busy as a beaver" I really knew nothing about beavers.

2. Now I know a little I've just read an article about them.

3. A beaver's four front teeth are constantly growing the beaver wears them down by gnawing trees to make dams.

4. A beaver's teeth are sharp a beaver can cut down a small willow in only a few minutes.

5. The tree suddenly begins to totter then the beaver dashes for safety.

6. Finally all is quiet again then the beaver returns to work.

7. A family of beavers work hard they can fell a thousand trees in a year.

8. A beaver has a flat tail he uses it in many ways.

9. He stands up to gnaw a tree his tail serves as a prop.

10. He slaps his tail against the water his tail sounds an alarm.

☐EXERCISE 7

1. One Christmas I got a new hockey stick I was about eleven.

2. I thought I could play better with a new stick therefore I was inspired.

3. We played with a tennis ball on the street we called it street hockey.

4. The goalie wore a baseball glove on one hand he wielded a hockey stick with the other.

5. We hit that tennis ball hard he tried to keep us from shooting it past him.

6. It got really cold in the winter then we flooded the backyard.

7. Finally the ice became solid my brother and I put on our skates.

8. We played with a real puck we pretended we were stars of the Maple Leafs.

9. The whole neighborhood gathered at our "rink" we felt like real pros.

10. Those were exciting games they left some great memories.

☐EXERCISE 8

1. I watched a "National Geographic Special" last night I learned about a world that I didn't know existed.

2. That world is the rain forests they form a band around the earth along the equator.

3. The rain forests get from 100 to 400 inches of rain a year there is sometimes too much water.

4. Wasps sometimes need to dry out their nests they simply drink the water and spit it out over the edge of the nest.

5. Insects swarm over the trees therefore the trees have to protect themselves against the insects.

6. The acacia tree is protected by ants the ants live in the tree.

7. Other insects attack the acacia then the ants attack the invaders and save the acacia.

8. One insect in the rain forest has unusual skin the skin is so nutritious that it can't be wasted.

9. The insect sheds its skin periodically then the insect eats every bit of it.

10. I'd like to learn more about the rain forests they are colorful and amazing.

JOURNAL WRITING

Now that you are aware of independent and dependent clauses, you can vary your sentences. Write three sentences, each containing two independent clauses connected by one of the following words. Be sure to use the correct punctuation—comma or semicolon.

and	for	or
but	however	then
consequently	nevertheless	

Now rewrite the three sentences using one independent and one dependent clause in each. Use some of the following dependent words. If you put the dependent clause first, put a comma after it.

after	if	until
although	since	while
because	unless	

MORE ABOUT FRAGMENTS

We've seen that a dependent clause alone is a fragment. Any group of words that doesn't have a subject and verb is also a fragment.

> Spent too much time on video games (no subject)
> Julio wondering about his girlfriend (no proper verb). Although *ing* words look like verbs, no *ing* word by itself can ever be the verb of a sentence. It must have a helping verb in front of it.
> Walking along the busy street (no subject and no proper verb)
> The letter that I had been expecting (no verb for an independent clause)

To change these fragments into sentences, we must give each a subject and an adequate verb:

> He spent too much time on video games. (We added a subject.)
> Julio was wondering about his girlfriend. (We put a helping verb in front of the *ing* word to make a proper verb.)
> Walking along the busy street, he met an old friend. (We added an independent clause.)
> The letter that I had been expecting finally came. (We added a verb to make an independent clause.)

Sometimes you can simply tack a fragment onto the sentence before or after it.

> Wondering why he hadn't phoned me.   I finally phoned him.
> Wondering why he hadn't phoned me, I finally phoned him.

Or you can change a word or two in the fragment and make it into a sentence.

> I wondered why he hadn't phoned me.

Are fragments ever permissible? Increasingly, fragments are being used in advertising and in other kinds of writing. In Exercises 4 through 6 you'll find advertisements that make use of fragments effectively to give a dramatic pause. But such fragments are used by writers who know what they're doing. The fragments are used intentionally, never in error. Until you're an experienced writer, stick with complete sentences. Especially in college writing, fragments should not be used.

EXERCISES

Put a period after each of the following that is a sentence. Make each fragment into a sentence either by adding an independent clause before or after it or by changing some words in it. Sometimes changing just one word will change a fragment into a sentence.

☐EXERCISE 1

1. Thinking we had missed the turn several miles back

2. Leaving me standing there holding the bag

3. Not just kids my own age but younger and older people too

4. Never believing anyone would come to my rescue

5. Whether we won or lost

6. Going to meetings that served no purpose

7. He decided to take charge of his life

8. Doing only the things that he wanted to do

9. Confidence that was built up after each win

10. If she were someone whom I could sit down and talk to

☐EXERCISE 2

1. Learning to say no has been difficult for me

2. Writing a clear thesis statement and backing it up with reasons

3. She looked in shop windows at the many things that she did not want

4. Begin at the beginning

5. If you do things for others without being asked

6. Something that will take years of experience to learn

7. Make your own decisions instead of letting someone else make them

8. Making a summary is excellent training in writing clearly

9. Writing a journal is good training too

10. Constantly striving to improve my writing

☐EXERCISE 3

1. My decision to look up all the words I don't know

2. Keep calm

3. Something that I had always wanted to do

4. While I still have time to finish my paper

5. Make out a study schedule

6. Which is what I should have done long ago

7. That the Mounties always get their man

8. Making the most of every opportunity

9. That the Nile is the longest river in the world

10. Making that decision changed my life

In the following excerpts from advertisements, the writers have chosen to use fragments. Although the fragments are effective in the ads, they wouldn't be acceptable in formal writing. On a separate sheet rewrite each ad, turning it into acceptable college writing.

☐EXERCISE 4

We need someone with the confidence of a surgeon, the dedication of a marathoner and the courage of an explorer. We have a unique opportunity for someone special.

A chance to spend two years in another country. To live and work in another culture. . . .

The person we're looking for might be a farmer, a forester, or a retired nurse. Or maybe a teacher, a mechanic, or a recent college graduate.

We need someone to join over 5,000 people already working in 60 developing countries around the world. To help people live better lives. . . .

If this sounds interesting to you, maybe you're the person we're looking for. A Peace Corps volunteer. . . .

—Peace Corps

□EXERCISE 5

Come to Canada. The Endless Surprise. Around the corner. Down the road. Just over the hill. Wherever you turn, your Canadian vacation is a medley of fascinating histories and colourful cultures. Where honoured customs live on amid the modern. Old-world beside the cosmopolitan. And where your pleasure and comfort is always our first concern.

—Canada

□EXERCISE 6

Who cares? Who cares about smoggy skies and polluted lakes. About empty cans and trash littering our countryside. About plants and trees dying in our forests. And animals too. Who cares? Woodsy Owl, the Nation's new battler for a clean environment cares. And so should you. Join Woodsy in the fight against pollution. GIVE A HOOT! DON'T POLLUTE.

—American Automobile Association

Review of Run-together Sentences and Fragments

Six Sentences That Show How to Punctuate Clauses

I gave a party. Everybody came. — (two independent clauses)

I gave a party; everybody came.

I gave a party; moreover, everybody came. — (two independent clauses connected by a word such as *also, consequently, finally, furthermore, however, likewise, moreover, nevertheless, otherwise, then, therefore, thus*)

I gave a party, and everybody came. — (two independent clauses connected by *and, but, for, or, nor, yet, so*)

When I gave a party, everybody came. — (dependent clause at beginning of sentence)

Everybody came when I gave a party. — (dependent clause at end of sentence) The dependent words are *after, although, as, as if, because, before, even if, even though, ever since, how, if, in order that, since, so that, than, that, though, unless, until, what, whatever, when, whenever, where, whereas, wherever, whether, which, whichever, while, who, whom, whose, why.*

If you remember these six sentences and understand the rules for their punctuation, most of your punctuation problems will be taken care of. It is essential that you become familiar with the italicized words in the above table. If your instructor reads some of the words, be ready to tell which ones come between independent clauses and which ones introduce dependent clauses.

Put periods and capital letters in these student paragraphs so there will be no run-together sentences or fragments.

1. Robert Frost is undoubtedly the most beloved American poet. People who are indifferent to most poetry can often quote "Birches" or "Stopping by Woods on a Snowy Evening." He writes about the countryside and the country people of Vermont and about his own choice to take the road less traveled by.

2. There's a place set deep in the woods of northern Minnesota that is very special to me. Every time I go there, I'm surrounded with feelings of serenity. The quietness of the area is something that I don't find anywhere else. There's an occasional cry of a hawk circling up above, and sometimes I hear chipmunks scurrying around in the leaves on the ground. These noises always make me feel closer to nature. I sometimes wish that I could be as free as that hawk or as carefree as that chipmunk.

3. I began wrestling seriously in my freshman year. The wrestling coach was walking around and talking to the kids playing football. He was looking for recruits for the upcoming wrestling season. Several of my friends had decided that they would go out for the team. I decided wrestling would be a good way to keep busy through the winter. Looking back over my wrestling years, I feel it was good for me. I learned that through hard work I could accomplish my goals. My career in wrestling is something that I can take pride in.

Here are the first four paragraphs of Martin Luther King, Jr.'s speech "I Have a Dream," given to 200,000 people gathered in front of the Lincoln Memorial in Washington on August 28, 1963. As King spoke, the audience could see the huge statue of Lincoln in the background.

The four paragraphs are printed here without the periods and capital letters that separate the sentences. Read the speech aloud and put in the periods and capital letters. (King does not use semicolons. And where you might expect a comma, he often begins a new sentence with *So* or *But*.) Correct your work using the original speech at the back of the book.

"I Have a Dream . . ."
Martin Luther King, Jr.

Five score years ago, a great American, in whose symbolic shadow we stand, signed the Emancipation Proclamation this momentous decree came as a great beacon light of hope to millions of Negro slaves who had been seared in the flames of withering injustice it came as a joyous daybreak to end the long night of captivity

But one hundred years later, we must face the tragic fact that the Negro is still not free one hundred years later, the life of the Negro is still sadly crippled by the manacles of segregation and the chains of discrimination one hundred years later, the Negro lives on a lonely island of poverty in the midst of a vast ocean of material prosperity one hundred years later, the Negro is still languished in the corners of American society and finds himself an exile in his own land so we have come here today to dramatize an appalling condition

In a sense we have come to our nation's Capital to cash a check when the architects of our republic wrote the magnificent words of the Constitution and the Declaration of Independence, they were signing a promissory note to which every American was to fall heir this note was a promise that all men would be guaranteed the unalienable rights of life, liberty, and the pursuit of happiness

It is obvious today that America has defaulted on this promissory note insofar as her citizens of color are concerned instead of honoring this sacred obligation, America has given the Negro people a bad check, a check which has come back marked "insufficient funds" but we refuse to believe that the bank of justice is bankrupt we refuse to believe that there are insufficient funds in the great vaults of opportunity of this nation so we have come to cash this check—a check that will give us upon demand the riches of freedom and the security of justice we have also come to this hallowed spot to remind America of the fierce urgency of *now* this is no time to engage in the luxury of cooling off or to take the tranquilizing drug of gradualism *now* is the time to make real the promises of Democracy *now* is the time to rise from the dark and desolate valley of segregation to the sunlit path of racial justice *now* is the time to open the doors of opportunity to all of God's children *now* is the time to lift our nation from the quicksands of racial injustice to the solid rock of brotherhood

Proofreading Exercise

See if you can find all nine errors in this student paper. You'll find errors in words confused, contractions, possessives, and punctuation. Challenge your instructor to find all nine on the first try. No answers are provided.

A DOLPHIN LESSON

[handwritten: material]

The stuff I'm learning in college doesn't have much to do with life—or so I thought. I learn about the Napoleonic Wars. I study Freud's theory of the id. I learn to do statistical analysis. I read Sandburg's poems. But Then I go out to have pizza with my friends, and we talk only about parties.

But last week something clicked.

Out at Marine World I saw some Atlantic bottle-nosed dolphins put on a show. With their sleek gray bodies, front flippers, and strong tails, they looked beautiful and friendly as they repeatedly surfaced and *[then]* than dived again into the water. Their performance was astounding. They "walked" on *[their]* there tails on the surface of the water, turned nose over tail in the air, jumped three times their body length in the air, spun in the air, jumped *[through]* threw hoops, and jumped over a rope stretched high across the pool. They performed faultlessly. Every minute was exciting.

But The best part came at the end when the trainer told how she trains them. It takes her six months to teach a dolphin to do an air spin and a year or more to get it ready for show business. She said she uses affection training and operant conditioning. Operant conditioning! I had just been reading in my psychology *[course]* coarse about B. F. Skinner's theory of operant conditioning—the theory that animals or, children, or adults can be trained by giving them rewards for good behavior.

And *[Here]* hear I was seeing the theory in practice! The trainer said, "When they do something we like, we give them something they like." When a dolphin does what the trainer wants, she gives it an affectionate pat and a small fish. If it doesn't do what she wants, she ignores it or sometimes even gives it a tiny bop on the snout.

So Here was my psychology course being used in real life. Maybe more of the things I'm learning in college relate to reality. I'll have to see.

[handwritten: material]

USING STANDARD ENGLISH VERBS

This chapter and the next are for those who need practice in using standard English verbs. Many of us grew up speaking a dialect other than standard English, whether it was in a farm community where people said *I ain't* and *he don't* and *they was* or in a black community where people said *I be* and *it do* and *they has*. Such dialects are effective in their place, but in college and in the business and professional world, the use of standard English is essential. Frequently, though, after students have learned to speak and write standard English, they go back to their home communities and are able to slip back into their community dialects while they are there. Thus they have really become bilingual, able to use two languages—or at least two dialects.

The following tables compare four verbs in one of the community dialects with the same four verbs in standard English. Memorize the standard English forms of these important verbs. Most verbs have endings like the first verb *walk*. The other three verbs are irregular and are important because they are used not only as main verbs but also as helping verbs. We'll be using them as helping verbs in the next chapter.

Don't go on to the exercises until you have memorized the forms of these standard English verbs.

REGULAR VERB: WALK

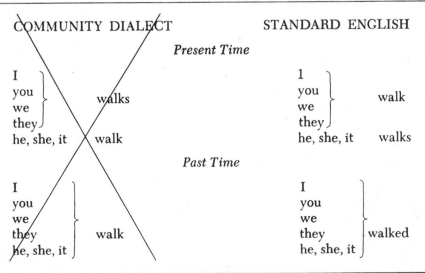

IRREGULAR VERB: HAVE

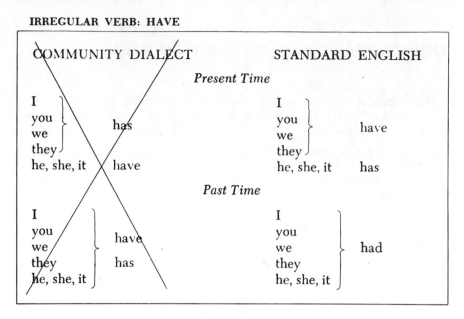

IRREGULAR VERB: BE

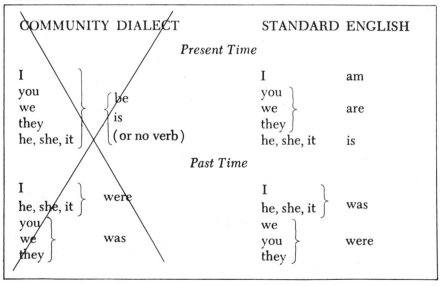

IRREGULAR VERB: DO

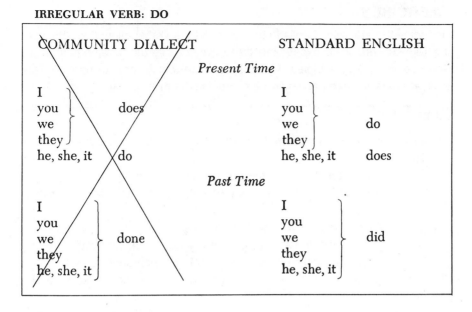

COMMUNITY DIALECT · STANDARD ENGLISH · *Present Time*

Community Dialect: I, you, we, they — does; he, she, it — do

Standard English: I, you, we, they — do; he, she, it — does

Past Time

Community Dialect: I, you, we, they, he, she, it — done

Standard English: I, you, we, they, he, she, it — did

Sometimes students have difficulty with the correct endings of verbs because they don't hear the words correctly. As you listen to your instructor or to TV, note carefully the *s* sound and the *ed* sound at the end of words. Occasionally the *ed* is not clearly pronounced, as in *He asked me to go,* but most of the time you can hear it if you listen.

Try reading the following sentences aloud, making sure you say every sound.

1. I intended to go to the library this afternoon.
2. He picks up his guitar and plays soft chords.
3. I just entered the biggest race in this county.
4. The child grasps my hand and asks me to play with him.
5. We crept along the trail but couldn't see any deer.
6. He decided he wanted to attend the athletic banquet.
7. She wanted a job but didn't get one.
8. I started studying last night at 10 and finished at 12.

Now read some other sentences aloud from this text, making sure that you sound all the *s*'s and *ed*'s. Listening to others and reading aloud will help you use the correct verb endings automatically.

A good way to learn to speak standard English is to make a pact with a friend that you will both speak only standard English when you are together. By helping each other, you'll soon find yourselves speaking more easily.

EXERCISES

Underline the standard English verb form. All the verbs follow the pattern of the regular verb *walk* except the three irregular verbs *have, be,* and *do.* Keep referring to the tables if you're not sure which form to use. Correct your answers for each exercise before going on to the next.

☐EXERCISE 1

1. Yesterday when I (walk walked) to class, I (happen happened) to see Tony.
2. Tony (doesn't don't) know what he (want wants) to be.
3. Last year he (drop dropped) out of college, but this fall he (return returned).
4. He (do does) better now in all his courses.
5. He (ask asked) me to listen to the history paper he had written.
6. He read it to me, and that (help helped) him catch some errors.
7. We (finish finished) class early, and afterward I (talk talked) to the instructor.
8. We (discuss discussed) my term paper, and her comments (help helped) me.
9. She (say said) that she (enjoy enjoyed) reading my paper.
10. I (work worked) hard on that paper. All the students (work works) hard in that class.

☐EXERCISE 2

1. Later that afternoon Tony (ask asked) me to go out for a snack.
2. It (please pleased) me that he (ask asked) me.
3. We (walk walked) down to the Snack Bar and (order ordered) pizza.
4. Tony (like likes) pizza now, but last year he always (order ordered) chili.
5. We (was were) at the Snack Bar until six o'clock.
6. Then I (had has) to go home because I (need needed) to study.
7. I always (do does) all my homework.
8. I (has have) to work because I (want wants) an A in that course.
9. I (did done) all my homework last night before I (watch watched) TV.
10. When I (work works) hard, I (am be) satisfied.

☐EXERCISE 3

1. One day last month I (happen happened) to witness a car accident.
2. A police officer (walk walked) up to me and (ask asked) my name.
3. He (suppose supposed) I had seen the accident and would be a witness.
4. I (learn learned) that the trial might take several days.
5. I (ask asked) if I could be excused.

6. He said no and (walk walked) away.
7. Therefore I (had have) my first day in court last week.
8. It (interest interested) me very much.
9. I (am be) glad I had to go.
10. I (learn learned) a lot that day.

☐EXERCISE 4

1. André and I (jog jogged) all the way to the cafeteria yesterday.
2. We (was were) out of breath when we (arrive arrived) there.
3. André and I both (like likes) to ski.
4. We (want wanted) to go skiing Saturday, but it (was were) too warm.
5. Since it (be is) snowing today, we (hope hopes) to go tomorrow.
6. We (like likes) downhill better than cross country.
7. There (be is) a good ski slope only five miles away.
8. We (plan plans) to ski all day tomorrow.
9. Then we (intend intends) to come home in time for dinner.
10. After that if we (aren't, not be) too tired, we (be are) planning to study.

In these sentences cross out the community dialect words and write the standard English ones above.

☐EXERCISE 5

1. I attend a music camp last summer.

2. I plays the drums now, but I play the trombone last year.

3. I expects to go to the camp again next summer.

4. We work hard there last summer, and we learn a lot.

5. It be fun to work with so many other musicians.

6. Yesterday I practice six hours. I likes to practice every day.

7. I enjoys playing in the school band too.

8. I plans to major in music and to become a professional musician.

9. I hopes to make my living that way someday.

10. If I changes my mind, I still has a good hobby for the rest of my life.

☐EXERCISE 6

1. I done my biology paper yesterday.

2. I learn a lot about the value of wasps.

3. I used to think wasps just be insects that sting.

4. I have learn that wasps destroys harmful caterpillars.

5. Wasps stings only when they be frightened.

6. Unlike bees, most wasps dies at the beginning of winter.

7. Only a few queen wasps sleeps through the winter.

8. Then in the spring they be laying eggs, and a new generation start.

9. Now that I be finished with my paper I can relax.

10. You going with me to the movies tonight?

JOURNAL WRITING

In your journal write about something that interests you at the moment using verbs you may formerly have had trouble with.

WRITING ASSIGNMENT

Continue with your writing assignments.

USING HELPING VERBS AND IRREGULAR VERBS

In the last chapter you studied the present and past forms of the regular verb *walk*. Other forms of regular verbs may be used with helping verbs. Here is a table showing all the forms of some regular verbs and the various helping verbs they are used with.

REGULAR VERBS

BASE FORM	PRESENT	PAST	PAST PARTICIPLE	*ING* FORM
(Use after *can, may, shall, will, could, might, should, would, must, do, does, did*.)			(Use after *have, has, had*. Or use after some form of *be* to describe the subject or to make a passive verb.)	(Use after some form of *be*.)
ask	ask *(s)*	asked	asked	asking
dance	dance *(s)*	danced	danced	dancing
decide	decide *(s)*	decided	decided	deciding
enjoy	enjoy *(s)*	enjoyed	enjoyed	enjoying
finish	finish *(es)*	finished	finished	finishing
happen	happen *(s)*	happened	happened	happening
learn	learn *(s)*	learned	learned	learning
like	like *(s)*	liked	liked	liking
need	need *(s)*	needed	needed	needing
open	open *(s)*	opened	opened	opening
start	start *(s)*	started	started	starting
suppose	suppose *(s)*	supposed	supposed	supposing
walk	walk *(s)*	walked	walked	walking
want	want *(s)*	wanted	wanted	wanting

Sometimes a past participle is used after some form of the verb *be* (or verbs that take the place of *be* like *appear, seem, look, feel, get, act, become*) to describe the subject.

He is satisfied.
He was confused.
He has been disappointed.
He appeared pleased. (He was pleased.)
He seems interested. (He is interested.)

He looked surprised. (He was surprised.)
He feels frightened. (He is frightened.)
He gets bored easily. (He is bored easily.)

Usually these past participles are called describing words that describe the subject rather than being called part of the verb of the sentence. What you call them doesn't matter. The only important thing is to be sure you use the correct form of the past participle (*ed* for regular verbs).

Note that when there are several helping verbs, it is the last one that determines which form of the main verb should be used: she *should* finish soon; she should *have* finished yesterday.

When do you write *ask, finish, suppose, use*? And when do you write *asked, finished, supposed, used*? Here's a rule that will help you decide.

Write *asked, finished, supposed, used*

1. when it's past time:

He *asked* her for a date last night.
She *finished* her paper yesterday.
When I saw you, I *supposed* you had had lunch.
I *used* to like her.

2. when some form of *be* (other than the word *be* itself) comes before the word:

She is *finished* with her paper now.
I am *supposed* to give you this note.
I am *used* to getting up early.

3. when some form of *have* comes before the word:

He has *asked* her to go out with him.
She had *finished* her paper last night.

IRREGULAR VERBS

All the verbs in the table on page 107 are regular. That is, they're all formed in the same way—with an *ed* ending on the past form and on the past participle. But many verbs are irregular. Their past and past participle forms change spelling instead of just adding an *ed*. Here's a table of some irregular verbs. (The present and the *ing* forms aren't usually given in a list of principal parts because they're formed easily from the base form and cause no trouble.) Refer to this list when you aren't sure which verb form to use. Memorize all the forms you don't know.

BASE FORM	PAST	PAST PARTICIPLE
be	was, were	been
become	became	become
begin	began	begun
break	broke	broken
bring	brought	brought
buy	bought	bought
build	built	built
catch	caught	caught
choose	chose	chosen
come	came	come
cost	cost	cost
do	did	done
draw	drew	drawn
drink	drank	drunk
drive	drove	driven
eat	ate	eaten
fall	fell	fallen
feel	felt	felt
fight	fought	fought
find	found	found
fit	fitted *or* fit	fitted *or* fit
forget	forgot	forgotten *or* forgot
forgive	forgave	forgiven
freeze	froze	frozen
get	got	got *or* gotten
give	gave	given
go	went	gone
grow	grew	grown
have	had	had
hear	heard	heard
hold	held	held

BASE FORM	PAST	PAST PARTICIPLE
hurt	hurt	hurt
keep	kept	kept
know	knew	known
lay (to place)	laid	laid
lead (rhymes with "bead")	led	led
leave	left	left
lie (to rest)	lay	lain
lose	lost	lost
make	made	made
meet	met	met
pay	paid	paid
read (pronounced, "reed")	read (pronounced "red")	read (pronounced "red")
ride	rode	ridden
ring	rang	rung
rise	rose	risen
run	ran	run
say	said	said
see	saw	seen
sell	sold	sold
shake	shook	shaken
shine (to give light)	shone	shone
shine (to polish)	shined	shined
sing	sang	sung
sleep	slept	slept
speak	spoke	spoken
spend	spent	spent
stand	stood	stood
steal	stole	stolen
strike	struck	struck
swim	swam	swum
swing	swung	swung
take	took	taken
teach	taught	taught
tear	tore	torn
tell	told	told
think	thought	thought
throw	threw	thrown
try	tried	tried
wear	wore	worn
win	won	won
write	wrote	written

EXERCISES

Write the correct form of each verb. Refer to the tables and explanations on the previous pages if you aren't sure which form to use after a certain helping verb. Do no more than 10 sentences at a time before checking your answers.

☐EXERCISE 1

1. (like, meet) I have always _____ train trips because I
   have _____ such interesting people.

2. (meet, build) Yesterday I _____ a man who designs
   model airplanes and even _____ them.

3. (suppose) His models are _____ to be the top of the line.

4. (meet, teach) On another trip I _____ a girl who has
   _____ disabled children for three years.

5. (devote, teach) She seemed _____ to her work and loves
   all the children she has _____ .

6. (give) Another person whom I met _____ flute lessons
   now and has _____ flute lessons for many years.

7. (become, design) Then last week I _____ acquainted with
   an engineer who _____ bridges.

8. (concern) She is _____ about not damaging the environment.

9. (catch) I have _____ the morning train to Jacksonville
   every weekend this spring.

10. (suppose, surprise) I was _____ to meet my cousin at the
    train station yesterday, but I was _____ to find my uncle
    there too.

☐EXERCISE 2

1. (intend, be) One of my friends _____ now to go into law
   enforcement, and another _____ majoring in business.

2. (plan, do) Another friend _____ to drop out of college
   soon because he _____ not like studying.

3. (attend) Two of my friends _____ Westchester Community College now.

4. (have) One of them _____ a job on weekends as well.

5. (wonder, do) I _____ if he _____ not find that difficult.

6. (say, do) He _____ , however, that it _____ not bother him.

7. (intend, hope) He _____ to transfer to a four-year college in the fall and _____ to graduate in two more years.

8. (be) Where _____ you last night? All of us _____ at the lecture except you.

9. (miss, be) It did not matter to me that you _____ it, but we _____ all expecting you.

10. (be, have) The lecture _____ one of the best I _____ ever heard.

☐EXERCISE 3

1. (have) Last year I _____ a good relationship with my counselor.

2. (wish, have) I _____ that I _____ the same counselor this year.

3. (know, make) My counselor last year _____ how to listen, and he always _____ time for me.

4. (understand) He _____ the importance of listening.

5. (offer, make) He would seldom _____ advice or _____ judgments.

6. (solve, talk) But I could often _____ my problems just by _____ to him about them.

7. (be) Sometimes a person with little training can _____ a good counselor.

8. (be) The most important quality for a counselor _____ the ability to listen.

9. (use) Now I _____ that counselor's technique.

10. (have, spend) When my small son _____ a problem, I _____ plenty of time listening.

Cross out the community dialect expressions and write the standard English ones above.

☐EXERCISE 4

1. It surprise me when my brother tell me he going back to school.

2. I guess he find out it hard to keep a job if you ain't finish school.

3. He work for a while at a grocery store.

4. Then he get laid off.

5. Now he be a year behind his friends.

6. He be a junior when they graduate.

7. He say he don't mind.

8. He want to play football this fall.

9. He hope he make the team.

10. I hopes so too.

☐EXERCISE 5

1. I learn a lot in class this morning. Why wasn't you there?

2. I didn't get my paper finish, and I be too embarrass to go.

3. You should have came anyway.

4. I know I should of. I be there next time.

5. You be going to the game tonight?

6. Yes, I be going with Clayton. He have to sell tickets, so we be going early.

7. What time do the game start?

8. It don't start till eight. You needing a ride?

9. No, I be going with Jermaine.

10. I see you at the game then.

AVOIDING DIALECT EXPRESSIONS

Although verbs cause the most trouble for those who have grown up speaking a dialect other than standard English, certain other expressions, more common in speech than in writing, should be avoided.

DIALECT	STANDARD ENGLISH
anywheres, nowheres, somewheres	anywhere, nowhere, somewhere
anyways	anyway
hisself, theirselves	himself, themselves
this here book, that there book, those there books	this book, that book, those books
them books	those books
he did good, she sang good	he did well, she sang well
my brother he plays ball	my brother plays ball
I be finished	I am finished
ain't	am not, isn't, aren't, hasn't, haven't

The following dialect expressions are called double negatives:

haven't none, haven't got none	have none, haven't any
haven't no, haven't got no	have no, haven't any
haven't never	have never, haven't ever
haven't nothing	have nothing, haven't anything
wasn't no	was no, wasn't any
wasn't never	was never, wasn't ever
ain't got no	have no, haven't any

EXERCISES

Cross out the dialect expressions and write the standard English ones above.

☐EXERCISE 1

1. I'd like to go, but I ain't got no time.

2. I haven't done none of my homework for tomorrow.

3. This here book be hard to read, and anyways it's not interesting.

4. My friend he did good on the test last week.

5. He should be proud of hisself because that test hard.

6. Did you read all them books we was suppose to read?

7. I never read none of them.

8. I watch TV last night and didn't do no reading.

9. I ain't watching no TV tonight.

10. I want to do good on that there test tomorrow.

☐EXERCISE 2

1. Me and my brothers be planning to take a trip somewheres this summer.

2. But we ain't decided yet where we be going.

3. My brother Torrence he want to go fishing in Wisconsin.

4. I ain't never like fishing.

5. My other brother don't want to go nowheres we been before.

6. I want to find one of them atlases what show you where the state parks is.

7. I never been to none of them.

8. I'd like to go to one of them if it ain't too far.

9. Anyways we got lots of time to decide.

10. I probably let my brothers suit theirselves about where we be going.

JOURNAL WRITING

Write three sentences using verbs you have missed in the exercises or in your papers.

WRITING ASSIGNMENT

Continue with your writing assignments. Have someone dictate to you your list of spelling words on the inside back cover. Can you spell them all correctly now?

Proofreading Exercise

Can you correct the eight errors in this student paper? There are errors in words confused, contractions, possessives, and run-together sentences. No answers are provided at the back of the book.

BEETLES

Beetles! I thought there were two or three kinds!

Of coarse I new that insects make up the largest group of animals in the world. Almost a million species have been described but the actual number of living species could be from two to five million. In one square yard of rich moist surface soil, 500 to 2,000 insects may be found.

Ive now learned that beetles are the largest order of insects. They make up about 40 percent of known species. About 250,000 species of beetles exist. Some have brilliant metallic colors, showy patterns, or striking forms and there size varies from a fraction of a millimeter to almost a fifth of a meter. Most of the colorful beetles live in the tropics and there the native women make necklaces and other ornaments from the beetles beautiful shell-like wings.

Progress Test

This test covers everything you've studied so far. One sentence in each pair is correct. The other is incorrect. Read both sentences carefully before you decide. Then write the letter of the correct sentence in the blank.

_____ 1. A. I've joined the bowling league it's fun.
        B. His principal interest these days is swimming.

_____ 2. A. Working all that time and getting nothing for it.
        B. Doesn't he make quite a bit of money too?

_____ 3. A. I have chose this field because I like nursing.
        B. His car broke down, and he spent the night in the desert.

_____ 4. A. Whether I win or lose isn't important.
        B. You're new clothes are better than any you've had in the past.

_____ 5. A. She doesn't want to lose her self-confidence.
        B. When my brother arrived, he ask me to phone you.

_____ 6. A. He was suppose to plan the trip for the two teams.
        B. I chose this course because I knew I needed it.

_____ 7. A. When you can't spell, you're in trouble.
        B. Our car wouldn't start, we were left stranded.

_____ 8. A. She did good on her comprehensive test.
        B. I worked for hours; then I finally finished.

_____ 9. A. She chose warm clothes for her trip.
        B. We was sure that woman was your mother.

_____ 10. A. Never having been in a track meet before.
        B. The puppy wouldn't eat its food.

_____ 11. A. If at first you don't succeed, try again.
        B. When she came in the door, I knew what had happen.

_____ 12. A. Working steadily, he soon finished painting the room.
        B. He studies best the night before a exam.

_____ 13. A. I jumped in my car and was off to the races.
        B. I enjoyed competing however I didn't win any prize.

_____ 14. A. It don't make any difference to me whether you come or not.
        B. I'm not sure who's to blame.

_____ 15. A. They was standing in the rain for an hour.
        B. Finally the bus came, and they got in.

MAKING SUBJECTS, VERBS, AND PRONOUNS AGREE

All parts of a sentence should agree. In general if the subject is singular, the verb should be singular; if the subject is plural, the verb should be plural.

> <u>Each</u> of the girls <u>has</u> her own bank account.
> <u>Both</u> of the girls <u>have</u> their own bank accounts.
> <u>Brian</u> and <u>Loretta</u> <u>have</u> a good friendship.
> There <u>were</u> fifty <u>people</u> in the classroom.
> <u>Many</u> of my friends <u>are</u> in that class.

The following words are singular and take a singular verb:

(*one* words)	(*body* words)	
one	anybody	each
anyone	everybody	either
everyone	nobody	neither
no one	somebody	
someone		

> <u>One</u> of my friends <u>is</u> from Mexico.
> <u>Everybody</u> in the class <u>has</u> to give a report.
> <u>Either</u> of the candidates <u>is</u> acceptable.

The following "group" words take a singular verb if you're thinking of the group as a whole, but they take a plural verb if you're thinking of the individuals in the group:

audience	family	kind
band	flock	lot
class	group	number
committee	heap	none
crowd	herd	public
dozen	jury	team

> The jury *is* ready . . . . The jury *are* still arguing.
> The team *is* on the field . . . . . The team *are* suiting up.
> A dozen rolls *is* plenty . . . . . . A dozen *are* planning to go.
> My family *is* behind me . . . . . My family *are* all scattered.

Here are some subject-verb pairs you can *always* be sure of. No exceptions!

you were	(*never* you was)
we were	(*never* we was)
they were	(*never* they was)
he doesn't	(*never* he don't)
she doesn't	(*never* she don't)
it doesn't	(*never* it don't)

Not only should subject and verb agree, but a pronoun also should agree with the word it refers to. If the word referred to is singular, the pronoun should be singular; if that word is plural, the pronoun should be plural.

Each of the boys has *his* own room.

The pronoun *his* refers to the singular subject *Each* and therefore is singular.

Both of the boys have *their* own rooms.

The pronoun *their* refers to the plural subject *Both* and therefore is plural.

Today many people try to avoid sex bias by writing sentences like the following:

If anyone wants a ride, he or she can go in my car.
If anybody calls, tell him or her that I've left.
Somebody has left his or her textbook here.

But those sentences are wordy and awkward. Therefore some

people, especially in conversation, turn them into sentences that are not grammatically correct.

> If anyone wants a ride, they can go in my car.
> If anybody calls, tell them that I've left.
> Somebody has left their textbook here.

Such ungrammatical sentences, however, are not necessary. It just takes a little thought to revise each sentence so that it avoids sex bias and is also grammatically correct:

> Anyone who wants a ride can go in my car.
> Tell anybody who calls that I've left.
> Somebody has left a textbook here.

Another good way to avoid the awkward *he or she* and *him or her* is to make the words plural. Instead of writing, "Each of the students was in his or her place," write, "All the students were in their places."

EXERCISES

Underline the correct word. Check your answers 10 at a time.

☐EXERCISE 1

1. Every one of the students in this class (get gets) to class on time.
2. If they (are is) late, they (miss misses) the one-sentence quiz given at the beginning of the hour.
3. The instructor dictates a sentence, and each of the students (write writes) it on a piece of paper and (hand hands) it in.
4. The sentence (include includes) some of the points that (are is) in the day's assignment.
5. The instructor then quickly (sort sorts) the papers into two groups—correct and incorrect.
6. One of the girls always (get gets) (her their) quiz correct.
7. Two of the boys usually (get gets) (his theirs) correct too.
8. Most of the students (like likes) those quizzes because they're short.
9. Even though the quiz (doesn't don't) take long, it's effective.
10. It (give gives) a good idea of a student's progress.

☐EXERCISE 2

1. One of my new interests (are is) geology.
2. Last month I found a couple of fossils that (was were) in the sediment of an old creek bed.

3. They show the outline of some plants that (was were) in this area millions of years ago.
4. I have a book about fossils that (give gives) a lot of information.
5. The exhibits in our college museum also (include includes) fossils.
6. Some of the exhibits (show shows) both plant and animal fossils.
7. A knowledge of both geology and biology (are is) necessary for a study of fossils.
8. The study of fossils (reveal reveals) the geologic history of an area.
9. The rock formations in many national parks (show shows) fossils.
10. One of my goals (are is) to see some of those formations.

☐EXERCISE 3

1. One of the best courses I'm taking this year (are is) typing.
2. Some of my friends (take takes) the same course.
3. All of us (wish wishes) we had learned to type earlier.
4. Typed papers usually (get gets) better grades.
5. Most of my friends now (type types) their papers.
6. One of my friends (has have) even typed her brother's papers.
7. It (doesn't don't) take as much time to type as to write longhand.
8. Two of the men in our class (take takes) computer programming.
9. Each of them (find finds) (his their) typing skills essential.
10. All the students who can't type (wish wishes) they could.

☐EXERCISE 4

1. Each of my sisters (has have) a weekend job to pay for (her their) tuition.
2. One of them (are is) a bagger at Safeway.
3. The other (drive drives) a delivery truck for Macy's.
4. Both of them (has have) had these jobs for about a year.
5. Some of my friends (has have) had trouble finding jobs.
6. Several of them (has have) been out of work all summer.
7. It (doesn't don't) look as if they'll get anything.
8. One thing that (help helps) to get a job is experience.
9. Another thing that (help helps) (are is) knowing the right person.
10. And of course one of the big factors (are is) persistence.

☐EXERCISE 5

1. No one in our family (has have) ever been to Yellowstone National Park.
2. For a long time all of us (has have) wanted to see it.
3. The stories about it (has have) impressed us, and each of us (are is) eager to visit it.
4. Therefore all of us (are is) planning to drive to Yellowstone in June.
5. Many of my friends (has have) been there, and one of my friends (are is) going in August.

6. The one thing all of us (want wants) to see most is Old Faithful.
7. Although it's not the largest nor even the most powerful geyser in the park, its fame and popularity (come comes) from its relative regularity of eruption.
8. Ever since it was discovered, in 1870, it has erupted every hour, although the time (varies vary) from 61 to 67 minutes.
9. Lately, however, because of earthquakes nearby, the timing of the eruptions (are is) not quite so faithful.
10. I was interested to learn that the term *geyser* (come comes) from an Icelandic word meaning "to gush."

☐EXERCISE 6

1. One of my brothers (want wants) especially to see some of the other geysers.
2. In the park there (are is) more than a hundred active geysers.
3. This concentration of geysers (are is) the greatest in the world.
4. Only in New Zealand and Iceland (are is) there other active geyser regions of any consequence.
5. All of us (look looks) forward to seeing the animals of the park too: the bears, bison, deer, moose, elk, and coyotes.
6. My sister, who is interested in plants, (want wants) to learn about the flora of the area.
7. The main trees in Yellowstone (are is) lodgepole pines, and along the stream banks (grow grows) cottonwoods and willows.
8. All of us (plan plans) to take advantage of the interpretive programs and listen to campfire talks.
9. Each of us (has have) something different we want to see.
10. But all of us (intend intends) to stay together in our sight-seeing.

☐EXERCISE 7

1. I especially want to see the petrified forests, which (are is) unique among the petrified forests of the world.
2. In most petrified forests, like the Petrified Forest National Park in Arizona, the trees (lie lies) horizontally.
3. The reason for their lying flat on the ground is that most of them (has have) been carried into the area by streams.
4. In Yellowstone the petrified trees (stand stands) upright just where they grew millions of years ago.
5. Yellowstone's petrified forests are also the largest known and (cover covers) more than 40 square miles.
6. All of us (are is) eager to take some of the self-guiding trails.
7. Along those trails (are is) hot springs, mud pots, and mud geysers.
8. We have all been reading some books about the park and (hope hopes) to have enough background to get the most from our trip.

9. Our plan to camp out and cook our own meals (suit suits) all of us.
10. Since Yellowstone is our oldest national park, all of us (think thinks) it's time we saw it.

☐EXERCISE 8

1. Everybody in our family (are is) going to the races today.
2. Not one of us (want wants) to miss them.
3. There (are is) 10 horses in the featured race.
4. All of them (has have) been well trained.
5. Each of them (seem seems) to like to race.
6. Everyone in our family (has have) picked a favorite horse.
7. Luckily it (doesn't don't) look like rain today.
8. Therefore each of us (are is) planning to walk to the stadium.
9. It (doesn't don't) take more than five minutes to walk there.
10. Then all of us (are is) going to be free from parking worries.

JOURNAL WRITING

Write about something that interests you using at least four words from your Spelling List on the inside back cover of this book.

CHOOSING THE RIGHT PRONOUN

Of the many kinds of pronouns, the following cause the most difficulty:

SUBJECT GROUP	NONSUBJECT GROUP
I	me
he	him
she	her
we	us
they	them

A pronoun in the Subject Group may be used in two ways:

1. as the subject of a verb:

He is my counselor. (*He* is the subject of the verb *is.*)

Meg is older than *I.* (The sentence isn't written out in full. It means "Meg is older than *I* am." *I* is the subject of the verb *am.*) Whenever you see *than* in a sentence, ask yourself whether a verb has been left off the end of the sentence. Add the verb, and then you'll automatically use the correct pronoun. In both writing and speaking, always add the verb. Instead of saying, "She's smarter than (I me)," say, "She's smarter than I am." Then you can't fail to use the correct pronoun.

2. as a word that means the same as the subject:

That was he in the blue car. (*He* means the same as the subject *That.* Therefore the pronoun from the Subject Group is used.)

It was she who phoned. (*She* means the same as the subject *It.* Therefore the pronoun from the Subject Group is used.)

Modern usage allows some exceptions to this rule however. *It is me* and *it is us* (instead of the grammatically correct *it is I* and *it is we*) are now established usage; and *it is him, it is her,* and *it is them* are widely used, particularly in informal speech.

Pronouns in the Nonsubject Group are used for all other purposes.

In the following sentence, *me* is not the subject, nor does it mean the same as the subject. Therefore it comes from the Nonsubject Group.

He came with Amanda and *me.*

A good way to tell which pronoun to use is to leave out the extra name. By leaving out *Amanda,* you will say, *He came with me.* You would never say, *He came with I.*

> We saw Kimberly and *him* last night. (We saw *him* last night.)
> The firm gave my wife and *me* a trip to the Virgin Islands. (The firm gave *me* a trip.)

EXERCISES

Underline the correct pronoun. Remember the trick of leaving out the extra name to help you decide which pronoun to use. Use the correct grammatical form even though an alternate form may be acceptable in conversation.

□EXERCISE 1

1. Our instructor asked Jessica and (I me) to organize a panel discussion.
2. Since Lew is such a good speaker, we asked (he him) and Robert to be the leaders.
3. (He Him) and Robert got some pointers from the instructor.
4. Between you and (I me), I think it was a good program.
5. Everyone told Jessica and (I me) that it was interesting.
6. Several students wanted to know when Jessica and (I me) would plan another panel.
7. Most of (we us) students think we should have panel discussions often.
8. (We Us) two began thinking of a subject for another panel.
9. Then our instructor asked whether Jessica and (I me) could get one ready in two weeks.
10. Naturally both Jessica and (I me) were pleased.

□EXERCISE 2

1. My roommate and (I me) have made a new agreement.
2. Both (he him) and (I me) had low grades this past semester.
3. Now we realize it's up to both (he him) and (I me) to do something about it.
4. We've decided that neither (he him) nor (I me) will turn on the TV after dinner.
5. If (we us) two have the entire evening to study, our grades should improve.
6. During the first week of our agreement, it was really hard for both (he him) and (I me).
7. But by the second week (we us) two really followed our plan.

8. And the semester grades for both (he him) and (I me) were a surprise.
9. (He Him) and (I me) each got an A and a couple of B's.
10. Now the rest of the year is going to be no problem for (we us) two.

☐EXERCISE 3

1. Carol and (I me) went to a play at the university last night.
2. Carol thought Vicki would be there, and at intermission we saw (she her) and Bob.
3. Bob and (I me) have always been good friends.
4. They came over and spoke to Carol and (I me) and asked us to go out for pizza afterward.
5. When we went out for pizza, Bob and (I me) fought over the check.
6. Then they rode home with Carol and (I me) in my car.
7. They asked Carol and (I me) to go skiing with them next weekend.
8. It didn't take long for Carol and (I me) to accept.
9. (Carol and I, Me and Carol) both like to ski.
10. (We Us) four are sure to have a great weekend.

☐EXERCISE 4

1. (Jason and I, Me and Jason) have parts in the play being put on by the Drama Department.
2. It's something new for both (he him) and (I me).
3. It's been a struggle for Jason and (I me) to learn all our lines.
4. But now both (he and I, him and me) are sure of them.
5. Neither Jason nor (I me) have ever missed a rehearsal.
6. The director complimented Jason and (I me) on our faithfulness.
7. During the scenes when we're not on stage Jason and (I me) play pinochle.
8. The last game we played was a tie between (he him) and (I me).
9. The entire production has been fun for Jason and (I me).
10. Now both (he him) and (I me) are looking forward to the next play.

☐EXERCISE 5

1. (My brother and I, Me and my brother) take turns shoveling our walks.
2. He is younger than (I me).
3. He thinks the family car should be available to both (he and I, him and me).
4. It was a problem that my dad and (I me) had to work out.
5. Dad and (I me) sat down to talk it over.
6. Dad thought the car should be available equally to my brother and (I me).
7. My brother and (I me) now have an agreement about it.
8. There never has been any trouble between (we us) two.
9. Oh, when we were little, (we us) two used to have fights.
10. But now (he and I, him and me) can always come to an agreement.

MAKING THE PRONOUN REFER TO THE RIGHT WORD

When you write a sentence, *you* know what it means, but your reader may not. What does this sentence mean?

Kelly told her instructor that she had made a mistake.

Who had made a mistake? We don't know whether the pronoun *she* refers to *Kelly* or to *instructor*. The simplest way to correct such a faulty reference is to use a direct quotation:

Kelly said to her instructor, "I've made a mistake."

Here is another sentence with a faulty reference:

I've always enjoyed helping teach preschoolers, and now I'm actually going to be one.

Going to be a preschooler? There's no word for *one* to refer to. We need to write

I've always enjoyed helping teach preschoolers, and now I'm actually going to be a preschool teacher.

Another kind of faulty reference is a *which* clause that doesn't refer to any specific word, thus making it difficult to tell what part of the sentence it refers to.

He finally landed a job which gave him some self-confidence.

Was it the job that gave him self-confidence or the fact that he finally landed a job? The sentence should read

Finally landing a job gave him some self-confidence.

or

The job that he finally landed gave him some self-confidence.

EXERCISES

Most—but not all—of these sentences aren't clear because we don't know what word the pronoun refers to. Revise such sentences to make the meaning clear. Remember that using a direct quotation is often the easiest way to clarify what a pronoun refers to. Since there are more ways than one to rewrite each sentence, yours may be as good as the one on the answer sheet.

☐EXERCISE 1

1. When Curt showed his father the dented fender, he was upset.

2. He said he would have to get it repaired.

3. She showed us a conch shell and explained how they live in them.

4. The parents take turns supervising the park playgound, where they have free use of the swings and slides.

5. He told his instructor that he didn't think he understood the novel.

6. His instructor said that maybe he hadn't read it carefully enough.

7. The clerk told his boss he was too old for the job.

8. When the professor talked with Roland, he was really worried.

9. She told her girlfriend that her record collection needed reorganizing.

10. She asked the job applicant to come back after she had given more thought to the question.

☐EXERCISE 2

1. His motorcycle hit a parked car, but it wasn't damaged.

2. As I went up to the baby's carriage, it began to cry.

3. Rebecca told her mother that her wardrobe was completely out-of-date.

4. As soon as the carburetor of my car was adjusted, I drove it home.

5. I couldn't find the catsup bottle, and I don't like a hamburger without it.

6. His father said he would have to get a bank loan.

7. Susanne told Cynthia that she had failed the exam.

8. She was shy, and it kept her from moving ahead in her profession.

9. He finished his paper, turned off the typewriter, and took it to class.

10. When we couldn't find the cake plate, we decided my husband must have eaten it.

☐EXERCISE 3

1. When the dentist pulled the child's tooth, it screamed.

2. I finished my exam, put down my pen, and handed it in.

3. I'm interested in politics and would like to become a politician.

4. I decided to take a different job which my parents disapproved of.

5. When I opened the dog's carrying case at the airport, it ran away.

6. The cars streamed by without paying any attention to the stalled motorist.

7. John told Max that his parakeet was loose in his room.

8. I finally made up my mind to major in math which wasn't easy.

9. When Debbie phoned her mother, she was quite ill.

10. He asked the salesperson to come back when he wasn't so rushed.

☐EXERCISE 4

1. He told his father that his car needed a tune-up.

2. After I read about Tom Dooley's career in medicine, I decided that that was what I wanted to be.

3. After Alfredo talked to the boss, he was enthusiastic about the project.

4. He loves to wrestle and spends most of his time doing it.

5. The park commission established a hockey rink where they can play free.

6. The doctor told the orderly he had made a mistake.

7. She tried to persuade her sister to take her car.

8. My car hit a truck, but it wasn't even scratched.

9. She told her mother she was working too hard.

10. As we approached the robin's nest, it flew away.

☐EXERCISE 5

1. She told her daughter that she had always been too shy.

2. Erica's mother let her wear her fur coat to the party.

3. He told his dad that he had made a terrible mistake.

4. She slammed her cup into the saucer and broke it.

5. I enjoy figure skating and would like to be one if I could.

6. The president told the chief accountant that he had made an error in reporting his income.

7. In Hawaii they have June weather the year around.

8. When her sister came home from college, she was excited.

9. He told his father he thought he should go back to college for a year.

10. His father told him he didn't have enough money.

WRITING ASSIGNMENT

As you get back your writing assignments, are you keeping a list of your misspelled words on the inside back cover of this book?

CORRECTING MISPLACED OR DANGLING MODIFIERS

A modifier gives information about some word in a sentence, and it should be as close to that word as possible. In the following sentence the modifier is too far away from the word it modifies to make sense:

Playing with a ball of string, we sat and watched our kitten.

Was it *we* who were playing? That's what the sentence says because the modifier *Playing with a ball of string* is next to *we*. Of course it should be next to *kitten*.

We sat and watched our kitten playing with a ball of string.

Here's another misplaced modifier:

We saw a deer and a fawn on the way to the shopping center.

Were the deer and fawn going to the shopping center? Who was?

On the way to the shopping center we saw a deer and a fawn.

The next example has no word at all for the modifier to modify:

At the age of nine, my dad was transferred to Alabama.

The modifier *At the age of nine* is dangling there with no word to attach itself to, no word for it to modify. We can get rid of the dangling modifier by turning it into a dependent clause.

When I was nine, my dad was transferred to Alabama.

Here the clause has its own subject—*I*—so that there's no chance of misunderstanding the sentence.

EXERCISES

Most—but not all—of these sentences contain misplaced or dangling modifiers. Some you may correct simply by shifting the modifier so it will be next to the word it modifies. Others you'll need to rewrite. Since there is more than one way to correct each sentence, your way may be as good as the one at the back of the book.

☐EXERCISE 1

1. Garbed in a brief bikini, he watched her strolling along.

2. My brother-in-law took me to the hospital after breaking my leg.

3. Glowing in the dark garden, we watched hundreds of fireflies.

4. After finishing the English assignment, that pizza tasted great.

5. After cleaning the cage and putting in fresh water and seed, my canary began to sing.

6. Sound asleep in the hammock, I discovered my boyfriend.

7. Jerking the leash, I made my dog heel.

8. At the age of six, my mother had another baby.

9. I gave away that blue suit to a charity that I didn't care about anymore.

10. While answering the doorbell, my cookies burned to a crisp.

☐EXERCISE 2

1. Hundreds of colorful tropical fish could be seen cruising in the glass-bottom boat.

2. While playing on the floor, I noticed that the baby seemed feverish.

3. After being wheeled out of the operating room, a nurse asked me how I felt.

4. While watching the football game, Mark's bike was stolen.

5. The bank will make loans to responsible individuals of any size.

6. Rounding a bend in the road, a huge glacier confronted me.

7. I could see six lakes flying at an altitude of 10,000 feet.

8. Having finished mowing the lawn, the lawn chair looked comfortable.

9. Before planting my garden, I consulted a seed catalog.

10. Having broken my right arm, the instructor let me take the test orally.

☐EXERCISE 3

1. After doing all the outside reading, the term paper almost wrote itself.

2. Flitting among the apple blossoms, I spotted a monarch butterfly.

3. After drinking a lot of coffee, the lecture was less boring.

4. Standing there being milked, we thought the cows looked contented.

5. The Museum of Science and Industry is the most interesting museum in the city that I have visited.

6. She was going out with a man who owned a Corvette named Harold.

7. We gave all the meat to the cat that we didn't want.

8. Speeding down the slope, our toboggan hit a rock.

9. Determined to learn to write, the textbook was slowly mastered.

10. After eating a quick lunch, our bus left for Palatine.

☐EXERCISE 4

1. The little town is in the middle of a prairie where I was born.

2. You may visit the National Cemetery where noted people are buried every day except Friday from nine until five.

3. At the age of three I saw my first circus.

4. She put the clothes back in the traveling bag that she had not worn.

5. Although almost ten years old, he still hangs onto his old car.

6. Completely smashed, I saw that my little car was beyond repair.

7. Barking furiously, I went to see what was the matter with my puppy.

8. Sitting there looking out over the water, her decision was finally made.

9. Crying pitifully, I tried to find the child's mother.

10. Being a boring conversationalist, I always try to avoid him.

☐EXERCISE 5

1. I bought a secondhand car from a man with generator trouble.

2. I read that the hit-and-run driver had been caught in the evening paper.

3. We gave all the newspapers to the Boys Scouts that have been lying around for months.

4. She left the meat on the table that was too tough to eat.

5. A report was made about the holdup by the police.

6. Twittering delightfully, I watched the wren building its nest.

7. Being a conceited fool, I didn't much care for his company.

8. After smelling up the whole house, I finally gave my dog a bath.

9. While watering the geraniums, a bee stung me.

10. Being unsure of the way to correct dangling or misplaced modifiers, my instructor gave me a low grade.

JOURNAL WRITING

Make up a sentence with a dangling or misplaced modifier, and then write the correction.

Proofreading Exercise

Can you correct the eight errors in this student paragraph? You may find errors in words often confused, run-together sentences, fragments, or agreement of subject and verb. No answers are provided.

THE DENVER MINT

Are family all went on a trip to Denver last summer we wanted to see the Rockies for the first time. We did a lot of sightseeing but the most interesting place was the Denver Mint. Coins our made in two places in the United States those two places are Philadelphia and Denver. Therefore all of us was eager to see the Denver Mint. It produces 20 to 40 million coins a day. A river of money! A coin goes from a sheet of nickel alloy threw a rumbling stamping machine into a bag for shipping. We stood and watched for a long time. It was exciting to see a coin in the making.

USING PARALLEL CONSTRUCTION

Your writing will be clearer if you use parallel construction. That is, when you make any kind of list, put the items in similar form. If you write

She likes cooking, weaving, and to make pottery.

the sentence lacks parallel construction. The items don't all have the same form. But if you write

She likes cooking, weaving, and making pottery.

then the items are parallel. They all have the same form. They are all *ing* words. Or you could write

She likes to cook, to weave, and to make pottery.

Again the sentence has parallel construction because the items all have the same form. They all use *to* and a verb. Here are some more examples. Note how much easier it is to read the column with parallel construction.

LACKING PARALLEL CONSTRUCTION	HAVING PARALLEL CONSTRUCTION
They were looking for a house with six rooms, a full basement, and it should have an all-electric kitchen.	They were looking for a house with six rooms, a full basement, and an all-electric kitchen. (All three items can be read smoothly after the preposition *with*.)
She is intelligent, outgoing, and she likes to help people.	She is intelligent, outgoing, and helpful. (All three words describe her.)
Because I worked hard, had a good attendance record, and I often suggested new ideas, I was promoted.	Because I worked hard, had a good attendance record, and often suggested new ideas, I was promoted. (All three items can be read smoothly after *Because I*.)
I did all my math, studied my Spanish, and then there was that composition to write.	I did all my math, studied my Spanish, and then started my composition. (All items begin with a verb in past time.)

The supporting points for a thesis statement should always be parallel. For the following thesis statements, the supporting points in the left-hand column are not all constructed alike. Those in the right-hand column are; they are parallel.

NOT PARALLEL	PARALLEL
Playing in the college orchestra has been a valuable experience.	Playing in the college orchestra has been a valuable experience.
1. I've improved my playing. 2. Made friends. 3. Trips.	1. I've improved my playing. 2. I've made good friends. 3. I've had out-of-town trips.
My decision to study at the library was wise.	My decision to study at the library was wise.
1. I have no distractions. 2. Spend more time. 3. No fridge.	1. I have no distractions. 2. I spend my allotted time. 3. I have no fridge to tempt me.

Using parallel construction will make your writing more effective. Note the effective parallelism in these well-known quotations:

With malice toward none, with charity for all, with firmness in the right as God gives us to see the right . . .

—Abraham Lincoln

It was the best of times, it was the worst of times, it was the age of wisdom, it was the age of foolishness, it was the epoch of belief, it was the epoch of incredulity, it was the season of Light, it was the season of Darkness, it was the spring of hope, it was the winter of despair . . .

—Charles Dickens

Let both sides seek to invoke the wonders of science instead of its terrors. Together let us explore the stars, conquer the deserts, eradicate disease, tap the ocean depths, and encourage the arts and commerce.

—John F. Kennedy

EXERCISES

Most—but not all—of these sentences lack parallel construction. Cross out the part that is not parallel and write the correction above.

☐EXERCISE 1

1. I like living in Bellevue because I can go fishing, sailing, or take a ski trip without driving very far.

2. Sacramento has a great climate, excellent parks, and you can go to good plays and concerts.

3. He can ski, swim, and he has even learned to sail a boat.

4. The goals of this course are critical reading, careful writing, and being able to think clearly.

5. I haven't decided whether to go into medicine or be a lawyer.

6. I like hiking, mountain climbing, and I especially like camping out.

7. It's not only what you do but the way in which it's done.

8. Expecting a phone call, dreading it, and yet wanting it, I sat there all evening.

9. The orchestra leader asked us to come to practice at 7:00, that we should get our instruments tuned immediately, and to be ready to start practicing at 7:15.

10. I admire her. I love her. I find that I need her.

☐EXERCISE 2

1. Whatever the weather, whatever your mood, even though you have obligations, save a few minutes to vote on Election Day.

2. He is succeeding through hard work, persistence, and maybe he's also having a bit of luck.

3. I am learning how to study, the way to organize my time, and how to concentrate.

4. The speed-reading course has taught me not only to read faster but also comprehending more of what I read.

5. The visitors to the island were impressed with the quiet friendliness of the people, the lack of hard-sell tactics in the stores, the absence of billboards and neon lights, and of course they liked the balmy weather.

6. The speaker said that applause before a speech is faith, during a speech is hope, and after a speech is charity.

7. In Mount Rainier National Park in Washington are flower-covered meadows, luxuriant alpine forests, and there are also lots of birds and animals.

8. The park is famed for its 40 square miles of glaciers that are still active but that are only a remnant of the vast rivers of ice of the past.

9. Glaciers move from a fraction of an inch to as much as 100 feet a day depending on the thickness of the ice, the atmospheric temperature, and it also depends on the degree of slope down which the glacier is moving.

10. The National Park Service administers 367 areas covering 80 million acres in 49 states. The areas include national parks, national monuments, battlefields, national seashores, and also included are national cemeteries.

☐EXERCISE 3

1. Since we had always wanted to see Williamsburg, since we both had time off last month, and since we had saved enough money, we made the trip.

2. Reading about Williamsburg, planning our trip, and then to get our route worked out kept us busy.

3. We liked visiting the reconstructed village because we could visit the cooper, the silversmith, and watch a shoemaker.

4. An eighteenth-century shoemaker might work 12 hours, average two pair of shoes, and he would earn praise for his speedy work.

5. When goods were shipped in the eighteenth century, they were put in barrels, in kegs, and buckets were also used.

6. The cooper learned not only to make open buckets but designing closed containers as well.

7. The barrels and kegs were used to store goods as well as shipping them.

8. Eighteenth-century music was performed on harpsichord, violin, and flute.

9. The crape myrtle in Williamsburg is an interesting tree because it seems to have no bark, blooms beautifully in the heat of summer, and it has a strange growth pattern.

10. The Raleigh Tavern was a popular meeting place, a center for business deals, and auctions were held there too.

□EXERCISE 4

1. I've been reading that the railroad industry is dying, that we used to have almost 270,000 miles of track in service, that now we have only 129,000 miles, and the number is dropping fast.

2. Analysts predict that by the year 2000 we'll be down to 100,000 miles, and as the lines are dropped from service, the railroad corridors rapidly deteriorate.

3. Some corridors are chopped up for development; some are plowed under for agriculture; and some simply dumping areas for trash.

4. Railroad corridors were often constructed on new land that had never felt the plow, that was part of original prairies and valleys, and is today part of our natural heritage.

5. The corridors often went through mountain valleys, beside rivers, deserts, and through other scenic areas.

6. Today these corridors can be turned into trails for nature study, areas for wildlife protection, or conservation of endangered species.

7. Or they can be turned into recreation trails for hiking, biking, walking, skiing, or for horseback riding.

8. About 564 rail trails with a total of 6,800 miles have already been created in 45 states.

9. Changing rails into trails turns railroad loss into natural area gain.

10. Fortunately, "rail-to-trail" advocates are now trying to save this part of our natural heritage, are planning for an "emerald necklace" linking the various parts of our country, and fast gaining public support.

Underline the examples of parallelism in these paragraphs.

☐EXERCISE 5

In April of 1884—that's right, 1884, not 1984—Thomas Stevens began a bicycle trip from Oakland, California, to Boston. Stevens, then called a wheelman, had a bicycle with a big front wheel 50 inches in diameter and a small rear wheel 17 inches in diameter. It wasn't easy to mount or to ride, but Stevens started on his journey across deserts, mountains, streams, and fields. He saw wild horses, cougars, and wolves, and he was once pursued by a pack of coyotes. The only way he could get across the Sacramento River was by pedaling across a railroad trestle. As he felt the bumping of the huge front wheel from tie to tie, he wondered whether he would ever get to the other side. Then about halfway across he heard the whistle of a freight train. He climbed down to a support beam beneath the track, braced himself on the beam, hung on to his 75-pound bicycle, watched the raging river below, and heard the freight train roaring above him. But he survived. When some Indians saw him pedaling across the vast prairie, they left him entirely alone because they didn't know what to make of him. When he stopped in a Nevada town to rest, the people couldn't understand how a vehicle with only two wheels could be ridden without falling over. After 103 days Stevens reached Boston. He had traveled 3,700 miles. To say that he had ridden his bicycle that far wouldn't be quite accurate because for about a third of the way the terrain was so rough that he had had to carry, push, shove, or drag his 75-pound steed. In Boston he was given a magnificent welcome as the first person to cycle across the United States.

☐EXERCISE 6

It used to be that when I dialed 411, Information, an operator would answer, listen to my request, leaf through the pages of her directories until she found the number I wanted, and then read it to me. It was a personal call. Today when I dial 411, Directory Assistance, almost anywhere in New Jersey, for example, 356 operators are there to take my call. Each operator handles four calls a minute, and an expert operator can complete 1,400 calls a day. A computer decides which operator has been free the longest—measured in milliseconds—and gives my call to that operator. Within six seconds the operator speaks to me, listens to my request, plucks my desired number from millions of listings, and has it read to me by a computer. The time between my dialing 411 and my receiving the requested number has been only 22 seconds. It's not personal service anymore, but it's mighty efficient.

Source: *Smithsonian,* November 1986

Make the supporting points of these thesis statements parallel.

□EXERCISE 7

1. Recycling cans and bottles has been worthwhile.
   1. It has reused valuable resources.

   2. Prevents littering.

   3. It has made Americans conscious of ecological problems.

2. Air bags should be standard equipment on new cars.
   1. They are more effective than seat belts.

   2. They would reduce injuries.

   3. Worth the cost.

3. My summer job on the playground for the disabled was valuable.
   1. It provided funds for my first year of college.

   2. It provided experience for my career.

   3. Opportunity to do something for society.

4. A camping trip in Estes Park gave me some new insights.
   1. I now know I'm capable of coping with hardship.

   2. New interest in nature.

   3. Ecology.

5. Improving one's vocabulary is important.
   1. It will lead to improvement in academic grades.

   2. Lead to a more successful career.

   3. Give one personal satisfaction.

JOURNAL WRITING

Write two sentences with parallel construction, one telling why you think you'd enjoy a certain career and the other telling why you'd like to live in a certain place.

CORRECTING SHIFT IN TIME

If you begin writing a paper in past time, don't shift now and then to the present; and if you begin in the present, don't shift to the past. In the following paragraph the writer starts in the present and then shifts to the past and then back to the present again.

> In Eudora Welty's short story "A Worn Path," old Phoenix Jackson encounters all sorts of hazards on her long walk to Natchez to get some medicine for her grandson. But she overcame them all and at the doctor's office was given not only the medicine but also a nickel, which she plans to spend on a paper windmill for her grandson.

It should be all in the present:

> In Eudora Welty's short story "A Worn Path," old Phoenix Jackson encounters all sorts of hazards on her long walk to Natchez to get some medicine for her grandson. But she overcomes them all and at the doctor's office is given not only the medicine but also a nickel, which she plans to spend on a paper windmill for her grandson.

Or it could be all in the past:

> In Eudora Welty's short story "A Worn Path," old Phoenix Jackson encountered all sorts of hazards on her long walk to Natchez to get some medicine for her grandson. But she overcame them all and at the doctor's office was given not only the medicine but also a nickel, which she planned to spend on a paper windmill for her grandson.

EXERCISES

These sentences have shifts in time, either from past to present or from present to past. Make all the verbs in each sentence agree with the first verb used. Cross out the incorrect verb and write the correct one above it.

☐EXERCISE 1

1. Only a few feet in front of me I saw a quail, and I walk quietly forward, hoping not to frighten it away.

2. After I finished studying, I decide to jog a few miles.

3. We were enjoying the game tremendously, and then it begins to rain.

4. I tried to keep a study schedule, but sometimes I give up.

5. I closed my book, had a snack, and then decide to call it a day.

6. I wanted to register for that course, but it was full, so I register for this one.

7. He thought he wanted a job, but then he finally come back to college.

8. I added something to my knowledge of nature today; I learn the difference between cumulus and nimbostratus clouds.

9. In *The Grapes of Wrath* John Steinbeck wrote about the dust bowl days. He describes how one family left their home in Oklahoma and migrated to California.

10. When I was seven, I ran away and stayed away until dark; then I come home.

These selections shift back and forth between present and past time. Change the verbs to agree with the first verb used.

☐EXERCISE 2

1. Eric Berne's *Games People Play* shows how people play games instead of acting frankly. It explained that people play the game of Blemish by pointing out other people's faults in order to enhance their own image.

2. Mark Twain gives us a saga of the Mississippi River in his novel *The Adventures of Huckleberry Finn*. The story was told by Huck and recounts the adventures of the two most famous boys in American literature.

3. Hans Selye, a world authority on stress, says that life without stress would be boring and meaningless, but he also said that it must be the right kind of stress.

4. My friends decided to drive to Pasadena to see the Rose Parade, but when they got there, the crowds were so great that they can't get near, and they have to settle for watching the parade on TV.

5. On the day in 1937 when the Golden Gate Bridge was finally completed and opened to the public, a mob of pedestrians makes a mad dash to be the first to cross the bridge.

6. An article in *Discover* says that 42,000 mites live in every ounce of dust under our beds. It also said that the mites live by eating the 50 million skin scales our bodies shed every day.

7. Walking catfish, an introduced species in Florida, use their fins as legs and can breathe on land. They cross roads and fields in search of a new environment while other fish couldn't leave the marshy water they were in.

☐EXERCISE 3

The planners of the 1893 Chicago World's Fair wanted something spectacular that would beat the Eiffel Tower of the 1889 Paris Exposition. Finally George Ferris, Jr., decided to accept the challenge and built a giant steel wheel 250 feet in diameter that was suspended between steel towers and that could carry 36 cars, each seating 60 people, making a total of 2,160 riders. Everyone said that people would be afraid to ride in such a contraption, but by the end of the fair one and a half million people had paid the price of 50 cents to take a ride. After the fair was over, George Ferris had financial reversals, but still he leaves to posterity his name—in Ferris wheels.

☐EXERCISE 4

I've been reading about some of the changes the various presidents made in the White House when they moved into it. Thomas Jefferson had the backyard wooden "necessary" of John Adams torn down in 1800 and replaced upstairs by two "Water Closets . . . prepared so as to be cleaned constantly by a pipe throwing Water through them at command from a reservoir above." Then Andrew Jackson decides to have running water put in the White House. James Polk had the first gaslights installed in 1848.

Benjamin Harrison had electric lights installed in 1891, but he forbade members of his family to touch the light switches lest they be electrocuted. A fearless servant has to snap them on and off.

☐**EXERCISE 5**

Having heard about the unusual Boston Children's Museum, I decided to visit it. Children were everywhere, running, screaming, laughing. With no "Do Not Touch" signs to stop them, they were climbing, feeling, pushing, pulling, and operating the exhibits. Some children were taking off their shoes to go into an authentic Japanese house; some were filling a gas tank; some were examining a house sliced in two from cellar to attic to show its plumbing, gas lines, and electric lines.

Still other children were experimenting in the "What If You Couldn't?" room. One little girl is finding her way blindfolded with a white cane. One boy is tapping out his name on a Braille typewriter. One is trying to propel a wheelchair along a gravel path and up a slight incline. Another is walking with metal crutches. Thus they are gaining an understanding of and a compassion for the disabled.

In this museum the children were all educating themselves by doing.

The following student papers shift back and forth between past time and present. Change the verbs to agree with the first verb used, thus making the whole paper read smoothly.

☐**EXERCISE 6**

MY BEARSKIN BLANKET

One cold March evening I came home late and got ready for bed. I think I must have switched myself onto automatic as I went through the familiar routine of taking off my clothes, brushing my teeth, and setting my clock radio. At least I know I must not have been very aware of anything.

I turned out the lights, crawled into bed, and reach for my bearskin blanket, which keeps me toasty warm on the coldest of nights. I reach but can't find it. I check the floor to see if it has fallen off the bed. Nothing. My mind wakes out of its half-asleep-already state. I pause and try to think where in my room it was. I shook my head and peered into the darkness, but I can't see a thing.

"Something strange here," I thought.

I get up, grope for the light switch, and see that my desk drawers are all open and ransacked. And there is no bearskin blanket anywhere.

"What's been going on? Someone's been in my room," I thought.

Now my mind races as I scan the room. My stereo was still there, and my TV is OK, and I didn't have anything else valuable, but someone has been in my room. I found a few other things missing: my camera, some change from a jar, and a half bottle of wine from the cupboard. I was furious. I had left my door unlocked, so I really was angry at myself too. But the worst part was the idea that someone has been looking through my things. I felt as if my privacy had been invaded.

Well, after a few days of rage, I finally calmed down and give up ever recovering my bearskin blanket. Now I lock my door when I go out.

☐EXERCISE 7

THE DAY I FLEW

I had always wanted to fly a plane, so I grab at my chance. I had saved the money for lessons, and I had enough enthusiasm to fly a jumbo jet.

That first time I flew I remember the sensation of leaving the ground and feeling the air pull us off the runway and float us upward and cushion us from the effects of gravity. It was an amazing sensation, a feeling of escaping the ground and leaving gravity behind. It was a wonderful feeling to hear the engine drone as we moved higher and see the earth get smaller below.

My instructor let me do most of the flying even on my first lesson. It seems so easy and yet so impossible that a little plane could get off the ground. I kept trying to remember just what kept us up, and I nervously try to reassure myself that airplanes do work and we aren't going to suddenly fall out of the sky.

I learn to turn left and right and go up or down. In only half an hour I learn the thrill of flying. Then I am reminded how much more there is to flying when my instructor asks me if I know where we are. It has been only a few minutes since we were over the airport, but now I have no idea how to get back.

"There's a lot more to learn," he said as he took over and flew us back. He was right. I learned a lot more in future lessons, but that first time I flew will always be special to me.

JOURNAL WRITING

Write a brief paragraph telling about something that happened to you recently. Then describe the same incident as if it is happening to you at this moment.

CORRECTING SHIFT IN PERSON

You may write a paper in

First person—*I, we*
Second person—*you*
Third person—*he, she, they, one, anyone, a person, people*

but don't shift from one group to another.

Wrong:	In writing a paper, *one* should first write a thesis statement; otherwise *you* may have difficulty organizing your paper.
Right:	In writing a paper, *one* should first write a thesis statement; otherwise *one* may have difficulty organizing the paper.
Right:	In writing a paper, *you* should first write a thesis statement; otherwise *you* may have difficulty organizing your paper.

Wrong:	Few *people* get as much enjoyment out of music as *they* could. *One* need not be an accomplished musician to get some fun out of playing an instrument. Nor do *you* need to be very advanced before joining an amateur group of players.
Right (but stilted):	Few *people* get as much enjoyment out of music as *they* could. *One* need not be an accomplished musician to get some fun out of playing an instrument. Nor does *one* need to be very advanced before joining an amateur group of players.

(Too many *one*'s in a paragraph make it sound stilted and formal. Sentences can be revised to avoid using either *you* or *one*.)

Better:	Few *people* get as much enjoyment out of music as *they* could. It's not necessary to be an accomplished musician to get some fun out of playing an instrument. Nor is it necessary to be very advanced before joining an amateur group of players.

Also, too frequent use of the expressions *he or she* and *him or her* can make a paper sound awkward. Turn back to page 120 to see how a sentence can be revised to avoid sex bias without using those expressions.

Wrong:	A student should not cut classes; otherwise *you* may miss something important.
Right (but awkward):	A student should not cut classes; otherwise *he or she* may miss something important.
Better:	Students should not cut classes; otherwise *they* may miss something important.

Often students write *you* in a paper when they don't really mean *you, the reader*.

You could tell that the speaker wasn't well prepared.

Such sentences are always improved by getting rid of the *you*.

It was obvious that the speaker wasn't well prepared.

Sometimes, however, a shift to *you* is permissible. The paper beginning on page 202 shifts in the next-to-the-last sentence to *your* and *yourself*. The shift seems more natural than using the correct *my*, and *myself*.

As a rule, though, a shift in person should be avoided.

EXERCISES

Change the pronouns (and verbs when necessary) so that there will be no shift in person. Cross out the incorrect words and write the correct ones above. Sometimes you may want to change a sentence from singular to plural to avoid using the awkward *he or she*. Sentences 7 and 10 that follow are examples.

☐EXERCISE 1

1. I enjoy jogging because you feel so good when you quit.

2. I like living in Florida because you have good weather all year.

3. All those who intend to graduate should order your gowns immediately.

4. I used to think my parents were fussy, but as you get older you become more tolerant.

5. If one has done all these exercises, you should get a perfect score on the final.

6. When we opened the door that morning, you could see rabbit tracks in the snow.

7. Often a person can find work if you are willing to take what you can get.

8. We were on the plane for four hours, and you get tired of sitting that long.

9. When we looked down, you could see the little farms growing smaller and smaller.

10. A beginning driver should stay out of heavy traffic until you have more experience.

When students write *you* in a paper, they usually don't mean *you the reader*. Getting rid of the *you* will usually get rid of wordiness too.

☐EXERCISE 2

1. After you finish that course in psychology, you're a different person.

2. You need to exercise every day if you want to keep fit.

3. I like being with a person you can be perfectly frank with.

4. I spent two days in Williamsburg, but you really need more time if you want to see everything.

5. If you want to succeed in college, you need a good vocabulary.

6. You should have seen the fancy costume she wore to the masquerade.

7. When our instructor gives an assignment, he expects you to finish it by the next day.

8. After an escape like that, you felt lucky to be alive.

9. When you watch TV for a whole evening, you realize how much violence is on the programs.

10. When we started the car, you could hear that something was wrong with the motor.

□EXERCISE 3

1. I've been windsurfing for the last two years.

2. I love the feeling of sailing along on a surfboard under wind power.

3. I have a short board that goes so fast that I can jump off waves and soar through the air for a few moments.

4. It's an amazing feeling to fly like a kite.

5. Then if you're careful, you gently touch down on the water again and sail away.

6. But if you haven't done it right, you crash into the water.

7. Then you have to start all over again.

8. It's worth a few crashes though for the times that you soar in the wind.

9. You won't find windsurfing easy at first.

10. But for me it's the perfect sport.

Revise these paragraphs to avoid the shift in person.

□EXERCISE 4

Can the use of headphones cause hearing loss? Many people think hearing loss is just a part of aging, but doctors now warn that it's a result of damage done in early years. Loud noises cause hearing loss by damaging and eventually killing the sensory cells in our ears. The widespread use of headphones is one cause of later hearing loss. It's been found that when headphones are taken off, they're often running many times louder than what is considered the danger level. Other causes of hearing loss are power mowers and motorcycles. Doctors say you should wear earplugs when you mow your lawn or ride a motorcycle. Another cause is traffic noise although it's not as loud as it was a few years ago because the noise levels of jet engines and trucks have been lowered. We need to be aware of these sounds that can damage our hearing beyond repair.

☐EXERCISE 5

When I think of museums, I think of the Smithsonian in Washington, D.C., and the Field Museum in Chicago, but I've just learned that there are hundreds of little museums all over the country. For example, in Phoenix, Arizona, the Hall of Flame contains fire-fighting vehicles dating back to 1725 as well as thousands of badges, helmets, and uniforms. In Eatonton, Georgia, the Uncle Remus Museum, housed in two former slave cabins, has artifacts concerning Joel Chandler Harris and his stories about Br'er Rabbit and Br'er Fox. The Barbed Wire Museum in La Crosse, Kansas, has the world's most complete collection of barbed wire with more than 500 varieties. When you walk into the Grocery Hall of Fame in Vancouver, British Columbia, it's like walking into a corner store of 50 years ago with about 10,000 products on display. In the American Museum of Fly Fishing in Manchester, Vermont, you'll see the rods used by Daniel Webster, Ernest Hemingway, and Bing Crosby. I intend to see a few of these museums someday.

☐EXERCISE 6

In 1986 Los Angeles held its third Marathon. The Marathon, unlike most sports, includes ordinary people and not just great athletes. Almost 15,000 people ran the 26.2 miles, some coming from as far away as Brazil and New Zealand. Of course the winners were experienced runners, covering the 26.2 miles in slightly over two hours whereas many of the general runners made it in about four. But as the sponsors said, everyone was a winner. You would have been amazed to see 15 disabled people in wheelchairs racing the 26.2 miles. Their chairs had been built especially for racing and weighed only about 14 pounds. One of the wheelchair racers from Edmonton, Alberta, was the winner in their group.

☐EXERCISE 7

The construction of the Washington Monument, honoring the first president of the United States, was begun in 1848, but from the beginning there was disagreement about the plans. Then with the coming of the Civil War, construction ceased, and for almost 26 years the monument stood as an incomplete stump. Finally work was resumed, and the monument was completed in 1884. The new marble, however, was a slightly different hue from the first marble used, and today you can see the line marking the division between the two parts. Within the monument 898 steps lead to the top, but you can also make the ascent in an elevator in about 70 seconds.

JOURNAL WRITING

1. Write a brief paragraph telling someone how to learn to spell. It will, of course, be a "you should" paragraph.
2. Then write the same paragraph to yourself—an "I should" paragraph.
3. Finally write the same paragraph using "students should" and using the pronoun *they*.

CORRECTING WORDINESS

Good writing is concise writing. Don't say something in ten words if you can say it as well, or better, in five. "In this day and age" isn't as effective as simply "today." "At this point in time" should be "at present" or "now."

Another kind of wordiness comes from saying something twice. There's no need to say "in the month of July" or "7 A.M. in the morning" or "my personal opinion." July *is* a month, 7 A.M. *is* morning, and my opinion *is* personal. All you need to say is "in July," "7 A.M.," and "my opinion."

Still another kind of wordiness comes from using expressions that add nothing to the meaning of the sentence. "The fact of the matter is that I'm tired" says no more than "I'm tired."

WORDY WRITING	CONCISE WRITING
an unexpected surprise	a surprise
a person who is honest	an honest person
as a general rule	as a rule
brown in color	brown
due to the fact that	because
each and every	each
enclosed herewith	enclosed
end result	result
free gift	gift
he is a person who	he
important essentials	essentials
in order to	to
past history	history
refer back	refer
repeat again	repeat
serious crisis	crisis
small in size	small
surrounded on all sides	surrounded
usual custom	custom
the field of electronics	electronics
there are many boys who	many boys
there is no doubt but that	no doubt
two different kinds	two kinds
very unique	unique

Thomas Jefferson said, "The most valuable of all talents is that of never using two words when one will do."

EXERCISES

Cross out words or rewrite parts of each sentence to get rid of the wordiness. Doing these exercises can almost turn into a game to see how few words you can use without changing the meaning of the sentence.

☐EXERCISE 1

1. A player who had experience would have had an idea about what to do.

2. The girl who had roomed with me during my college years now was going to make a trip to see me.

3. Personally I think that the field of electronics is a good field to go into.

4. In the month of May two of the members of our family have birthdays.

5. The story I am going to tell you is a story that I heard from my grandfather.

6. It seems to me that the government should be able to work out some way to speed up the judicial process in the courts of our land.

7. What I'm trying to say is that I think justice should be swift and sure.

8. I grew up as a child in an ordinary small town.

9. Owing to the fact that I had a lot of work to do, it wasn't possible for me to accept their invitation.

10. I was unaware of the fact that she was leaving.

☐EXERCISE 2

1. History is a subject that interests me a great deal.

2. The professor is a man who makes his subject interesting to everyone.

3. I have no doubt but that he spends a great deal of time preparing each lecture and getting ready to present it to the class.

4. This polish will double the life of your shoes and make them last twice as long.

5. A personal friend of mine has a very unique invention.

6. There was a lot of objection on the part of the taxpayers.

7. It was 5 A.M. in the morning when we started, and we got there at 6 P.M. that evening.

8. In the month of August most of the employees of this institution of ours take a vacation.

9. The fact of the matter is that I have not had time to prepare an agenda for the program for our meeting this afternoon.

10. I want to repeat my final conclusion again.

☐EXERCISE 3

1. The purple martin circled around and around the martin house for half an hour and then disappeared from view.

2. He was arrested for driving his car in an intoxicated condition.

3. At the present time modern present-day medicine has practically wiped out polio from our country.

4. There were a number of spectators who couldn't get seats.

5. It is my opinion that the grandstand is not as large as it should be.

6. As you may be aware, a fly has a little suction cup on each of its six feet, and this enables it to walk on the ceiling without falling off.

7. The hardest exam that I had last semester was a psychology exam.

8. That exam included a number of questions about things that I had forgotten about completely.

9. The magpie is a bird that is quite large and has a black head, a long greenish tail, and white wing patches on its wings.

10. She is a person who will always do whatever she promises that she'll do.

☐EXERCISE 4

1. In spite of the fact that I hadn't eaten since morning, I wasn't hungry.

2. I'm hoping that I'll be able to find a job in the not-too-distant future.

3. Owing to the fact that there was no announcement of the meeting, not many people came.

4. There were 10 people who were planning to come.

5. Within a period of three months, six of the people in the department have handed in their resignations.

6. I learned to identify three different kinds of ivy on the field trip that I went on this morning.

7. I've gained 10 pounds in weight since I first began this diet.

8. Each and every person who attended the opening of the new store received a free gift.

9. I'm convinced of the fact that I use entirely too many words in many of the sentences that I write.

10. There is no doubt but that many people do the exact same thing.

These paragraphs are from a university publication about a new library. On a separate sheet, revise them to get rid of the wordiness. The material as it stands has 241 words; the revision at the back of the book has 126—just about half as many. Can you make a revision that concise and still keep the essential information? Finish your revision and count the words before you check with the one at the back of the book.

☐EXERCISE 5

1. Whatever has been accomplished has been made possible because of the cooperation of the university administration, faculty, students, and the library staff working together.

2. Periodicals do not circulate because of the heavy use by all students, and this provision guarantees that they will always be available. Many divisions provide photoduplication facilities so that articles from the periodicals can be easily reproduced.

3. The Information Center is a general reference area which assists faculty and students in the use of the card catalogue, basic reference books, bibliographies, and indexes. There is an orientation program for the purpose of instructing students on library procedures as well as the Inter-Library Loan service.

4. The Reserve Reading Room houses and circulates those books and materials which the faculty has chosen as required reading for current courses.

5. In the Music Division there are at present ten listening stations, and six of these are equipped with cassette recorders which can be used to record a particular piece of music so that the listener can play it back several times in order to study it.

6. Much of the material essential to a new library is no longer available in printed form. Technology has overcome this problem with the development of microfilms, microcards, and microfiche. The library contains over one million items of microfilms, and the students soon discover the very attractive rooms which house the latest equipment for accommodating these items, as well as microprint machines if copies are required.

AVOIDING CLICHÉS

A cliché is an expression that has been used so often it has lost its originality and effectiveness. Whoever first said "light as a feather" had thought of an original way to express lightness, but today that expression is outworn and boring. Most of us use an occasional cliché in speaking, but clichés have no place in writing. The good writer thinks up new ways to express ideas.

Here are a few clichés. Add some more to the list.

better late than never
busy as a bee
crazy as a loon
down in the dumps
few and far between
fresh as a daisy
go from bad to worse
in seventh heaven
not my cup of tea
put his foot down
safe and sound
sick as a dog

sink or swim
thank my lucky stars
the last straw
under the weather

Clichés are boring because the reader always knows what's coming next. What comes next in these expressions?

all work and no . . .

bring home the . . .

burning the midnight . . .

easier said than . . .

fighting a losing . . .

fit to be . . .

On a separate sheet rewrite these sentences to get rid of the clichés.

☐EXERCISE 1

1. We had planned to go to the lake, and I was up bright and early, raring to go.
2. But my wife was sleeping like a log, and our son was dead to the world.
3. I started the breakfast, but I was all thumbs and couldn't get the orange juice can open to save my life.
4. Finally I did get the breakfast on the table and called the others. I was determined to get rolling, come hell or high water.
5. When they finally came downstairs, they were hungry as bears, but they complained that the toast was cold.
6. I told them they were making a mountain out of a molehill and that they should be grateful for small favors.
7. Eventually we got in the car and took off, but as luck would have it, we had gone only a mile when it began raining cats and dogs.
8. Finally though, the skies cleared, and we got to the lake safe and sound.
9. Our son immediately jumped into the lake because he swims like a fish.
10. My wife soon followed him, but I just sat on the beach like a bump on a log and took a well-earned rest.

JOURNAL WRITING

One way to become aware of clichés so that you won't use them in your writing is to see how many you can purposely put into a paragraph. Write a paragraph describing your difficulties trying to make an eight o'clock class every morning. Use all the clichés possible while still keeping your account smooth and clear. What title will you give your paragraph? Why, a cliché of course. Writing such a paragraph should make you so aware of clichés that they'll never creep into your writing again.

Review of Sentence Structure

Only one sentence in each pair is correct. Read both sentences carefully before you decide. Then write the letter of the *correct* sentence in the blank. You may find any of these errors:

run-together sentence
fragment
wrong verb form
lack of agreement between subject and verb
wrong pronoun
faulty reference of pronoun
dangling modifier
lack of parallel construction
shift in time or person

_____ 1. A. They invited Juan and me to go along.
    B. They invited Juan and I to go along.

_____ 2. A. He ask his parents for more money, and they gave it to him.
    B. They gave an award to him and his brother.

_____ 3. A. One cannot make people learn; you can only show them the way.
    B. I've worked really hard and think I'll pass the course.

_____ 4. A. The director asked Kristin and me to help with the publicity.
    B. I can't decide whether to be a secretary, a nurse, or go into teaching.

_____ 5. A. Having washed the car, I found the swimming pool inviting.
    B. Kirk told the professor that his watch was wrong.

_____ 6. A. Have you finish your assignment yet?
    B. He invited my brother and me to go for a ride in his boat.

_____ 7. A. Most of the class were prepared for the exam.
    B. I finished my math then I spent the rest of the evening watching TV.

_____ 8. A. Racing down the hill, I fell and sprained my ankle.
    B. I made the lunch, set the table, and then I sat down to wait.

_____ 9. A. Having prepared a tasty lunch, the table looked beautiful.
    B. We got an invitation from him and his wife.

_____ 10. A. A list of required readings was posted in the library.
    B. I rewrote my paper, typed it, and proofread it, and then I ran for class.

_____ 11. A. Making the most of every opportunity that came his way.
 B. When I turned in for the night, I fell asleep immediately.

_____ 12. A. There's no use complaining it's too late now.
 B. I certainly didn't choose an easy course.

_____ 13. A. The instructor gave A's to both Melissa and me.
 B. Sticking to a strict diet, my weight gradually came down.

_____ 14. A. Most of my friends are going to work this summer.
 B. I was driving along at the speed limit when I see a cop following me.

_____ 15. A. She cleared the table, washed the dishes, and then she dusted the living room.
 B. Of course they blamed my friend and me.

_____ 16. A. She told her sister she was too late.
 B. Our team had worked hard but couldn't compete with them.

_____ 17. A. Getting a B made me happy and caused me to have more self-confidence.
 B. Each of my sisters have their own phone now.

_____ 18. A. When one writes a thesis statement, you should make the points parallel.
 B. I worked until midnight and even then didn't finish.

_____ 19. A. She's beautiful, talented, and has lots of money.
 B. The car belongs to my fiancé and me.

_____ 20. A. Graduating from college, and then being unable to find a job.
 B. Each of my three friends has a scholarship.

_____ 21. A. I had been studying since morning I had to have a break.
 B. I wish they'd invite my husband and me sometime.

_____ 22. A. The rain dampen the heads but not the spirits of the cheering crowd.
 B. I enjoy math and psychology, but I find history and English difficult.

_____ 23. A. Each of his children is interested in music.
 B. Having worked hard all semester, my grades improved.

_____ 24. A. The instructor asked Jill and me to lead a group discussion.
 B. I came around a turn in the road, and there I see a pheasant in front of me.

_____ 25. A. You was here before I was, so you should go in first.
 B. They offered my wife and me their cottage for a week.

Proofreading Exercise

Can you correct the seven errors in this paragraph? No answers are provided at the back of the book.

A LIVING CURIOSITY

The ostrich is one of natures living curiosities. It's a bird, but it can't fly. It gets away from it's enemies because its long legs make it a good runner with a speed of up to 65 km an hour. Also its enemies have difficulty approaching it because its huge eyes can see danger a long way off. Its eyes weigh more then its brain and are larger than the eyes of any other animal. Its the largest bird in existence. The adult male stands about 2.5 meters high with almost half its height in its long neck. Ostrich eggs weigh a kilogram apiece and are the largest eggs laid by any animal. The ostrich can swim but it has difficulty drinking because it can't swallow as other animals do. It has to take water into its mouth by a shoveling motion and then raise its head and neck to let the water flow down its throat. In any group of ostriches you will always find a dominant male holding his tail high to show his superiority. The other males simply let there tails droop.

Punctuation and Capital Letters

3

3 Punctuation and Capital Letters

PERIOD, QUESTION MARK, EXCLAMATION MARK, SEMICOLON, COLON, DASH

Every mark of punctuation should help the reader. Just like red and green signals at an intersection, marks of punctuation will keep the reader, like the traffic, from getting snarled up.

Here are the rules for six marks of punctuation. The first three you have known for a long time and have no trouble with. The one about semicolons you learned when you studied independent clauses (p. 76). The ones about the colon and the dash may be less familiar.

Put a period at the end of a sentence and after most abbreviations.

Mr.	A.D.	Dr.	Wed.	sq. ft.
Ms.	etc.	Jan.	P.M.	lbs.

Put a question mark after a direct question (but not after an indirect one).

What time is it? (the exact words of the speaker)
He asked what time it was. (not the exact words)

Put an exclamation mark after an expression that shows strong emotion.

Help! I'm lost!

Put a semicolon between two closely related independent clauses unless they are joined by one of the connecting words *and, but, for, or, nor, yet, so*. (Refer to pp. 76–77 for more information about the semicolon.)

The day was bitter cold; we didn't venture outdoors.
I need to study; therefore I'm going to the library.

Actually you can write quite acceptably without ever using semicolons because a period and capital letter can always be used instead of a semicolon.

The day was bitter cold. We didn't venture outdoors.
I need to study. Therefore I'm going to the library.

Put a colon after a complete sentence when a list or long quotation follows.

In the trunk of our car were the following items: two sleeping bags, a camp stove, a bag of provisions, and a cooler. (*In the trunk of our car were the following items* is a complete statement. You can hear your voice fall at the end of it. Therefore we put a colon after it before adding the list.)

In the trunk of our car were two sleeping bags, a camp stove, a bag of provisions, and a cooler. (*In the trunk of our car were* is not a complete statement. It needs the list to make it complete. Therefore, since we don't want to separate the list from the first part of the sentence, no colon is used.)

The professor closed his lecture on writing with a quotation from Donald M. Murray: "Maple syrup is the product of boiling 30 or 40 gallons of sap to get one of syrup, and in writing there's a great deal of sap that needs to be boiled down." (*The professor closed his lecture on writing with a quotation from Donald M. Murray* is a complete statement. Therefore we put a colon after it before adding the quotation.)

Donald M. Murray said, "Maple syrup is the product of boiling 30 or 40 gallons of sap to get one of syrup, and in writing there's a great deal of sap that needs to be boiled down." (*Donald M. Murray said* is not a complete statement. Therefore we don't put a colon after it.)

Use a dash to indicate an abrupt change of thought or to throw emphasis upon what follows. Use it sparingly.

And then came the last act—what a letdown.

A Portuguese proverb says that visits always give pleasure—if not in the coming, then in the going.

EXERCISES

Add to these sentences the necessary punctuation—period, question mark, exclamation mark, semicolon, colon, dash. Not all sentences require additional punctuation. Also your answer may differ from the one at the back of the book because either a semicolon or a period with a capital letter may be used between two independent clauses.

☐EXERCISE 1

1. We've bought a place in the country it's only a mile from town.
2. It's a run-down farmhouse it's really only a shell.
3. We enjoy remodeling we'll make something of it.
4. Our outdoor hobbies are gardening and hiking.
5. Our indoor hobbies are these painting, decorating, and furniture refinishing.
6. We'll make use of all our interests not a talent will be wasted.
7. Sure, it will take work it will take money too.
8. Eventually it should pay off at least that's what we're counting on.
9. We'll work at it slowly there's no hurry.
10. Meantime we'll enjoy our surroundings we like the country.

☐EXERCISE 2

1. Did you know there are more than half a million snowflakes in each cubic foot of snow.
2. And did you know that glaciers are formed by snowflakes being compressed for thousands of years into hard ice.
3. Snow delights children it often annoys or inconveniences adults.
4. People think of snow as sterile actually it teems with microorganisms.
5. There are various kinds of snow the Eskimos have more than two dozen words for snow.
6. The U.S. record for snowfall in a period of 24 hours was 75.8 inches in Silver Lake, Colorado, in 1921.
7. Snow begins with ice crystals they are formed in the clouds.
8. They may have various shapes their basic shape is determined by the temperature of the air in which they grow.
9. Several ice crystals may join to form a snowflake the snowflake may be as large as an inch in diameter.
10. No two snowflakes are alike most are six-pointed however.

☐EXERCISE 3

1. Don't you collect aluminum cans the recycling center pays good money for them.
2. Last week I made four dollars on them some weeks I make more.

3. I took a sack out to the park and filled it with empties in 25 minutes.

4. One man told me that he found 300 cans in a forest preserve another found almost that many in vacant lots.

5. Some people hunt mushrooms others hunt aluminum cans.

6. It's not only the money that interests me I like cleaning up our environment.

7. I can't pass by an aluminum can on a forest path I just have to pick it up.

8. I'm taking a course in ecology it has opened my eyes.

9. Our environment is suffering from three things air pollution, water pollution, and unsightly waste.

10. When will people become involved in the cleanup.

☐EXERCISE 4

1. I always thought that spiders were pests now I've learned that they're useful.

2. Among the harmful insects that spiders destroy are the following mosquitoes, flies, grasshoppers, and garden insects.

3. Spiders are found in almost all parts of the world they're the spinners and engineers of nature.

4. Their webs are marvels of geometric design their suspension bridges over streams are amazing.

5. Spider thread is stronger than silkworm thread it can't be obtained, however, in large enough quantities to make cloth.

6. Spiders use their thread in the following ways to spin webs, to catch insects, to line their nests, and to make cocoons for their eggs.

7. About 40,000 kinds of spiders live throughout the world some are the size of a pinhead some are eight inches long.

8. A spider that loses a leg is in no difficulty it simply grows a new one.

9. The female is larger than the male sometimes she eats her mate.

10. Spiders are important in the balance of nature they shouldn't be thoughtlessly killed.

☐EXERCISE 5

1. Are you tired of the long winters some geologists say the winters are getting shorter.

2. In North America 20,000 years ago, ice and snow covered the land the year round there were summers though.

3. The summers were simply too cool to melt the winter snow therefore the snow piled up year after year.

4. In the cold summers only mosses and lichens could grow a few fast-blooming plants also appeared.
5. Today we have remnants of that ice age the Antarctic and Greenland.
6. Most of Greenland is covered by an ice cap the Antarctic also is covered by a sheet of ice.
7. And we have icebergs they are the broken-off ends of glaciers.
8. Some are tiny others are mountains a mile across.
9. The part below the water is as much as seven times larger than the part above the water also the part below may extend farther than the visible part.
10. The *Titantic* struck part of an iceberg not visible above the water the ship went down near Newfoundland in 1912 with 1,513 people on board.

☐EXERCISE 6

1. Do you enjoy driving slowly along a country road.
2. Most states are busy building efficient highways one state, however, is also preserving some old country roads.
3. The idea was first presented to the people of Wisconsin in 1973 they gave the proposal their enthusiastic support.
4. The legislature liked the idea too the governor then signed the Rustic Roads Act into law.
5. Now the state has 27 rustic roads moreover requests for more are growing.
6. Along these roads are remnants of the past old stone barns, old mills, log buildings, rusting farm plows and hay rakes, as well as fields of wildflowers.
7. The rustic character of the road is never changed plank bridges are kept, and if one wears out, it is simply replaced with another.
8. Life goes on as it always has visitors can drive along and enjoy the countryside, sharing it with squirrels, deer, beavers, and turtles.
9. Travelers will never see any signs of commercialism billboards, signs, motels, souvenir shops.
10. Wisconsin now has two kinds of roads those for leisurely travel and those for people in a hurry.

☐EXERCISE 7

1. I've been learning some word roots it's a good way to increase one's vocabulary.
2. Words didn't just happen they grew from roots.
3. Yesterday I learned four roots CRED, LOGY, PATH, and TELE.
4. CRED means "to believe" about 15 common words contain that root.

5. Something that is *credible* is believable anything that is *incredible* is not believable.
6. A *creed* is a statement of one's beliefs *credentials* are documents that cause others to believe in one.
7. LOGY means "study of" it is found at the end of hundreds of words.
8. For example, GEO means "earth" therefore *geology* is a study of the earth.
9. ARCH means "ancient" therefore *archeology* is a study of ancient cultures.
10. ASTR means "star" *astrology* is a pseudoscience claiming to tell the future by the stars.

□EXERCISE 8

1. Another root I've learned is PATH it means "feeling."
2. SYM means "together" therefore *sympathy* is literally a feeling together with someone.
3. ANTI means "against" thus *antipathy* is a feeling against someone or something.
4. The root TELE meaning "far" is found in many common words *telephone, telegraph, television, telescope,* and *telepathy*.
5. A *telephone* (PHON sound) lets one hear far sounds a *telegraph* (GRAPH to write) is literally an instrument for far writing.
6. *Television* (VIS to see) lets one see pictures from afar a *telescope* (SCOP to look) lets one look at far objects.
7. *Telepathy* (PATH feeling) is the supposed communication between two people far apart that is, they sense each other's feelings from afar.
8. Other words containing the root TELE are *telegram, telemetry,* and *telephoto*.
9. I now intend to learn more roots they help me remember difficult words.
10. They also surprise me I find more meaning in words I already know.

Punctuate these student paragraphs.

□EXERCISE 9

Have you ever bicycled 87 miles in one day. I have it's not easy. Last year I took part in the Annual Great Bicycle Ride across Iowa. Oh, my poor knees. After the first day I was ready to give up by the next morning though I was eager to continue. There were

9,000 of us ranging in age from an 83-year-old man to a couple of 12-year old girls, we rode the 495 miles across Iowa in seven days. At the start all of us dipped the rear wheels of our bikes in the Big Sioux River at the western border of Iowa, seven days later we dipped our front wheels in the Mississippi at the eastern border. The people in the Iowa towns were friendly and welcomed us at every stop. Of course we brought money to their towns, but that wasn't the reason that they welcomed us it was just plain Iowa friendliness.

□EXERCISE 10

I always thought of coconut as that white stringy stuff in cookies and cream pies, then during my week in Hawaii I discovered that coconut means something more coconut milk. Coconuts are as big as volleyballs and grow on palms, they either fall to the ground, or small boys climb the tree for them. I was told that a coconut palm begins to bear in about seven years and that it then produces nuts for 70 or 80 years. I bought a coconut from a man on the street who was selling them, he took a machete and chopped away at the outer husk and then through the hard shell until he opened a small hole for me to drink from. Somehow the milk tasted cool and refreshing even though the coconut had been in the hot sun all day, the only size coconuts come in is king size, so I sure didn't have to buy another one in order to quench my thirst.

JOURNAL WRITING

Write two sentences, the first requiring a colon and the second not requiring a colon, in which you list the things you have to do this coming weekend. Make sure, of course, that the items are parallel.

WRITING ASSIGNMENT

Continue your writing assignments from the latter part of the book.

COMMAS (Rules 1, 2, and 3)

Students often sprinkle commas through their papers as if they were shaking pepper out of a pepper shaker. Don't use a comma unless you know a rule for it. But commas are important. They help the reader. Without them, a reader would often have to go back and reread a sentence to find out what the writer meant.

Actually you need only six comma rules. MASTER THESE SIX RULES, and your writing will be easier to read. The first rule you have already learned (p. 77).

ALWAYS USE A COMMA BEFORE ~ "BUT"
USE A COMMA IF THE C.C, JOINS TWO COMPLETE SENTENCES

1. **Put a comma before *and, but, for, or, nor, yet, so* when they connect two independent clauses.**

   They started to play Scrabble, and that ended their studying.
   I may try out for the next play, or I may wait until the following one.

But be sure such words do connect two independent clauses. The following sentence is merely one independent clause with one subject and two verbs. Therefore no comma should be used.

   He wanted to try out for the play but didn't have the time.

USE A COMMA AFTER AN INTRODUCTORY CLAUSE
SINCE, BECAUSE, AFTER, ALTHOUGH, BEFORE, WHEN
WHILE, WHENEVER

2. **Put a comma between items in a series.**

   She ordered ice cream, cake, and an éclair.
   He opened the letter, read it hastily, and gave a shout.

Some words "go together" and don't need a comma between them even though they do make up a series.

   The tattered old plush album had belonged to her grandmother.
   Large bright blue violets bordered the path in the woods.

The way to tell whether a comma is needed between two words in a series is to see whether *and* could be used naturally between them. It would sound all right to say *ice cream and cake and an éclair*. Therefore commas are used between the items. But it would not sound right to say *tattered and old and plush* album or *Large and bright and blue violets*. Therefore no commas are used. Simply put a comma where an *and* would sound right.

It's permissible to omit the comma before the *and* connecting the last two members of a series, but more often it's used.

If an address or date is used in a sentence, treat it as a series, putting a comma after every item, including the last.

> He was born on May 17, 1966, in Madison, Wisconsin, and grew up there.
> She lived in Winnipeg, Manitoba, for two years.

When only the month and year are used in a date, the commas are omitted.

> In May 1984 he moved to Chester, Viriginia.

3. **Put a comma after an introductory expression that doesn't flow smoothly into the sentence, or before an afterthought that is tacked on.** It may be a word, a group of words, or a dependent clause.

> No, I'm not interested.
> Well, that's finished.
> Racing to the finish line, she won the 100-meter dash.
> When I entered, the house was in darkness.
> It's important, isn't it?

When you studied dependent clauses, you learned that a dependent clause at the beginning of a sentence needs a comma after it. In the fourth example above, you can see that a comma is necessary. Otherwise the reader would read *When I entered the house* . . . before realizing that that was not what the writer meant. A comma prevents misreading.

EXERCISES

Punctuate these sentences according to the first three comma rules. Correct your answers 10 at a time.

☐EXERCISE 1

1. You always have two choices.
2. You always have had ,and you always will have.
3. You could have gone to college, or you could have taken a job.
4. You chose college and you still have two choices.
5. You can choose to work ,or you can choose to slide.
6. If you choose to work, you still have two choices.
7. You can work for a grade ,or you can work to learn.

8. If you choose to learn, you still have two choices.
9. You can do something with your learning, or you can forget it.
10. As far as you can see into the future, you'll always have two choices.

☐EXERCISE 2

1. One night a friend showed me some constellations in the sky, and I learned a lot.
2. I already could find the Big Dipper, but that was about all.
3. She showed me the Little Dipper, and now I can even find Polaris at the end of the Little Dipper handle.
4. Polaris is the North Star, but I had never before had any idea of its location.
5. She showed me Cassiopeia, and I learned to find it by looking for a large letter W.
6. Since I was really interested, I got a book about constellations the next day.
7. Now I can find Boötes, for it looks like an ice cream cone, with the star Arcturus at the bottom of the cone.
8. According to that book, Arcturus is a giant star with a diameter of 400,000,000 miles.
9. The constellation Hercules, the warrior, and Pegasus, the winged horse, are part of Greek mythology, and I've learned their stories.
10. The constellations are now beginning to have personalities for me, and on a clear night I can find familiar constellations like old friends.

☐EXERCISE 3

1. No matter what the devastation nature always makes a comeback.
2. After the eruption of Mount Saint Helens 150 square miles of countryside lay dead.
3. Everything was covered with gray ash and no green was seen anywhere.
4. But only two months after the eruption small ferns pushed through the ash.
5. A year later tiny fir trees pink fireweed and lupine appeared.
6. Animals began reestablishing themselves too: pocket gophers elk and deer.
7. And ladybugs black ants and honeybees were found at work.
8. People too began to come back for there was cleaning up to do.
9. Some salvaged the fallen timber and others prepared for the tourists.
10. It may take years but the area around Mount Saint Helens will someday be green again.

□EXERCISE 4

1. I've been reading about the history of some common things and I've had some surprises.
2. I thought ice cream was a modern invention but I've discovered that it's had a long history.
3. Alexander the Great enjoyed a chilled mixture of milk honey and fruit juice in 335 B.C.
4. The first ad for ice cream appeared in 1777 and in 1848 a hand-cranked ice-cream freezer was patented.
5. The freezer was a large wooden bucket filled with chipped ice and in the center was the container with the cream sugar eggs and vanilla.
6. The ingredients had to be stirred constantly by a dasher turned by a crank and this stirring made the ice cream freeze smoothly.
7. In the early part of this century every household had an ice-cream freezer and before a meal someone always got the job of cranking the freezer.
8. After perhaps half an hour the ice cream was frozen and one of the children was then given the treat of licking the dasher.
9. The homemade ice cream melted rapidly but that never caused a problem.
10. Before it had a chance to melt it was gone.

□EXERCISE 5

1. When we think of birds we usually think of frail little creatures.
2. Actually birds are stronger than humans in many ways and they have set records beyond human capability.
3. For example in 1987 a tiny semipalmated sandpiper weighing less than an ounce set a new record for the fastest long-distance flight.
4. It was banded and released by researchers in Massachusetts.
5. Within four days it had reached Guyana South America 2,800 miles away.
6. A human runner of course could not even approach such a record.
7. Although most birds fly at low altitudes even small birds can fly as high as 21,000 feet.
8. In comparison humans begin to experience shortness of breath and exhaustion at 14,000 feet.
9. Smaller birds fly 25 to 30 miles an hour but larger birds can fly at speeds of more than a mile a minute.
10. Setting the distance record the Arctic tern flies 11,000 miles each way between its breeding ground in the Arctic and its winter home in the Antarctic.

☐EXERCISE 6

1. I always thought totem poles were just freestanding poles but now I know they had many uses.
2. When I visited the Museum of Anthropology in Vancouver I saw many totem poles and learned that the Northwest Coast Indians used them in various ways.
3. A totem pole might be a corner post of a house or it might be a post to support the roof.
4. A pole with an opening at the base was an entrance to a plank house and other poles simply stood against exterior or interior walls.
5. Some poles were large freestanding memorial poles in honor of deceased high-ranking people and inside such poles might be coffins with human remains.
6. A family totem pole might display figures from family legends or it might have representations of a raven bear beaver frog or a supernatural bird with a huge beak.
7. Humans were also represented and the size of the head was always exaggerated.
8. The southern and central groups of the Northwest Coast Indians carved human figures with heads one-third the body height but the northern group enlarged the head to one-half the body height.
9. Besides having such personal uses some totem poles stood on seashores or riverbanks to welcome visitors.
10. Carved from the trunks of red cedar trees the totem poles tell us something of the history and customs of the Northwest Coast Indians.

☐EXERCISE 7

1. Carl Sandburg was born in Galesburg Illinois on January 6 1878.
2. Between the ages of 13 and 17 he was successively a driver of a milk wagon porter in a barbershop sceneshifter in a theater and truck operator at a brick kiln.
3. Then he went west, where he harvested wheat in the Kansas wheat fields washed dishes at hotels in Kansas City Omaha and Denver and worked as a carpenter's helper in Kansas.
4. Eventually he went to college became a newspaper reporter and began writing poetry.
5. After the publication of his poem "Chicago" he became recognized.
6. Some critics objected to phrases like "Hog Butcher for the World" but the country generally came to accept Sandburg.
7. He chose to write about ordinary things and the public liked his themes.
8. Soon he became one of the best liked poets in the country and he is still a favorite poet of Illinois.

9. Of all his poems "Fog" is the one most people memorize.
10. Although he is best known for his poetry he also wrote an excellent biography of Lincoln.

☐EXERCISE 8

1. We heard a carillon recital from the Bok Singing Tower at Lake Wales Florida.
2. The carillon was designed built and installed in 1928 by an English company.
3. The carillon's 53 tuned bronze bells range in size from 17 pounds to 22,000 pounds and they play a chromatic scale.
4. It's considered one of the finest carillons in the United States and people come from great distances to hear it.
5. Whereas the history of carillons in Europe dates back more than 300 years it is only in this century that carillons have become popular on this continent.
6. Today many college campuses have carillons and many town halls and churches have carillons also.
7. Because the carillons vary in size and complexity they vary in the way they are played.
8. Large carillons for example are often played by a carillonneur who sits at an organlike manual and plays the bells.
9. The bells of other carillons are simply played electronically and still others do not have bells but are just recorded carillon programs.
10. Most carillons strike the hour and many play the Westminster chimes every quarter hour.

☐EXERCISE 9

The Guinness Book of World Records hasn't always been around. It had its beginning in 1951 when some sportsmen in Ireland disagreed about which was the fastest-flying game bird. Sir Hugh Beaver, managing director of Guinness Breweries, said it was the golden plover but he was unable to prove his point because no book contained the information. He decided to create his own book and four years later he published *The Guinness Book of World Records*. In 1974 the book became the world's all-time best-selling copyright book and thus earned its own place in *The Guinness Book of World Records*. By 1990 it had a cumulative sale in 39 languages in excess of 65 million copies and its sales are increasing by 50,000 copies a week.

COMMAS (Rules 4, 5, and 6)

4. Put commas around the name of a person spoken to.

> I hope, Michelle, that you're going with me.
> David, you're an hour late.

5. Put commas around an expression that interrupts the flow of the sentence (such as *however, moreover, finally, therefore, of course, by the way, on the other hand, I am sure, I think*).

> I hope, of course, that the rumor isn't true.
> We decided, therefore, to leave without him.
> The entire trip, I think, will take only an hour.

Read the preceding sentences aloud, and you'll hear how those expressions interrupt the flow of the sentence. Sometimes, however, such expressions flow smoothly into the sentence and don't need commas around them. Whether an expression is an interrupter or not often depends on where it is in the sentence. If it's in the middle of a sentence, it's more likely to be an interrupter than if it's at the beginning or the end. The expressions that were interrupters in the preceding sentences are not interrupters in the following sentences and therefore don't require commas.

> Of course I hope that the rumor isn't true.
> Therefore we decided to leave without him.
> I think the entire trip will take only an hour.

Remember that when one of the above words like *however* comes between two independent clauses, that word always has a semicolon before it. It may also have a comma after it, especially if there seems to be a pause between the word and the rest of the sentence (see p. 76).

> I wanted to go; however, I didn't have the money.
> Everyone liked the speaker; furthermore, they asked her to return.
> I'm going out for track; therefore I'm spending hours running.

Thus a word like *however* or *therefore* may be used in three ways:

1. as an interrupter (commas around it)
2. as a word that flows into the sentence (no commas needed)
3. as a connecting word between two independent clauses (semicolon before it and often a comma after it).

6. Put commas around nonessential material.

Such material may be interesting, but the main idea of the sentence would be clear without it. In the following sentence

Kay Carter, who edits the college paper, chaired the meeting.

the clause *who edits the college paper* is not essential to the main idea of the sentence. Without it, we still know exactly who the sentence is about and what she did: *Kay Carter chaired the meeting.* Therefore the nonessential material is set off from the rest of the sentence by commas to show that it could be left out. But in the following sentence

The young woman who edits the college paper chaired the meeting.

the clause *who edits the college paper* is essential to the main idea of the sentence. Without it the sentence would read: *The young woman chaired the meeting.* We would have no idea which young woman. The clause *who edits the college paper* is essential because it tells us which young woman. It couldn't be left out. Therefore commas are not used around it. In this sentence

The suit I'm wearing, which I bought two years ago, is still my favorite.

the clause *which I bought two years ago* could be left out, and we would still know the main meaning of the sentence: *The suit I'm wearing is still my favorite.* Therefore the nonessential material is set off by commas to show that it could be left out. But in this sentence

The suit that I bought two years ago is still my favorite.

the clause *that I bought two years ago* is essential. Without it, the sentence would read: *The suit is still my favorite.* We'd have no idea which suit. Therefore the clause couldn't be left out, and commas are not used around it.

The trick in deciding whether material is essential is to say, "Interesting, but is it necessary?"

EXERCISES

Look back now at Rules 4 and 5. Punctuate the next two exercises according to those two rules.

☐EXERCISE 1

1. Yes Gregg I know the car needs washing.
2. I'm too busy this evening however to wash it.
3. It will have to wait therefore until tomorrow.
4. Therefore it will have to wait until tomorrow.
5. However much I'd like to wash it I'm simply too busy now.
6. I wish Felipe that I could be out surfing now.
7. Surfing however won't get you a college degree Gregg.
8. Neither will watching television Felipe.
9. Well there's nothing to do I guess but turn it off.
10. Yes we can't go on this way.

☐EXERCISE 2

1. I heard a lecture on maturity yesterday by a psychologist who I understand has written a book on the subject.
2. Maturity the lecturer explained is the ability to establish helping relationships.
3. The immature person is usually egocentric and gives no thought to others.
4. The mature person on the other hand is concerned about the development, the well-being, and the happiness of others.
5. The great difference in people therefore is in their maturity and their ability to care.
6. He said furthermore that maturity is essential for settling any quarrel.
7. In any disagreement he said there is just one question to ask, and that question is, "What's important here?"
8. Only one of the two people disagreeing needs to be mature he said in order to solve the problem.
9. The one mature person can distinguish the important from the unimportant the lecturer continued and can then use that knowledge to settle the quarrel.
10. The basis of all good relationships it seems is maturity.

The rest of the exercises include not only Comma Rules 4 and 5 but also Comma Rule 6. Make sure you understand the explanation of Rule 6 before you begin the exercises.

□EXERCISE 3

1. This weekend we're going to our cottage which we all love.
2. We go there mainly to play chess which is our favorite game.
3. I don't know how old the game of chess is; I know however that it's ancient.
4. The origin of games which have always been a part of civilization is unknown.
5. Carvings on Egyptian tombs that date from 250 B.C. show board games being played.
6. And a game board dating from 1090 B.C. with squares and pieces for playing has been found in Egypt.
7. The games of hopscotch, blindman's buff, and tug-of-war which we think of as modern were actually played by the children of ancient Rome.
8. Furthermore an illuminated manuscript from the Middle Ages has pictures in the margins showing figures throwing dice and walking on stilts.
9. Surprisingly among the games Shakespeare mentions are hide-and-seek and blindman's buff.
10. Hey Sybil how about going to the cottage with us for a game of chess?

□EXERCISE 4

1. Avalanches I thought were accidents of nature that could not be prevented.
2. Now however I have learned that their hazards can at least be lessened.
3. Snow safety workers have developed techniques that control avalanches to some extent.
4. They study the factors that can start an avalanche: the kind of snow, the amount of snowfall, and the force of the wind.
5. Then they shoot explosives into a likely spot and start small avalanches which are not so destructive as large ones.
6. Ski patrollers who carry hand charges of explosives in their jackets scour any area where there has been heavy snow.
7. A resort area 25 miles southeast of Salt Lake City is the spot that has more avalanches than any other populated area on this continent.
8. The thousands who ski there are undoubtedly safer today because of the new methods of avalanche control.
9. But this continent doesn't have the hazardous avalanches that occur in the Alps.
10. In Switzerland for example in the winter of 1950–51 which was the worst avalanche year in modern times 279 people were killed by avalanches.

☐EXERCISE 5

1. The idea that touching a toad may cause warts is a superstition.
2. A toad's skin however is dry and covered with warts.
3. A frog's skin on the other hand is moist and smooth.
4. The toad which spends most of its life on land has feet that are not fully webbed for swimming.
5. The toad flicks out its tongue which is long and sticky to catch insects.
6. When a toad sings, its vocal sac enlarges into a balloon that is larger than its head.
7. The toad's song which is used to attract females is heard in May and June.
8. The female lays thousands of eggs which look like strings of beads.
9. In a few days the eggs hatch into tiny tadpoles which are often eaten by other creatures.
10. Those that survive turn into little toads which are at first no bigger than a shirt button.

☐EXERCISE 6

1. The reason students can't write some people say is that they haven't been taught enough grammar.
2. They should some think learn to diagram sentences the way their grandparents did.
3. Authorities tell us however that extensive drill on grammar has virtually no effect on writing skills.
4. Too much drill on grammar can in fact be harmful because it will take time that should be spent on writing.
5. Of course students need to know the fundamentals of grammar.
6. But more important than a lot of grammar drill we are told is giving students more opportunity to write.
7. The standardized test which can be graded by a computer has almost replaced the essay exam.
8. What is necessary it seems clear is for students to write more in all their classes and not only in English classes.
9. When students write about a subject, they learn more undoubtedly than if they merely read about it and answer some true-false questions.
10. S. I. Hayakawa said that one doesn't know anything clearly unless one can state it in writing.

☐EXERCISE 7

1. The traditional Japanese home we must admit was more artistic than most American homes.

2. Its beauty lay of course in its simplicity.
3. The traditional Japanese living room was decorated with one picture which was changed frequently so that it would not become monotonous.
4. One picture and one vase of flowers were as a rule the sole ornaments in the room.
5. Cushions and a small table were of course brought in when needed.
6. Our American homes in comparison are cluttered.
7. We keep adding to our possessions and of course displaying them.
8. Western ways however are rapidly gaining popularity in Japan.
9. Before long most of the traditional simplicity of Japanese decoration will be forgotten.
10. And along with it I fear will go the simple Japanese life.

☐EXERCISE 8

1. Anthropologist Mary Leakey widow of famed Louis Leakey has made some new discoveries in Africa about the origin of humans.
2. Forty years ago she and Louis excavated for a time in Laetoli a remote area of Tanzania but found little of interest.
3. They moved on to Olduvai Gorge 25 miles to the north where they made most of their discoveries.
4. Now however Mrs. Leakey has returned to Laetoli and has uncovered jawbones, teeth, and other fossils.
5. Her greatest find is the footprint of a creature that was a direct ancestor of humans.
6. The footprint according to radioactive dating was made more than three million years ago.
7. It's wider than the footprints of Neanderthal man which were left 80,000 years ago and which had always been accepted as the earliest human footprints.
8. Now a still more recent discovery is a skeleton that was found in Ethiopia in 1974 by Donald Johanson.
9. This skeleton which was named "Lucy" after a Beatles' song is 3.5 million years old and is the oldest, most complete, best-preserved skeleton of any erect-walking human ancestor ever found.
10. The bones of all these finds belonged to erect walkers who were not human but who were the ancestors of humans.

☐EXERCISE 9

1. The world was shocked quite naturally at the disaster in the pesticide plant in India in 1984.

2. But fully as frightening according to the environmentalists is the ever-growing buildup of poisonous wastes in our land.
3. Some 90 billion pounds of toxic waste according to the Environmental Protection Agency are produced annually in the United States.
4. This waste is produced by giant companies of course but also by small companies such as local dry cleaners.
5. Only 10 percent of the chemical wastes regardless of their potency are disposed of properly.
6. The rest which are dumped into rivers, abandoned mine shafts, swamps, or fields are endangering everyone.
7. There are according to the Natural Resources Defense Council as many as 50,000 toxic-waste dumps around the United States.
8. At least 14,000 of these it is estimated are or soon could be dangerous.
9. Their contents are slowly dripping into the soil or water supplies.
10. The full effects of these gradual seepages may not be felt for 10 or 15 years which is the time it takes for some cancers to develop.

Source: *Time,* December 17, 1984

JOURNAL WRITING

A question of punctuation arose in writing the Republican Party platform in 1984. The first draft said that Republicans "oppose any attempts to increase taxes which would harm the recovery." A revised draft said that Republicans "oppose any attempts to increase taxes, which would harm the recovery." Can you explain the difference in meaning between the two drafts? Write a paragraph giving your explanation.

Review of the Comma

THE SIX COMMA RULES

1. Put a comma before *and, but, for, or, nor, yet, so* when they connect two independent clauses.
2. Put a comma between items in a series.
3. Put a comma after an introductory expression or before an afterthought.
4. Put commas around the name of a person spoken to.
5. Put commas around an interrupter, like *however, moreover,* etc.
6. Put commas around nonessential material.

Add the necessary commas to these sentences.

1. When I have a lot of things to do I make a little list.
2. Somehow my list helps me get through even my most unpleasant tasks.
3. When I finish a job I cross it off my list but not until every job is crossed off can I stop.
4. Yes my friends making a little list is the way to get things done.
5. The tallest office building in the world is the Sears Tower on Wacker Drive in Chicago with 110 stories.
6. The earliest parking meters ever installed were those put in the business district of Oklahoma City Oklahoma on July 19 1935.
7. Frederick Stock the great conductor of the Chicago Symphony Orchestra always tried to fix the mistake and not the blame.
8. For every ton of newspaper that is recycled seventeen trees are not cut down.
9. Some experiments have been conducted with chimpanzees and the results are surprising.
10. A chimpanzee can aim a ball at a target almost as well as a person can but the chimpanzee can't concentrate as long.
11. If the first few shots are unsuccessful the person tries harder.
12. The chimpanzee however rapidly loses patience.
13. If the aiming tests are made too difficult the chimpanzee may even wreck the apparatus.
14. People who died in 1929—just over sixty years ago—had never heard of jet airplanes Polaroid cameras food freezers frozen vegetables radar V-8 engines electric razors electric typewriters drive-in movie theaters color television the United Nations the atomic bomb or bubble gum.

QUOTATION MARKS

Put quotation marks around the exact words of a speaker (but not around an indirect quotation).

> She said, "I'll go." (her exact words)
> She said that she would go. (not her exact words)

Whenever *that* precedes the words of a speaker (as in the last example), it indicates that the words are not a direct quotation and should not have quotation marks around them.

If the speaker says more than one sentence, quotation marks are used only before and after the entire speech.

> She said, "I'm ready. I'll be there in a minute. Don't go without me."

The words telling who is speaking are set off with a comma unless, of course, a question mark or exclamation mark is needed.

> "I'm ready," she said.
> "Come here!" she shouted.

Every quotation begins with a capital letter, but if a quotation is broken, the second part doesn't begin with a capital unless it's a new sentence.

> "The best way out," wrote Robert Frost, "is always through."
> "People always get what they ask for," wrote Aldous Huxley. "The only trouble is that they never know, until they get it, what it actually is that they have asked for."

Begin a new paragraph with each change of speaker.

> "Let's try some Carl Rogers psychology," he said.
> "Do you mean his idea about stating the other person's opinion?" she asked.
> "That's right," he said.

Put quotation marks around the name of a short story, poem, song, essay, TV program, radio program, or other short work. For a longer work such as a book, newspaper, magazine, play, record album, or movie, use underlining, which means it would be italicized in print.

> I like the song "Somewhere Out There."

Have you seen the movie *Jurassic Park*?

In our short story class we read James Joyce's "Eveline," which is found in his book *Dubliners*.

Do you read *National Geographic* magazine?

Bobby McFerrin's album *Simple Pleasures* has sold close to 1.5 million copies in the U.S.

Indent and single space, without quotation marks, all quotations of more than five lines.

In an article about some famous people who accomplished things in their spare time, Albert Payson Terhune writes:

> A down-at-heel instructor in an obscure college varied the drudgery he hated by spending his evenings and his holidays in tinkering on a queer device of his, at which his fellow teachers laughed. I don't recall the names of any of those teachers. Neither do you. But we have not forgotten who invented the telephone— in his spare time.

EXERCISES

Punctuate the quotations, and underline or put quotation marks around each title. Correct each group of 10 sentences before going on.

☐EXERCISE 1

1. A college education is one of the few things a person is willing to pay for and not get said William Lowe Bryan, former president of Indiana University.

2. Americans have more timesaving devices and less time than any other group of people in the world wrote Duncan Caldwell.

3. If all misfortunes were laid in a common heap said Socrates from which everyone would have to take an equal portion, most people would be content to take their own and depart.

4. Our guide said that the Cathedral of St. John the Divine in New York City is one of the two largest cathedrals in the world.

5. I have been brought up to believe that how I see myself is more important than how others see me said Anwar Sadat.

6. Speaking of his life of unceasing effort, the great pianist Jan Paderewski said before I was a master, I was a slave.

7. An excellent plumber is infinitely more admirable than an incompetent philosopher says John Gardner.

8. Alfred North Whitehead said that education is a movement of the mind from freedom through discipline to freedom again.

9. The secret of happiness is not in doing what one likes said James M. Barrie but in liking what one has to do.

10. The toastmaster said that marriage is oceans of emotions surrounded by expanses of expenses.

☐EXERCISE 2

1. In an art galley a man said to his wife I know what the artist is trying to say. He's trying to say he can't paint worth a damn!

2. The important thing in life is not the person one loves. It is the fact that one loves said Marcel Proust in his novel Remembrance of Things Past.

3. A diplomat is someone who remembers a lady's birthday but forgets her age said the speaker.

4. By working faithfully eight hours a day said Robert Frost you may eventually get to be a boss and work twelve hours a day.

5. My dad says that our forefathers didn't need as much machinery to run a farm as we need to mow a lawn.

6. Alexander Woollcott said all the things I really like to do are either immoral, illegal, or fattening.

7. More and more I come to value charity and love of one's fellow beings above everything else said Albert Einstein.

8. A man who uses a great many words to express his meaning is like a bad marksman who, instead of aiming a single stone at an object, takes up a handful and throws at it in hopes he may hit said Samuel Johnson.

9. A Sioux Indian prayer says Great Spirit, help me never to judge another until I have walked in his moccasins for two weeks.

10. In describing the Taj Mahal, Rufus Jones said only a few times in one's earthly life is one given to see absolute perfection.

☐EXERCISE 3

1. What's the most important thing you've learned in this class Brenda asked.

2. Learning to write a complete thesis statement Alex said because it's going to help me in my writing for other courses.

3. I know that's important Brenda replied but it's not most important for me.

4. What's most important for you Alex asked.

5. My biggest improvement has been learning to write concisely. My papers used to be so wordy.

6. That never was my problem he said my biggest achievement besides learning about thesis statements is that I finally decided to learn to spell.

7. And have you improved?

8. Tremendously he said I used to spell every word wrong now I just spell every other word wrong.

9. Come on! You're not that bad. I read one of your papers, and there wasn't a single misspelled word.

10. I'm getting there Alex said.

☐EXERCISE 4

1. Do commas and periods go inside the quotation marks Alex asked.

2. Of course Brenda replied they'd look lost on the outside.

3. I guess they would he said.

4. Is there anything more you want to know about punctuation she asked.

5. What do you do if you want to quote a whole paragraph from a book he asked.

6. If the quotation is more than five lines long, then you punctuate it differently from ordinary quotations she said.

7. How he asked.

8. You indent the whole quotation five spaces, single-space it, and forget about the quotation marks she said.

9. I suppose that makes it stand out clearly as quoted material.

10. Exactly she said.

☐EXERCISE 5

1. And what have you been doing with yourself Kevin wanted to know.

2. Oh, I've been doing a lot of reading for one thing Natalie said.

3. Still learning new words Kevin asked.

4. Sure, I'm always learning new words Natalie said yesterday I learned what *energize* means.

5. And what does it mean?

6. Well, the root *erg* means a unit of energy or work, and *energize* means to give energy to. For example, some people find cold showers energizing Natalie said.

7. I prefer to get my energy some other way Kevin said I suppose that same root *erg* is in *energy* and *energetic*.

8. Right. And it's also in *metallurgy,* which means working with metals. Another interesting word is *George*. *Geo* means earth, and *erg* means work. Therefore *George* is an earth worker or farmer.

9. I never knew that before Kevin said it really helps to know word roots.

10. It helps me Natalie replied.

☐EXERCISE 6

1. I had three chairs in my house: one for solitude, two for friendship, and three for society wrote Henry David Thoreau in his book Walden.

2. Sometimes wrote Thoreau as I drift idly on Walden Pond, I cease to live and begin to be.

3. If a man does not keep pace with his companions Thoreau said perhaps it is because he hears a different drummer.

4. Victor Hugo wrote the greatest happiness of life is the conviction that we are loved, loved for ourselves, or rather loved in spite of ourselves.

5. No matter what happens said Marcus Aurelius you can control the situation by your attitude.

6. It's very hard to take yourself too seriously when you look at the world from outer space said Astronaut Thomas K. Mattingly II.

7. If I could choose one degree for the people I hire, it would be English says a senior vice president of the First Atlanta Corporation. I want people who can read and speak in the language we're dealing with.

8. All of our people—except full-blooded Indians—are immigrants, or descendants of immigrants said Franklin Roosevelt.

9. Social benefits are denounced as handouts, but it is proposed to open up vast areas of public lands to developers in what may be the greatest giveaway in our history said Norman Cousins.

10. I used to read Newsweek, but now I read Time.

☐EXERCISE 7

1. In an article on the way pollutants are carried by air currents throughout the world, Michael H. Brown says a molecule you're inhaling now could have been expelled by a man in the seventeenth century or by a woman in China two weeks ago.

2. Last year I read Steinbeck's novel Grapes of Wrath.

3. My counselor says that words once spoken can never be un-said.

4. Falling to the chain saw at the rate of 170 acres a day said the lecturer the virgin woodlands of the Pacific Northwest—with their dependent communities of plants and wildlife—have become a battleground for loggers and environmentalists.

5. The essence of genius is to know what to overlook said William James.

6. A friend is a person with whom I may be sincere said Ralph Waldo Emerson before him I may think aloud.

7. There's a difference said a spokesperson for the Council of the Blind between people who can see and people who have vision.

8. My dad says that there are two kinds of people: single and worried.

9. For my birthday I was given a subscription to National Wildlife.

10. The famous book Bartlett's Familiar Quotations is being revised by Justin Kaplan.

JOURNAL WRITING

To practice using quotation marks, record a conversation you had with a friend recently. Start a new paragraph with each change of speaker.

CAPITAL LETTERS

Capitalize

1. The first word of every sentence.

2. The first word of every direct quotation.

> He said, "The tour starts at six."
> "The tour starts at six," he said, "and latecomers will be left behind." (The *and* isn't capitalized because it doesn't begin a new sentence.)
> "The tour starts at six," he said. "Latecomers will be left behind." (*Latecomers* is capitalized because it begins a new sentence.)

3. The first, last, and every important word in a title. Don't capitalize prepositions, short connecting words, the *to* in front of a verb, or *a, an, the*.

> *The New Grove Dictionary of Music and Musicians*
> *To Have and Have Not*

4. Names of people, places, languages, races, and nationalities.

Aunt Christine	English	Indian
Central America	Carnegie Hall	Chinese

5. Names of months, days of the week, and special days, but not the seasons.

September	Memorial Day	fall
Tuesday	Labor Day	winter

6. A title of relationship if it takes the place of the person's name. If *my* (or another possessive pronoun) is in front of the word, a capital is not used.

She talked to Uncle Fred.	*but* She talked to her uncle.
I phoned Mom this evening.	*but* I phoned my mom.

7. Names of particular people or things, but not general ones.

I spoke to Professor Hayes.	*but* I spoke to the professor.
We sailed on the Hudson River.	*but* We sailed on the river.
Are you from the South?	*but* We turned south.
I take Art 300 and History 101.	*but* I take art and history.
I go to San Mateo High School.	*but* I'm in high school now.
He goes to Fullerton College.	*but* He's going to college now.

EXERCISES

Add the necessary capital letters.

☐EXERCISE 1

1. Even if you've never been to New York city, you've heard of Carnegie hall.
2. It was built in 1891, but by 1967 it was in a sad state of repair; the plaster was cracked; the lobby was too small; and one had to climb several flights of stairs to the balcony, where the seats were creaky.
3. Some wondered whether it was worthwhile to restore such a victorian antique, but then people remembered the great names associated with it through the years.
4. Tchaikovsky had journeyed from russia for the opening of Carnegie hall in 1891, and Winston Churchill and Mark Twain had lectured from its stage.
5. Toscanini had conducted the New York philharmonic there, and Benny Goodman, Paderewski, Rubinstein, and the Beatles had played there.
6. Although Lincoln center in New York city now also has a great concert hall, the acoustics are not so good as those in Carnegie.
7. Therefore a restoration was undertaken at a cost of $50 million or about 25 times the cost of the original structure.
8. The original acoustics have been preserved, but now there are a glittering lobby and inviting staircases and elevators.
9. Also a beautiful marquee in front of the building on 57th street welcomes the patrons.
10. At the reopening in December 1986, tickets sold for as much as $500 compared to $2 when Carnegie hall first opened in 1891.

☐EXERCISE 2

1. I've been reading Kenneth Clark's *civilisation* for my art history course.
2. Art history 201 requires a lot of reading.
3. My english and history courses also require a great deal of reading.
4. English 410 is entitled literature of the renaissance.
5. Our instructor asked each of us to memorize a quotation from a renaissance author.
6. I've memorized John Donne's "No man is an island."
7. My course in Canadian history will count toward my major.
8. Our professor, who is a graduate of the university of Toronto, makes the course interesting.

9. Canada is a bilingual country with both english and french as official languages.
10. My term paper is on the early development of the land along the Mississippi river.

☐EXERCISE 3

1. Our family is planning a big reunion for Christmas day.
2. Aunt Nancy and uncle Karl, who live in the south, are coming.
3. My aunt and uncle who live in the east already have their reservations on United airlines.
4. My brother will be coming from Franklin, Massachusetts, where he has been attending Dean junior college.
5. My grandparents won't have far to come because they live over on second avenue.
6. And my sister works right here in town at Sears.
7. We hoped cousin Jim would come from Alvin, Texas, but he can't make it.
8. And dad's brother from Missoula can't come either.
9. The rest of us are sure to have fun because it's the first time we've all been together since memorial day two years ago.
10. Dad and mom are already making plans. My mother always produces a feast.

☐EXERCISE 4

1. Having a good counselor is one of the most important parts of college life.
2. Some counselors simply fill out your schedule and say, "see you next semester."
3. But every time I appear at her door, my counselor says, "good to see you again."
4. She always has an apt quotation to fit whatever problem I'm faced with.
5. "What happens," she said the first time I took a problem to her, "is not so important as how you react to what happens."
6. Another of her quotations that I'll always remember is this: "I learned a long while ago," said Eleanor Roosevelt, "not to make judgments on what other people do."
7. And another was by William Lyon Phelps: "this is the final test of a gentleman: his respect for those who can be of no possible service to him."
8. I've been lucky in my professors too. I had a professor for English last term who really helped me with my writing.
9. Now I have professor Reynolds, who makes our English 800 course interesting.
10. I hope I'll find the university as enjoyable as this community college.

□EXERCISE 5

1. Our table conversation is about nothing but college these days.
2. My mother is going to Diablo Valley college to prepare herself for a new career.
3. After finishing two years there, she plans to transfer to California state university in Long Beach.
4. Then in two more years she hopes to get her teaching credential.
5. Do you know Edna St. Vincent Millay's poem "My candle burns at both ends"?
6. We tell mom she's burning her candle at both ends.
7. We're all mighty proud of what mom's doing however.
8. Dad is taking evening classes at the community college too, but he isn't working for a degree.
9. He merely wants to improve his skills for his job at western tool works, inc.
10. Of course my brother and I are both in college, so college looms large in our table conversation.

□EXERCISE 6

1. When we graduated from high school last spring, my five good friends and I all went our separate ways.
2. Anita got a scholarship to Los Angeles Pierce college in Woodland Hills, California.
3. Candace decided to work for a year at the Ford motor company.
4. Alan first thought of going to DeVry institute of technology in City of Industry but then decided to go to Victor Valley college instead.
5. It didn't take Jerry long to make up his mind to go to Chabot college in Hayward, California, because his girlfriend was going there.
6. Lee decided to take a job with Benson landscaping company during the day and go to a community college in the evening.
7. I of course went to Weber state university in Ogden, Utah, as I had planned.
8. Now all of us look forward to getting together at Thanksgiving vacation.
9. We might even all meet on Thanksgiving day.
10. We're sure to reminisce about the good old days in high school.

□EXERCISE 7

1. The world's largest shopping mall is not in New York city or Chicago or Los Angeles. It's in Edmonton, Alberta, the northernmost of Canada's major cities.
2. The West Edmonton Mall is classed as the largest shopping mall in the world by the 1992 *Guinness book of world records*.

3. It has more than 800 stores, including 11 major department stores and 110 eating places, and it contains the world's largest indoor amusement park, the world's largest water park, and the planet's biggest parking lot.
4. Also in the mall are a skating rink, a spanish galleon in its own lake, and four submarines in the lagoon.
5. Its petting zoo includes siberian tiger cubs, miniature arabian horses, baby bears, baby moose, and one baby elephant.
6. Spending a day there is like going with Alice on her trip *Through the looking glass*.
7. Today we take shopping malls for granted, but they have been around for only about 30 years.
8. Mom and dad say they can remember when there were no shopping malls.
9. The first mall ever to be enclosed was the Southdale shopping center outside Minneapolis/St. Paul in 1956.
10. Now there are several thousand multilevel enclosed malls in north america and others scattered on every continent on Earth, except—for the moment—antarctica.

□EXERCISE 8

1. On Labor day weekend we went to visit my dad's parents, who live 600 miles north of here.
2. They used to live in the south, but they moved to the northwest two years ago.
3. You can see where they live by looking at an atlas. Here's the *Rand McNally world atlas*.
4. Then on our way home we decided to go fishing in the Huron river.
5. I had never fished in a river before. I had always fished in lakes.
6. One lake where I have fished is Duck lake in Michigan.
7. I went fishing there one fourth of July, and by the fifth of July I had my quota of fish.
8. The day after we came home we heard senator Berlis speak in the elks hall on conservation.
9. Some things he said applied to the river where we had been fishing.
10. Certainly it's true that there aren't as many fish in the Huron river as there used to be.

Review of Punctuation and Capital Letters

Punctuate these sentences and paragraphs. They include all the rules for punctuation and capitalization you have learned. Correct your answers carefully by those at the back of the book. Most sentences have several errors. Some have none.

☐EXERCISE 1

1. A comma is required when a dependent clause comes first in a sentence.

2. When a dependent clause comes first in a sentence put a comma after it.

3. The proper use of commas I've found prevents misreading.

4. Stop I'll go with you can you wait until 5 P.M.

5. In speaking of his childhood as one of seven children of a poor oil field worker in Texas Franklin Pollard says We had three rooms and a path.

6. She's attending community college of Philadelphia this summer.

7. He memorized William Butler Yeats' poem The Lake Isle of Innisfree.

8. When Eric Heiden was a sophomore at the university of Wisconsin in Madison he became the first skater to win three world championships in one year.

9. Heiden an 18-year-old skated his way to three world championships in one stunning season against the best speed skaters of Europe.

10. I think dad that I've finally decided on my major.

☐EXERCISE 2

1. Birds are not only fast fliers but also fast walkers an adult roadrunner which is only nine inches tall can keep pace with a human sprinter.

2. Life lived at its best is full of daily forgivin' and forgettin' said Edward Hill.

3. There are only two lasting things we can give our children roots and wings.

4. An Arabian proverb says I had no shoes and complained until I met a man who had no feet.

5. There are two kinds of pain the pain that leaves as soon as the wound heals and the pain that lasts a lifetime.

6. The United States is a bit presumptuous in calling itself America a big chunk of North America is Canada and a big chunk is Mexico and the United States is really just a swath across the middle of the continent.

7. After the breakup of the Soviet Union Canada became the largest country in the world.

8. Not more than one-third of Canada is developed much of the land is mountainous or rocky or located in an Arctic climate.

9. My brother loves to cook he says that he's at home on the range.

10. Commas are like pounds you either have too many or too few or you have them in the wrong places.

☐EXERCISE 3

1. A study has shown that children whose TV viewing was cut back to no more than one hour a day improved their grades in school and seemed happier they played more with other children and increased their concentration in school one child changed from a passive loner into a friendly playmate then when the study was concluded she went back to her former TV habits and became a loner again.

2. A hundred years ago when Edison was working on his first tin horn phonograph he wasn't even thinking about music he just wanted to make a dictating machine in fact it took almost a whole generation for musicians to get interested in recordings fortunately Edison lived long enough (until 1931) to get the first inkling of the big change his invention was making in the world of music

3. An Assyrian stone tablet of about 2800 B.C. makes the following statements our earth is degenerate in these latter days bribery and corruption are common children no longer obey their parents the end of the world is evidently approaching.

☐EXERCISE 4

1. Yesterday I had my first solo flight at the Flying Club it's an amazing feeling when your instructor tells you to go flying alone then after you take off you look around and find you really are alone at that point it's too late to change your mind you've got to land by yourself sooner or later it's a great sensation it's like the time you first rode a bicycle—quite a thrill.

2. The federal budget speaks in terms of billions but how much *is* a billion dollars if a man stood over a big hole in the ground and dropped in a $20 bill every minute day and night it would take him 95 years to throw a billion dollars into the hole.

3. There have been six basic changes in the tools people write with since the cave dwellers used sharp stones to scratch pictures on their stone walls first came the quill pen then came the lead pencil next came the fountain pen in about 1870 came the first typewriter by 1960 the electric typewriter was taking over and now it's the word processor.

Proofreading Exercise 1

Proofread this student paper. You will find only a few errors—13 in fact—but correcting those few errors will improve the paper (the shift to *your* and *yourself* in the last paragraph is not counted an error). This is the kind of careful proofreading you should do before you call your own papers finished. See if you can find all 13 errors before checking with the answers.

THE BIG GRIN ON MY FACE

One afternoon I was driving my car when I notice a pinging noise in my engine. In a few days the pinging grew to a thumping and then to a loud clunking that couldn't be ignored.

My knowledgeable friends broke the news to me that it was undoubtedly my main engine bearings and in the same breath they mentioned sums like four or five hundred dollars. Being a poor student, I had only two alternatives—walk or fix it myself.

Necessity force me to chose the latter alternative and I found myself up to my elbows in grease and grime for the next few days. With the help of a lot of free advice from friends, who claimed to be undiscovered mechanical geniuses, and the guidance of a library book on engines, I removed and disassembled the whole thing.

An engine is something I take for granted as long as it goes, and only when it fails, do I really appreciate how intricate and complicated it is. Their are all kinds of odd-shaped highly polished parts, each one for some function. My taking the engine apart was like a little boy fixing an alarm clock each new piece was so interesting and so completely unfathomable.

Then when it was all in pieces the reassembly with new parts began, along with the job of trying to remember where each nut and bolt belonged. This work was a lot slower and required more help but it was encouraging to watch the motor grow with each new piece.

Finally it was all connected in the car and ready to be tested. It had taken weeks of late evenings of work but now it was ready at last. My friends stood around offering final advice and checking to make sure I had remembered everything. I held my breath and turned the key—the engine started and turned, a little rough at first, but soon it ran smoothly.

"Eureka! I've done it!" I shouted.

I was overwhelm with a great feeling of accomplishment and I couldn't hide the big grin on my face.

There's an indescribable feeling of pride in having rebuilt your own engine yourself. It was worth it, not just for saving money but for the experience.

Proofreading Exercise 2

This student paper has been rewritten three times but still has 12 errors. You may have to read the paper several times to find all the errors. Challenge your instructor to find all 12 on the first try! No answers are provided at the back of the book.

THE ROLLING STONES

Although I've been a fan of the Rolling Stones for years, I never thought I'd see them perform in a live concert. Even when I learn that their tour of the United States would include two concerts at the local football stadium, I knew I wouldn't bother to wait in line all night for tickets that would sell out in a few hours. But a last-minute decision by the promoters to sell 3,000 extra tickets on the day before the second concert allowed me to get a ticket after all—and without waiting in line.

I arrive at the stadium three hours ahead of time, but two-thirds of the seats were all ready filled. Security at the gates was tight each person was frisked and police were everywhere. But the fans were all well-behaved and just out for a rollicking afternoon of music in the sun.

Across one entire end of the stadium, a huge stage with pastel-painted 40-foot screens had been erected. A high fence separated the crowd from the stage, and burly guards in yellow T-shirts were kept busy pushing over-eager fans off the fence.

Somehow the hours past, and the Stones finally appeared at about 4:30 P.M. The crowd of 90,000 was more than ready, and each song was greeted with a roar of recognition. Some people danced in the aisles others just tapped their feet. The music was great. Mick Jagger's singing matched his strutting and striding around the huge stage and Keith Richard's lead guitar was stunning. The rest of the band seem content to create the music and leave the visual effects to Jagger.

The stones clearly intended to give the fans their moneys worth, and they were still playing as the sun went down and as the huge banks of lights around the stage went into action. At one point, after darkness fell, the fans spontaneously lit matches or lighters so that the whole stadium seemed blanketed by fireflies.

As the end of the concert approached, the sky was lit up with a dazzling display of fireworks. For his final song, Jagger scrambled up the scaffolding of the stage to hop into the basket of a huge crane, which later deposited him, still singing, back on the stage. After a thundering encore, the Stones were lifted away in helicopters and the tired but satisfied crowd let out a final cheer and headed home.

Proofreading Exercise 3

Can you find the seven errors in this paragraph? No answers are provided.

THE CORN PALACE

The last place one would expect to find a Byzantine palace is on the plains of South Dakota, but their it stands in Mitchell, South Dakota, complete with domes, turrets, minarets, and kiosks. Built in 1892 to house the farmers' Corn Belt Exposition, it has been rebuilt several times and is the worlds only monument to corn. Three thousand bushels of corn are used each year to decorate the Corn Palace inside and out with huge scenic murals made entirely of corn and other grains and grasses. A artist sketches designs and than transfers the designs to huge panels, marking each part with the color needed. Farmers grow purple, red, blue, and white corn for the murals and workers cut the ears of corn in half lengthwise and nail them to the marked murals. During the last of September visitors come from great distances for Corn Palace Week. A 12-block-long carnival offers rides, games, and concessions, and inside the Corn Palace famous stars perform. When the festival is over the Corn Palace still stands on the South Dakota prairie but the squirrels and pigeons see to it that the murals have to be refurbished each year.

Comprehensive Test on Entire Text

In these sentences you'll find examples of all the errors that have been discussed in the entire text. Correct them by adding apostrophes, punctuation, and capital letters and by crossing out incorrect expressions and writing the corrections above. Most sentences have several errors. A perfect—or almost perfect—score will mean you have mastered the first part of the text.

1. We girls made the deserts for the party everyone like them.

2. The altos carried the melody the sopranos sung the accompaniment.

3. Joe Namath was a talented quarterback in high school his team won lots of championships.

4. When we got to the end of the detour we turn south and then West.

5. Which turned out to be the wrong thing to do.

6. Each of her trophies are displayed in it's proper place on the shelf.

7. Working hard that semester my grades improved.

8. I enjoy math social studies and gym but I find chemistry and english difficult.

9. Making the most of every opportunity that came her way.

10. He spends most of his time however reading comic books and you cant do that and get satisfactory grades.

11. I cant decide whether to get a job take a trip or whether I should just loaf this summer.

12. Yes personally I think Amys costume is more striking than Beverlys.

13. She took to many cloths along on her trip party dresses beachwear and half a dozen other outfits.

14. Her mother and father are sending her to a exclusive school but she dont appreciate it.

15. Leroy told his father he was embarrassed by his old car.

16. Their quiet pleased with there new car although it was to expensive.

17. Joan you was driving to fast when we past that cop.

18. We didnt like the amendment furthermore we refuse to vote for it.

19. James invitation to my girlfriend and me came as a surprise.

20. Each of the leaves are quite unique in their vein patterns.

21. Ive been wondering about you and hoping for a letter.

22. She memorized Masefield's poem Sea Fever from his book Salt Water Ballads.

23. John Masefield who became poet laureate of England was born on June 1 1878 in Ledbury Herefordshire England.

24. Life's always a struggle if anything's easy it's not likely to be worthwhile said Hubert Humphrey.

25. When you get to the end of your rope said Franklin D. Roosevelt tie a knot and hang on.

26. If I had known you was coming I would of prepared a special meal.

27. Last week they develop a plan and then they proceed to carry it out.

28. He decided to join Fritz and me on the golf course.

29. There house is in a better location than our's.

30. When you wind up a clock you start it when you wind up a speech you end it.

Writing

4

4 Writing

Writing is just talking to people. There are good and poor writers just as there are good and poor talkers.

You probably have friends who, when they start to tell you about what happened yesterday, get sidetracked and tell you things that have nothing to do with yesterday. Also they keep saying "You know" and "I mean" and other useless expressions.

Then you have friends who, when they start to tell you about what happened yesterday, stick to the point, tell you interesting things, and hold your attention every minute.

It's the same with writing. You can bore your reader or intrigue your reader. It takes practice, though, to become either a good talker or a good writer. We're going to consider some of the points to keep in mind if you want to be a good writer.

You learn to write by *writing*—not by reading long discussions *about* writing. Therefore the instructions in this section are brief. In fact, they are boiled down to just eight steps that you need to take to write good papers. Take these eight steps, one at a time, and you'll write more effectively and also more easily. Here are the steps:

EIGHT STEPS TO BETTER WRITING

   I. Do some free writing.
   II. Limit your topic.
   III. Write a thesis statement.
   IV. Support your thesis with reasons or points.
   V. Organize your paper from your thesis.
   VI. Organize each paragraph.
   VII. Write and rewrite.
   VIII. Proofread ALOUD.

I. DO SOME FREE WRITING

"Writing is good for us," Oliver Wendell Holmes said, "because it brings our thoughts out into the open, as a boy turns his pockets inside out to see what is in them." Try "turning your pockets inside out" by writing as fast as you can for five minutes. Write anything that comes into your mind. Put your thoughts down as fast as they come. What you write may not make sense, but that doesn't matter. Write fast. Don't stop a moment. Don't even take your pen off the page. If you can't think of anything to write, just write, "I can't think of anything to write," over and over until something occurs to you. Look at your watch and begin.

This free writing should limber up your mind and your pen so that you'll write more freely.

Now try another kind of free writing—focused free writing. Write for five minutes as fast as you can, but this time stick to one subject—music.

Look at your watch and begin.

Did you focus on music that long? Did you think not only of music you like but of music you don't like, of music your mother tried to teach you, of music you've heard on special occasions, of your struggles to play some instrument, of conflicts you've had with someone concerning music?

You didn't have time to include all those things of course. Now write for ten minutes and add more to your discussion of music.

Focused free writing is a good way to begin writing a paper. When you are assigned a paper, try writing for ten minutes putting down all your thoughts on the subject. It will let you see what material you have and will help you figure out what aspect of the subject (what topic) to write about.

II. LIMIT YOUR TOPIC

Finding the right topic is sometimes the hardest part of writing. For one thing, you need to limit your topic so that you can handle it in a paper of 300 to 500 words. The subject music, which you used for free writing, was obviously too big. You could limit it by saying

> My video collection
> Music I hate
> The important place music had in our high school

but even those topics are too big. Keep making your topic smaller

> Our high school marching band

and smaller

> My first week with our high school marching band

and smaller

> The day I made the marching band

Now you have a topic limited enough to write about in a short paper.

Usually the more you limit your topic, the better your paper will be, for then you'll have room to add plenty of specific details. And it's specific details that will interest your reader.

□EXERCISE 1

Make each of these topics more and more limited until it would be a possible topic for a short paper. Then compare your topics with those suggested at the back of the book.

1. Painting a room

　　Preparing to paint a room

　　New tools for painting a room

2. Looking for a job

_____

_____

3. Camping out

_____

_____

4. My trip to Washington, D.C.

_____

_____

The following two assignments emphasize the first two Steps to Better Writing—doing some free writing and limiting your topic.

In these two assignments we won't worry about paragraph structure and many of the things we'll consider later. Just present your ideas the way you would if you were talking to someone. Our only goal is to write something others will find interesting.

Assignment 1   A Moment I'd Like to Relive

What moment in your life, if you could live one moment over again, would you most enjoy reliving? It might be a moment when you won a sports event, a moment when you made a big decision, a moment when you achieved something you didn't think you could, a moment when you did something courageous. . . . It need not be a dramatic moment; it might be a very simple one, but it should be a moment that had great meaning for you.

First do some free writing telling about the experience. Put down all the details you can think of. For example, if you are going to tell about the time you won a trophy, you'll want to say more than that it was a great moment. You'll want to tell what you saw at that moment, what you heard, how you felt. If you are groping for details, think of your five senses—sight, hearing, smell, taste, and touch. Each of them may call forth some details you hadn't thought of before. Remember that it's specific details that will help your reader experience your moment with you.

When you've done all the free writing you can, then make sure your topic is limited. If you're writing about winning a trophy, you won't tell about the entire season but only about actually receiving the award.

Before you start to write, you might like to read a student paper on this assignment. At first this writer was having so much trouble with sentence structure and wordiness that the paper was difficult to read, but after four rewritings, it is now clear. The writer had something interesting to say, and it was worth her while to get rid of errors so that her paper can now be read easily.

I Told Her Off

When we moved from one side of Elk Grove to the other, all the children in our neighborhood seemed to have their own friends, and I wasn't one to go out of my way to meet people. From the first day of fourth grade until the beginning of junior high, I kept my mouth shut. Then I met Suzette.

Suzette tried to gain popularity by making fun of people, this time someone who wouldn't talk back, someone who was shy. She ridiculed me in front of her friends, who in turn ridiculed me in front of the whole school. She pointed out how I dragged my feet on the ground, how I had a soft voice, and how unattractive I was.

At the end of eighth grade came the most embarrassing moment of my life. At our junior high graduation, where my father was one of the speakers, Suzette had planned for everyone to clap for me. Although clapping is usually good, this time everyone, including my father, realized it wasn't meant for praise.

As I walked home that evening, I knew I couldn't take being ridiculed anymore. Despite my shyness I had to tell Suzette what I thought. The next day as I stood at her doorstep trying to get courage to ring the bell, I knew I wasn't shaking because of the cold. Suddenly, with the next shiver, my finger jerked far enough forward for the bell to ring. As the door opened, I must have looked confident because Suzette didn't. None of her friends were there to back her up, and the impossible happened. I told her how she had ruined three years of my life. I explained how, because I was shy, I had no close friends, no one to talk over my problems with.

I got my point across because Suzette ridiculed me no more. But what makes me feel even better is that if I hadn't spoken to Suzette, I would still be that shy little girl who wouldn't speak up for herself.

Now write your paper for this assignment. Imagine you're telling someone about your satisfying moment, and write what you would say. Remember that fully as important as making your paper mechanically correct is making it so interesting that your readers will enjoy it.

Finally, spend some time thinking of a good title. Just as you're more likely to read a magazine article with a catchy title, so your readers will be more eager to read your paper if you give it a good title. (And remember that every important word in a title is capitalized.) Which of these titles from student papers would make you want to read further?

It's Not Just Pumping Gas   A Place I Love
Ready! Wrestle!   Is There College After Marriage?
An Interesting Experience

Your paper should be typed, double-spaced, or written legibly in ink on 8½-by-11-inch paper on one side only. A 1½-inch margin should be left on each side of the page for your instructor's comments. The beginning of each paragraph should be indented about five spaces.

Part of the success of a paper depends on how it looks. The same paper written sloppily or neatly might well receive different grades. If, however, when you do your final proofreading, you find a word misspelled or a word left out, don't hesitate to make neat corrections in pen. So long as your paper gives a neat appearance, no one will mind a few minor corrections.

Assignment 2   A Place I Like to Remember

What place means more to you than any other place in the world? It might be a place you know now or one you knew in childhood—a playroom, your workshop, a backyard, a playing field . . .

Do some free writing to bring to your mind specific details that will help your reader see your place. Telling some things that happened there will also help your reader participate in your memory of it.

After you have done all the free writing you can, ask yourself whether your topic is limited enough. Take it through several steps of limiting to see whether you can turn it into a more manageable topic.

Here's a student paper, a third draft. With each draft the writer added specific details about what he saw and what he remembered. Now you can visualize the place and understand how the writer feels about it.

Muddy McBride

Sometimes I take a shortcut across McBride Park even though it's muddy now in the rainy weather. I walk through the old softball diamond. It seems bleak with the benches empty, their green paint peeling after a summer's softball season. Three muddy puddles in the field mark where the three bases used to be, and a bumpy little hill is all that's left of the pitcher's mound. The park is like a tree that has lost its leaves in the fall.

I can remember the excitement and the fun of those games. I can imagine my teammates sitting on the bench yelling at the other team, and I can almost see, behind the backstop, a few people who have come to watch. I can feel my turn to bat coming up, and I remember how I always felt. I'd stand beside the plate right where that puddle has been made by a whole season of batters and would wait for each pitch. I remember the cheers and yells that came with every hit I made in that hot summer sun.

But the windy weather is brisk now, and those sunny Sunday afternoons seem a long time ago. Now there's litter piled up against the backstop fencing, and the light drizzle of rain is all the cheering I hear. There aren't any fielders standing in the grass waiting for each hit. There are only some birds looking for worms that the rain has brought up.

I miss those softball games when I walk through muddy McBride.

Now write a description of your place that will help your reader picture it and feel its importance to you.

III. WRITE A THESIS STATEMENT

The most important thing to keep in mind, no matter what you are writing, is the idea you want to get across to your reader. It doesn't matter whether you are writing a paragraph or a longer piece, you must have in mind a single idea that you want to express to your reader. In a longer paper such an idea is called a thesis statement; in a paragraph it's called a topic sentence, but they mean the same thing—an idea you want to get across.

The limited topic on page 212, "The day I made the marching band," doesn't make any point. What about that day? What did it do for you? What point about that day would you like to present to your reader? You might write

Making the marching band gave me new confidence.

or

Making the marching band gave me something to work for.

or

The day I made the marching band I decided to major in music.

Now you have said something. **When you write in one sentence the point you want to present to your reader, you have written a thesis statement.**

All good writers have a thesis in mind when they begin to write. Whether they are writing articles, novels, short stories, poems, or plays, they have in mind an idea they want to present to the reader. They may develop it in various ways, but back of whatever they write is their ruling thought, their reason for writing, their thesis.

For any writing assignment, after you have done some free writing and limited your topic, your next step is to write a thesis statement. As you write it, remember that a thesis statement must be a sentence that you can explain or defend (not merely a topic or fact that needs no explanation).

IV. SUPPORT YOUR THESIS WITH REASONS OR POINTS

Now you're ready to support your thesis with reasons or points. That is, you'll think of ways to convince your reader that your thesis is true. How could you convince your reader that making the marching band gave you confidence? You might write

> Making the marching band gave me new confidence. (because)
> 1. It was the first competition I ever won.
> 2. I won over peers I had always felt inferior to.
> 3. It was an achievement to get into one of the best bands in the state.

The points supporting a thesis are not always reasons. They may be examples (to make your thesis clear), steps (in a how-to paper), descriptions (in a descriptive paper), or anecdotes (in a narrative paper). Whatever they are, they should convince your reader that your thesis is true for you.

□EXERCISE 2

Add supporting points (sentences) to these thesis statements.

I've decided to change my major to computer science.

1.

(reasons)   2.

3.

Acid rain is harming the country in many ways.

1.

2.

(examples) 3.

4.

I'm doing three things to improve my study habits.

1.

(steps)   2.

3.

Learning to write a good thesis statement with supporting points is perhaps the most important thing you can learn in this course. Most writing problems are not really *writing* problems but *thinking* problems. Whether you're writing a term paper or merely an answer to a test question, working out a thesis statement is always the best way to organize your thoughts. If you take enough time to think, you'll be able to write a clear thesis statement with supporting points. And if you have a clear thesis statement with supporting points, organizing your paper won't be difficult.

Of course not all writing follows this "thesis and support" form. Experienced writers vary their writing. Using this form, however, is an excellent way to begin learning to write because it will help you think logically, and logical thinking is important for all writing.

Assignment 3 Two Thesis Statements with Supporting Points

Think of some decision you're trying to make. Are you wondering what major to choose, whether to drop out of college for a time, whether to give up smoking, whether to try out for the next dramatic production? Think of a decision that really matters to you. Only then will you be able to write something others will care to read. When you've decided on a topic, write a thesis statement for *each side*. For example, if you're wondering whether to drop out of college for a semester, you might write

> I've decided to drop out of college for a semester and take a job.
> I've decided to stick with college.

These statements now need to be supported with reasons. You might write

> I've decided to drop out of college for a semester and take a job (because)
> 1. I need to make some money.
> 2. I want some experience in my field.
> 3. I might come back to college with a clearer purpose.

> I've decided to stick with college (because)
> 1. I don't want to waste time merely making money.
> 2. I'm now getting used to studying.
> 3. If I left, I might never come back.

Three reasons usually work well, but you could have two or four. Be sure all your reasons are sentences.

Now write your two thesis statements for the two sides of the decision you are trying to make, and under them write your supporting reasons.

I've decided _____

1.

2.

3.

I've decided _____

1.

2.

3.

Eventually, you'll write a paper on one of the two sides, but first we must consider two problems: how to organize a paper and how to organize a paragraph.

V. ORGANIZE YOUR PAPER FROM YOUR THESIS

Once you have worked out a good thesis with supporting points, organizing your paper will be easy.

First you need an introductory paragraph. It should catch your reader's interest and should either include or suggest your thesis statement. It may also list the supporting points, but usually it's more effective to let them unfold paragraph by paragraph rather than to give them all away in your introduction. (Your instructor may ask you to write your complete thesis statement with supporting points at the top of your paper so that it can be referred to easily.) Even if your supporting points don't appear in your introduction, your reader will easily spot them later if your paper is clearly organized.

Your second paragraph will present your first supporting point—everything about it and nothing more.

Your next paragraph will be about your second supporting point—all about it and nothing more.

Each additional paragraph will develop another supporting point.

Finally you'll need a brief concluding paragraph. In a short paper it isn't necessary to restate all your points. Even a single clincher sentence to round out the paper may be sufficient.

Paragraph 1.   Introduction arousing your reader's interest and indicating your thesis

Paragraph 2.   First supporting point

Paragraph 3.   Second supporting point

Additional paragraphs for additional supporting points

Concluding paragraph

Learning to write this kind of paper will teach you to write logically. Then when you're ready to write a longer paper, you'll be able to organize it easily. A longer paper may divide each of the supporting points into several paragraphs, and it may not present the thesis statement until later in the paper. But no matter how the material is presented, it will still have some kind of logical pattern.

Here are the introductory and concluding paragraphs from a student paper. Note that the introductory paragraph arouses the reader's interest and suggests the thesis statement. And the concluding paragraph simply wraps the paper up in one good sentence.

Introductory paragraph · My superman doesn't soar through the sky or leap tall buildings in a single bound. My superman is my dad. I think my dad is super because he shows that he cares with the little things he does.

(The paper tells in three paragraphs the kinds of little things the father does.)

Concluding paragraph · My dad may not change clothes in a telephone booth or rescue the earth from alien attack, but he's still superman to me.

VI. ORGANIZE EACH PARAGRAPH

Organizing a paragraph is easy because it's organized just the way an entire paper is. Here's the way you learned to organize a paper:

> Thesis statement in introductory paragraph
>> First supporting point
>> Second supporting point
>> Additional supporting points
> Concluding paragraph

And here's the way to organize a paragraph:

> Topic sentence
>> First supporting detail or example
>> Second supporting detail or example
>> Additional supporting details or examples
> Concluding sentence if needed

You should have at least two or three points to support your topic sentence. If you find that you have little to say after writing the topic sentence, ask yourself what details or examples will make your reader see that the topic sentence is true for you.

The topic sentence doesn't have to be the first sentence in the paragraph. It may come at the end or even in the middle, but having it first is most common.

Each paragraph should contain only one main idea, and no detail or example should be allowed to creep into the paragraph if it doesn't support the topic sentence. Note how the following paragraph is organized.

Amazing as it seems, one of the largest archeological treasures in the United States lies under the city of Phoenix. As new highways and shopping centers are being built, remains of the ancient Hohokam Indian culture are being found. The Hohokam, who lived in the area from about 300 B.C. to the fifteenth century A.D., had one of the most advanced Indian cultures in North America, but it is a culture we know little about. They lived in two dozen large towns in or near what is now Phoenix. Because modern houses in Phoenix are built without basements, only the top foot of soil has been disturbed, thus leaving archeological remains that may go as deep as nine feet. If Phoenix had been a city with deep basements, the remains would have been completely destroyed. But now, if developers will give archeologists a chance to do some probing, something may be learned about that ancient culture.

—Source: Daniel B. Adams, "Last Ditch Archeology," *Science 83*, Dec. 1983

The topic sentence states that one of the largest archeological treasures in the United States lies under the city of Phoenix. Sentences explaining that statement follow, and the final sentence gives added emphasis to it.

Assignment 4   Writing a Paragraph

For practice in writing paragraphs, choose one of these topic sentences and add support sentences. You may alter each topic sentence slightly if you wish.

1. The main reason I prefer to travel by car is that I see more.
2. For me, a job must be challenging, or I don't want it.
3. The first step in preparing a meal is to have a plan.
4. My psych course has taught me not to waste time on regrets.
5. I've learned not to make a big thing of small things.
6. A near accident made me a careful driver.
7. The most important thing I've learned in college is to concentrate.
8. Learning to use a thesis statement has improved my writing.

Transition Expressions

Transition expressions within a paragraph help the reader move from one detail or example to the next.

☐EXERCISE 3

Here are some transition expressions that would make the following paragraph read more smoothly. In each blank in the paragraph write the transition expression you think appropriate. Check your answers with those at the back of the book.

Also	Furthermore
As for me	First of all
Finally	Then too

Last summer we decided to take a family vacation and to drive to California. _____, we hadn't had a family vacation for four years, and we all thought it would be a great idea. _____, no one in our family had ever been west of the Rockies. _____, my brother wanted to see the campus at San Diego State University because he was hoping to go there in another year. _____, my mother had a friend living in Long Beach and had always wanted to visit her. _____, I was eager to see a new part of the country and thought I might even look for a job while we were out there. _____, my dad clinched the idea by saying that he'd pay all the expenses.

Transition expressions are also important throughout a paper. They help the reader move from one supporting point to the next. It is often a good idea to start each supporting paragraph in a paper with a transition expression such as

My first reason	Another example
Second	Then too
Also	Furthermore
Equally important	Finally
Even more important	

The easiest and most natural way to practice writing paragraphs is to write them as part of a paper. You'll have an opportunity to practice writing paragraphs in the assignments that follow.

Assignment 5   A Decision I Have Made

Return to the two thesis statements with supporting points about a decision you are trying to make (Assignment 3, p. 219). Choose one of those thesis statements to write about. Even if your mind is not really made up, you must choose one side for this assignment. You may mention in your introduction the arguments on the other side, but you must focus on one side if your paper is to be effective.

Before you write your paper, you may want to read how one student handled the question.

Wobbly Backbone

In high school I never studied. I didn't need to. I was on the football team. But I paid attention in class and used my wits at exam time. I got along OK, and I assumed I could slide by in college the same way. I told myself that I don't want to be a grind, that making friends is important, that going out for sports is good for my health, that watching TV will make me a well-rounded person. I got along just fine all fall—until the midterm grades came out. Wow! I got three D's and an F! I was stunned. Suddenly I began to do some deep thinking. Maybe making friends, participating in sports, and watching TV weren't so important after all. Suddenly, after a couple of days of pondering, I decided that for three reasons I'd better start to study.

First, getting that college degree is mighty important to me. No matter what field I go into, the degree will be a help. I'm thinking of law, and certainly for that career I'd need a lot of background knowledge.

Second, it's crazy to pay for something and not get it. I don't go into a store, try on a coat, plunk down my money, and then walk out without the coat. But right now I'm paying for an education and not getting it.

Third, and most important, it's about time I began to use my willpower. I've been coming into my room each evening, opening my books—and then snapping on the TV. I always tell myself that I'll just watch the news, but invariably I spend the entire evening on entertainment. I've simply had a weak and wobbly backbone.

Now I'm going to study. For four evenings a week there is going to be no TV. More important than gaining enough knowledge to pass my courses will be my finally training my willpower. I said that my decision is to study. I should have said that my decision is to train my willpower. Straighten up there, Backbone.

Now write a rough draft of your paper, giving enough specific details in each supporting paragraph to convince your reader that you've made the right decision.

Then Take Step VII, which follows.

VII. WRITE AND REWRITE

If possible, write your paper several days before it's due. Let it sit for a day. When you reread it, you'll see ways to improve it. After rewriting it, put it away for another day, and again try to improve it.

Great writers don't just sit down and write their books in a first draft. They write and rewrite. Hemingway said, "I wrote the ending to *A Farewell to Arms*, the last page of it, 39 times before I was satisfied." And Leo Tolstoy wrote, "I can't understand how anyone can write without rewriting everything over and over again."

Don't call any paper finished until you have worked through it several times. **REWRITING IS THE BEST WAY TO LEARN TO WRITE.**

Here is a student paragraph—a second draft. Note how the writer has improved the first draft by

1. crossing out unnecessary words or expressions
2. adding more specific words or details.

Can you see why the writer made each change? In the right-hand margin write the number (1 or 2) showing the reason you think the writer made the change. Analyzing the reasons for the changes will help you make appropriate changes in your own writing.

Water is the most amazing chemical compound on our earth. ~~I learned about it just last week when I read an article telling about it.~~ It is amazing because of the ~~great~~ number of ways in which it can appear ~~on earth~~. Perhaps the most artistic way it appears is in beautiful six-pointed snowflakes. ~~In winter~~ *I*t may also appear as a solid sheet of ice on which people love to skate. In cold climates it can**,** over the centuries**,** turn into glaciers which move at the rate of a few inches to *a number of* ~~several~~ feet a year. In the summer it may turn into the fury of a thunderstorm and then afterward into a beautiful

rainbow. In the larger spaces it may become *an ocean with* a pounding surf or a quiet

blue lake. ~~I learned that~~ *It* is made up of hydrogen and oxygen **,** and it

makes up about seven-tenths of our body weight. If we have to go without

water for long, we die. ~~The same is true for other animals and plants.~~ In

fact all life on earth would die if it weren't for that amazing water.

Now reread your paper on "A Decision I Have Made" and see what improvements you can make before you copy it in final form.

Here's a checklist of questions to ask yourself as you begin to rewrite:

1. Will my introductory paragraph make my reader want to read further?
2. Does each paragraph support my thesis statement?
3. Does each paragraph contain only one main idea?
4. Do I have enough specific details in each paragraph to support the topic sentence, and are all the details relevant?
5. Does my concluding paragraph sum up my paper in a persuasive way?
6. Are my sentences properly constructed and clear?
7. Have I avoided wordiness and clichés?
8. Have I checked all questionable spellings?
9. Is my punctuation correct?
10. Is my title interesting?

VIII. PROOFREAD ALOUD

Finally, read your finished paper ALOUD. If you read it silently, you're sure to miss some errors. Read it aloud slowly, word by word, to catch omitted words, errors in spelling and punctuation, and so on. Make it a rule to read each of your papers **aloud** before handing it in.

As you do the following assignments, be sure to take each of the **EIGHT STEPS TO BETTER WRITING.**

Assignment 6   Someone Who Has Influenced Me

What person, other than a parent, has been of great influence in your life? Has someone—perhaps a teacher or a counselor or a coach—encouraged you in athletics or music, influenced you in the choice of a career, given you confidence in yourself? Write a thesis statement saying that a certain person has influenced you, and organize under two or three main points the ways in which you were influenced. Then write your paper. Remember to include specific examples.

Assignment 7   In Praise of Something

Write a paper praising something. It might be a job you enjoyed, an activity such as dramatics or music from which you have benefited, a sport that has done something for you, a kind of motorcycle or car you think is superior.

Be sure to limit your subject. Basketball, for example, would not be a possible subject because it's too broad. You might limit it to what playing on a particular basketball team did for you. After limiting your subject, work out a good thesis statement with two or three supporting points. Then write your paper using plenty of specific details.

Before you hand your paper in, read it aloud *slowly* word by word to catch errors.

Assignment 8   Something I Can Do

What is something you can do well? Bake brownies? Make jewelry? Play chess? Do high dives? Play the trombone? Throw a Frisbee? Give your reader the benefit of your expertise and explain in several steps just how to master your skill.

Assignment 9   A Letter to Myself

One reason for writing is to gain knowledge about ourselves. For this assignment, instead of looking outward, look inward. Have a talk with yourself. What are some things you've been telling yourself you should or should not do? Ten minutes of free writing will be a good way to find out what material you have. Then work out a thesis statement and write a letter to yourself. One student began his letter, "Dear Ben, Why don't you wise up?" Then he went on to tell three things he knew he should be doing. It's always harder to analyze oneself than someone else, but it can be fun and perhaps productive.

Assignment 10   A Recent Accomplishment

What recent accomplishment are you proud of? It might be a great accomplishment or a small one. It might be something public or something no one else knows about. Tell why you're proud of what you've done.

Assignment 11   A Place I'd Like to Live

If you could live anywhere in the United States, what place would you choose? Why?

Assignment 12   Advice That Hits Home

Look through the quotations in Exercises 1, 2, 6, and 7 on pages 188–93 and find one that you could profit from following. Or find one that you have followed. Then write a thesis statement explaining either how you have benefited from the quotation or how you might benefit from it. Back up your thesis statement with supporting points, and write your paper.

Assignment 13   My Opinion on a Current Problem

Choose one of the following problems and present your arguments for one side. Write a carefully thought-out thesis statement, supported by reasons, before you begin to write your paper. In your introduction or conclusion you may want to mention briefly the reasons you can see for the opposite side.

A. A couple, both alcoholics and totally unable to care for their infant son, were forced by the court to place him in a foster home. Now, ten years later, the couple, completely rehabilitated, have asked the court to return their child to them. The foster parents, however, have come to think of the boy as their own son, and the boy has come to think of them as his real parents and would like to stay with them. If you were the judge in the court, what would your decision be, and why?

B. The most important football game of the season is coming up, with the outcome depending largely on one top player. Unfortunately that player, although he has put forth considerable effort, has been flunking chemistry all term and now has failed the final exam. He is eager to play because he hopes to have a career in professional football and knows that scouts from professional teams will be watching. If he receives an F or even an Incomplete, he will be ineligible. If you were the chemistry professor, what grade would you give him?

C. A bill is before Congress to create a national park in an area where a commercial lumbering company is ready to move in. The congressman from that district, a conservationist, strongly favors the park and would like to vote for the bill. His constituents, however, are writing him asking that he oppose the bill because they want the commercial lumbering company to come in and create jobs. If you were the congressman, what would you do?

WRITING A SUMMARY

A good way to learn to write concisely is to write 100-word summaries. Writing 100 words sounds easy, but actually it isn't. Writing 200- or 300- or 500-word summaries isn't too difficult, but condensing all the main ideas of an essay or article into 100 words is a time-consuming task—not to be undertaken the last hour before class. If you work at writing summaries conscientiously, you'll improve both your reading and your writing. You'll improve your reading by learning to spot main ideas and your writing by learning to construct a concise, clear, smooth paragraph. Furthermore, your skills will carry over into your reading and writing for other courses.

Assignment 14   A 100-Word Summary

Your aim in writing your summary should be to give someone who has not read the article a clear idea of it. First read the article, and then follow the instructions given after it. Note that difficult words are defined in the margin.

The Jeaning of America—and the World
Carlin C. Quinn

This is the story of a sturdy American symbol which has now spread throughout most of the world. The symbol is not the dollar. It is not even Coca-Cola. It is a simple pair of pants called blue jeans, and what the pants symbolize is what Alexis de Tocqueville called "a manly and legitimate passion for equality. . . ." Blue jeans are favored equally by bureaucrats and cowboys; bankers and deadbeats; fashion designers and beer drinkers. They draw no distinctions and recognize no classes; they are merely American. . . .

de Tocqueville (1805–1859)—a French historian who wrote about America

This ubiquitous American symbol was the invention of a Bavarian-born Jew . . . Levi Strauss. He was born in Bad Ocheim, Germany,

ubiquitous—present everywhere

in 1829, and during the European political tur-
moil of 1848 decided to take his chances in New
York, to which his two brothers already had emi-
grated. Upon arrival, Levi soon found that his
two brothers had exaggerated their tales of an
easy life in the land of the main chance. They
were landowners, they had told him; instead, he
found them pushing needles, thread, pots, pans,
ribbons, yarn, scissors, and buttons to house-
wives. For two years he was a lowly peddler,
hauling some 180 pounds of sundries door-to-
door to eke out a marginal living. When a mar-
ried sister in San Francisco offered to pay his way
West in 1850, he jumped at the opportunity, taking with him bolts of canvas he hoped to sell for
tenting.

eke out—to make with great effort
marginal—low quality

It was the wrong kind of canvas for that purpose, but while talking with a miner down from
the mother lode, he learned that pants—sturdy
pants that would stand up to the rigors of the
diggings—were almost impossible to find. Opportunity beckoned. On the spot, Strauss measured
the man's girth and inseam with a piece of string
and, for six dollars in gold dust, had them tai-
lored into a pair of stiff but rugged pants. The
miner was delighted with the result, word got
around about "those pants of Levi's," and Strauss
was in business. The company has been in business ever since.

mother lode—main vein of ore in a district

When Strauss ran out of canvas, he wrote his
two brothers to send more. He received instead
a tough, brown cotton cloth made in Nîmes,
France—called *serge de Nîmes* and swiftly short-
ened to "denim" (the word "jeans" derives from
Gênes, the French word for Genoa, where a similar cloth was produced). Almost from the first,
Strauss had his cloth dyed the distinctive indigo
that gave blue jeans their name, but it was not
until the 1870's that he added the copper rivets
which have long since become a company trade-
mark. The rivets were the idea of a Virginia City,
Nevada, tailor, Jacob W. Davis, who added them
to pacify a mean-tempered miner called Alkali
Ike. Alkali, the story goes, complained that the
pockets of his jeans always tore when he stuffed
them with ore samples and demanded that Davis
do something about it. As a kind of joke, Davis

took the pants to a blacksmith and had the pockets riveted; once again, the idea worked so well that word got around; in 1873 Strauss appropriated and patented the gimmick—and hired Davis as a regional manager.

appropriate—to take possession of
gimmick—device

By this time, Strauss had taken both his brothers and two brothers-in-law into the company and was ready for his third San Francisco store. Over the ensuing years the company prospered locally, and by the time of his death in 1902, Strauss had become a man of prominence in California. For three decades thereafter the business remained profitable though small, with sales largely confined to the working people of the West— cowboys, lumberjacks, railroad workers, and the like. Levi's jeans were first introduced to the East, apparently, during the dude-ranch craze of the 1930's, when vacationing Easterners returned and spread the word about the wonderful pants with rivets. . . .

ensuing—following

From a company with fifteen salespeople, two plants, and almost no business east of the Mississippi in 1946, the organization grew in thirty years to include a sales force of more than twenty-two thousand, with fifty plants and offices in thirty-five countries. Each year, more than 250,000,000 items of Levi's clothing are sold— including more than 83,000,000 pairs of riveted blue jeans. . . .

The pants have become a tradition, and along the way have acquired a history of their own—so much so that the company has opened a museum in San Francisco. There was, for example, the turn-of-the-century trainman who replaced a faulty coupling with a pair of jeans; the Wyoming man who used his jeans as a towrope to haul his car out of a ditch; the Californian who found several pairs in an abandoned mine, wore them, then discovered they were sixty-three years old and still as good as new and turned them over to the Smithsonian as a tribute to their toughness. And then there is the particularly terrifying story of the careless construction worker who dangled fifty-two stories above the street until rescued, his sole support the Levi's belt loop through which his rope was hooked. . . .

Smithsonian—a museum in Washington, D.C.

Though Levi Strauss & Co. has since become

Levi Strauss International, with all that the cor-
porate name implies, it still retains a suitably
fond regard for its beginnings. Through what it
calls its "Western Image Program," employing
Western magazine advertisements, local radio
and television, and the promotion of rodeos, the
company still pursues the working people of the
West who first inspired Levi Strauss to make
pants to fit the world.

A good way to begin a summary is to figure out the author's thesis,
the major idea the author wants to present to the reader. Usually it is
suggested in the first paragraph. Reread the first paragraph of the article, and decide what the author's main idea is. Write that idea down
BEFORE YOU READ FURTHER.

How honest are you with yourself? Did you write that thesis statement? If you didn't, WRITE IT NOW before you read further.

You probably wrote something like this: *An American symbol of equality now spreading throughout the world is a simple pair of pants called blue jeans.*

Using your thesis statement as your first sentence, summarize as briefly as you can the rest of the article, which is simply the history and present status of blue jeans. Your first draft may be 150 words or more. Now cut it down by including only essential points and by getting rid of wordiness. Keep within the 100-word limit. You may have a few words less but not one word more. By forcing yourself to keep within the 100 words, you'll get to the kernel of the author's thought and understand the article better.

When you have written the best summary you can, then, *and only then,* compare it with the summary on page 306. If you look at the model sooner, you'll cheat yourself of the opportunity to learn to write summaries because once you read the model, it will be almost impossible not to make yours similar. So do your own thinking and writing, and *then* compare.

Even though your summary is different from the model, it may be just as good. If you're not sure how yours compares, ask yourself these questions:

Did I include as many important ideas?
Did I omit all unnecessary words and phrases?
Does my summary read as smoothly?
Would someone who had not read the article get a clear idea of it
    from my summary?

Assignment 15   A 100-Word Summary

After you read this concise article, you may wonder how you can condense it more, but you can. Turn it into a 100-word summary that will include just the most essential parts—the parts you will be sure to remember. Difficult words are defined in the margin.

Iceman

(A condensation of an article that appeared in *Time*, October 16, 1992)

The world's oldest human being was discovered in the Alps in 1991. He is known as the Iceman because he was found remarkably preserved in a melting glacier. Radio carbon dating has determined that his body is about 5,300 years old—by far the oldest human body ever found intact. Some Egyptian mummies are older, but they had their brains and other vital organs removed before they were mummified. The Iceman also died literally "with his boots on," because with him were his clothes, a bow and arrow, and other equipment.

intact—in its original state

Most remains of ancient humans are found surrounded by funerary objects, but the Iceman was snatched from life completely outfitted with clothing and the instruments of everyday existence. He wore an unlined fur robe made of patches of deer skin, and for further protection he wore a woven grass cape and leather shoes stuffed with grass for warmth. The Iceman's fur quiver is the only quiver from the Neolithic period that has been found in the whole world. Its arrows are carved from wood branches, and he was also armed with a tiny flint dagger.

funerary—funeral

Among other surprises, the Iceman has shown that human haircuts and tattoos have been in vogue longer than anyone had suspected.

The Iceman was found by a man who was on a walking trip through the Alps. Hurrying to a hikers' shelter to report his find, he unknowingly started a series of blunders that almost deprived the world of a priceless treasure. For example, an Austrian policeman tried to force the body from the glacier with a sledge hammer, chewing up the Iceman's garments and ripping through his left leg. Word spread, and soon about two dozen curious people collected fragments of the Iceman's garments and some of his tools. Fortunately the temperature dropped overnight, and the body was again locked in ice.

Eventually the Iceman and his possessions were moved from the glacier and transported to the University in Innsbruck where, except for 30-minute intervals when he is removed for scientific experiments, he lives in a refrigerated room with a temperature he had grown accustomed to for more than 5,000 years.

Assignment 16   A 100-Word Summary

Write a 100-word summary of this Reader's Opinion article from *U.S. News & World Report*.

Turning Highway Rights into Wrongs
Dr. David Hochberg

I'm writing in the hope of reaching young people: Those of you who insisted on your "rights" prior to my treating you in the hospital and those whom I have yet to treat but who also insist on the right not to wear seat belts while racing cars, the right not to wear helmets while riding your motorcycles, the right to "one last beer before hitting the road," the right to defy the laws made for everyone's protection and safety that you seem to think were made specifically to hassle you.

I've met you in the emergency room at all hours. Usually you were supposed to be home in bed or studying, but instead you were out looking for kicks. Some of you I know personally but could not recognize because of injuries that deformed your handsome faces, twisted your graceful limbs—injuries that were the direct result of exercising "your rights."

Often, by the time I've arrived, some of your bravado has worn off as the pain sets in and the realization that you are really hurt takes hold. "Will I be all right, Doc?" you ask. "Will I have bad scars?" "Am I going to die?"

Most of you survived; some did not. One of the hardest nights of my life came when I had to tell a lady very close to me that her son was dead. I held her and watched the light go out of her eyes. I wondered how many other mothers in how many other emergency rooms were losing their children at that very moment. I knew the answer: *Too* many.

I stand by the stretcher of those who survive, assess your injuries and plan needed repairs. I ask a question I've asked a hundred times: "How come you weren't wearing your seat belt (or your helmet)?" Briefly, the bravado and the bluff return: "I've got my rights, Doc."

As you utter that declaration of independence, I can see the glaze in your eyes. It could be from alcohol or injury. I work swiftly to be certain that your injuries are not life threatening, and when you are stabilized I ask you the question again. That's when I hear all the feeble excuses—the myths that have been passed from one misinformed youth to the next: "I can't hear well with my helmet on." "I don't want to get trapped in the car by my seat belt."

Your puny reasons pour forth as I wipe the blood from your mouth and try to figure out how I am going to put your torn ear back on.

You keep telling me how dangerous seat belts can be while I am X-raying your broken bones and looking for evidence of internal injury.

Finally, I determine that you are not going to die but that it is going to take several hours to put your face back together. The windshield stopped you—not your seat belt. But, hey, you've got your rights!

Then I get angry and I want to scream at you. I don't. But now I can say what I wanted to tell you that night in the emergency room:
• What about the rights of the other people on the road—the ones you sometimes run into and maim along with yourselves?
• What about the rights of the emergency-room crews who are already overworked trying to stabilize the heart-attack victim and the young child with pneumonia?
• What about your parents' rights—their rights to assume that you are acting responsibly with your life and the lives of those with you? And what about the rights of those with you in the car?
• What about the rights of all your family and friends who anguish when they see you in needless pain?
• And what about *my* rights—my right to a full night's sleep before a full day's work without being dragged out of bed at 2 A.M. to go to the emergency room to patch up another maimed teenager?

I want to shake you and say, "Never mind *your* rights! *Listen* when we say: 'Please wear your seat belt. Please wear your helmet.' We are not trying to impose rules or take away your rights; we are saying, quite simply, 'We love you!' "

Assignment 17   A 100-Word Summary

Do you know how many sites there are in the National Park System? Here is an article from the *National Geographic* that gives a number of facts most of us didn't know. Write a 100-word summary.

The Best Idea America Ever Had
Paul C. Pritchard

"To conserve the scenery and the natural and historic objects and the wild life therein and to provide for the enjoyment of the same . . . unimpaired for the enjoyment of future generations." With a stroke of his pen, President Woodrow Wilson thus signed the National Park Service Act 75 years ago this month.

Thirty-six national parks were brought under a single federal agency by this law. Former British ambassador to the U.S. James Bryce called them "the best idea America ever had." In the words of J. Horace McFarland, one of the visionaries who helped establish our National Park Service in 1916, "It is the one thing we have that has not been imported." Other nations had preserved gardens and open spaces—but mainly for the privileged classes. Not so for the U.S. parks, which would be preserved for all.

The National Park System has grown to 357 sites covering 80 million acres, including national parks and monuments, wild and scenic rivers, seashores, historic sites, scenic trails, and battlefields. In addition to natural wonders, such as Yellowstone and Grand Canyon, the Park Service preserves pieces of our history and culture— British cannon surrendered at Yorktown, the derringer that killed Abraham Lincoln, Carl Sandburg's typewriter, even a type of shortlegged Hereford cattle bred by President Lyndon B. Johnson.

The service is acutely aware that its lands are among the last natural refuges for America's plant and animal diversity. More and more, it is being called upon to provide scarce habitat for thou-

National Geographic, August 1991. Reprinted by permission.

sands of species and to use the parks as laboratories for research in a world of dwindling wild places. The service's 12,000 employees include those investigating why rare saguaro cactuses are dying in the Southwest, seeking how to protect a shrinking population of sea turtles in the U.S. Virgin Islands, exploring how to get clean water to Florida's Everglades in the right volume, and managing a bison herd in Yellowstone that wanders outside the park.

These concerns reflect a growing sensitivity and sophistication in our understanding of the natural world. In Yellowstone, for example, where bleachers were once erected at the garbage dumps so tourists could watch grizzly bears feeding, the dumps have been closed, the bleachers have been razed, and thousands of dollars *raze*—to destroy to the have been spent to install bear-proof garbage ground cans. The bears have returned to their normal diet, and they are healthier.

As our understanding of nature has changed, so has the role of national parks. Most Americans probably still think of picture postcard vistas. *vista*—view But, in fact, most parks today focus on history or culture, and they often are within easy reach of cities and suburbs. And many of today's parks reflect our nation's evolving values and demographic mix.

In San Antonio, Texas, the Park Service is working with the Roman Catholic Church to preserve old missions, representing the heritage of Spanish colonial days. In California, Asian Americans have asked for a national park at Manzanar recognizing the internment during World War II *internment*— of American citizens of Japanese descent. In Mas- confinement sachusetts, restored 19th-century textile mills at the Lowell National Historical Park sit in a city of 103,000, the site of America's first planned industrial town.

Our park system has been called the "largest university in the world." The prime purpose of the system, says Yale University historian Robin Winks, "is to educate people, with the 357 park units as branch campuses." But this great university faces a number of challenges stemming from *stem*—develop as a overcrowding, understaffing, and budget con- consequence straints. In the 1970s our parklands were doubled *constraint*—restriction with the creation of many urban parks and the addition of more than 40 million acres of Alaska lands. But there has been no comparable increase in staff—this during a time when more people than ever, more than 250 million a year, are visiting parks. . . .

Under this stress, park rangers could become an endangered species, victims of too little pay and too much work. Surveys within the Park Service indicate that while many dedicated individuals continue to perform outstanding feats of public service, the general level of morale is at an all-time low. It's understandable. Many rangers who joined the service to be close to nature must increasingly deal with the problems of drug enforcement, vandalism, and pollution. Rangers' average starting salary is only $15,000. Lacking adequate housing, some have been forced to sleep in their cars; others subsist on food stamps. "The rangers of the National Park Service can't live on sunsets," says Representative Bruce Vento of Minnesota, chairman of the House Subcommittee on National Parks and Public Lands. . . .

This anniversary has rekindled concern for the well-being of the National Park Service. Americans care deeply about their natural and cultural heritage, and they admire the dedicated individuals who keep our parks open. Without such people . . . there could be no national parks.

Assignment 18   A 100-Word Summary

This article by Gilbert Grosvenor, president of the National Geographic Society, should be easy to summarize in 100 words.

A Few Thoughts on Penguins and Tourists
Gilbert M. Grosvenor

As our small group of tourists climbed the rocky slope of Half Moon Island, one of dozens of islands strung out along the west coast of the Antarctic Peninsula, I was struck by the air of absolute indifference assumed by the chinstrap penguins all around us. If I hadn't known better, I could have picked up one of the birds and taken it home with me—they showed that little fear.

That's precisely the problem, of course, posed by the tide of tourism now reaching remote places such as Antarctica. Unless visitors are carefully supervised, they are likely to disrupt the pristine worlds they come to enjoy.

Many nations are facing this issue. During the past 25 years the crowd of trekkers in Nepal has grown from 10,000 to 250,000 a year. Ecuador's Galápagos National Park handles more than 40,000 visitors annually. And tourism to Botswana, little heralded before the 1960s, now attracts more than 300,000 visitors a year, becoming a major source of foreign currency for that country.

Don't misunderstand me. I'm not against tourism in such places. On the contrary, I'm all for it. Because no one who witnesses the desolate beauty of Antarctica can fail to come back home as anything but an advocate for its preservation. No one who marvels at the sight of humpback whales playing in the shadow of icy cliffs, or Weddell seals snoozing on floes, or orcas slicing through the sea can tolerate the idea of beer cans in the snow. Or oil drills, for that matter, or mining equipment.

At the same time, we must be sure not to overwhelm Antarctica's seemingly unlimited space with even well-meaning disruption. While most of the approximately 3,000 casual visitors a year still arrive in ships run by responsible cruise lines, we must guard against future tour operations that might fail to comply with the accepted norms of Antarctic "ecotourism:" Stay away from protected areas, never disturb wildlife, leave no trash, take no souvenirs.

National Geographic, May 1991. Reprinted by permission.

. . .

The purity of Antarctica, after all, could change as rapidly as its weather. Returning to the ship one afternoon, our party was caught by a sudden gale that tossed our rubber rafts about and filled them with six inches of frigid water. Considering the ease with which uncontrolled waves of tourists could similarly swamp this fragile, unspoiled land, we shouldn't let the challenge catch us by surprise.

WRITING AN APPLICATION

Assignment 19   A Letter of Application

You may not need to do much writing in the career you have chosen, but almost certainly you will at some time need to write a letter of application. Write a letter of application now, either for a job this coming summer or for a job you might want to apply for after you finish college. Then write a separate résumé. Follow the forms given here.

Lincoln Hall
West Adams Street
Macomb, IL 61455
January 25, 1994

Tom Levy, Director
Argyle Lake State Park
Rural Route 1
Colchester, IL 62326

Dear Mr. Levy:

A friend of mine, Christopher Ransom, was one of the leaders in
your Summer Interpretive Program three years ago, and he has
told me so much about it that I'd like to apply for a position in
the program for the coming summer.

Chris explained that you try to keep your park visitors,
particularly young people, busy and happy by showing them how
to make things from natural sources. He said he took a group to a
clay bank and helped them make clay pottery, that he showed
them how to weave simple mats from blue stem grass, and that
he helped them make dye from walnut shells. Of course he also
took them on nature hikes and stargazing trips. All these are
activities I enjoy and am capable of leading.

My college courses in botany and biology have given me a
background in nature study, and last summer I gained some
experience in working with young people as a counselor at Camp
Timberidge of the YMCA in Glen Ellyn, where I helped with crafts
and nature study.

Since I'm majoring in biology and am planning to go into some
kind of conservation work eventually, the experience I would get
in your program would be valuable to me, and I hope that what I
can offer would be valuable to your visitors.

I have listed my training and experience on the attached sheet
and will be glad to come for a personal interview at your
convenience. I'll phone you soon to see if I can make an
appointment.

Sincerely,

Jack Doe

Jack Doe

RESUME

Jack Doe
Lincoln Hall
West Adams Street
Macomb, IL 61455
Tel. 000-000-0000

WORK EXPERIENCE
    1993 summer   Counselor at Camp Timberidge of the B. R.
                  Ryall YMCA in Glen Ellyn, IL
    1992 summer   Bagger at Krogers in Glen Ellyn, IL

EDUCATION
    1993–94   Freshman at Western Illinois University,
              Macomb, IL   Majoring in biology; minoring
              in special education
    1989–93   Student at Community High School, District 94,
              West Chicago, IL

ACTIVITIES
    1993–94   Participant in all field trips of Department of Bio-
              logical Sciences
              Member of the Varsity Swim Team

REFERENCES
    Professor Gordon R. Thurow
    Department of Biological Sciences
    Western Illinois University
    Macomb, IL 61455

    Professor Robert D. Henry
    Department of Biological Sciences
    Western Illinois University
    Macomb, IL 61455

    Judy Bucci
    Camp Director
    B. R. Ryall YMCA
    Glen Ellyn, IL 60137

WRITING AN EVALUATION

Assignment 20   An Evaluation of My Performance

Do five minutes of free writing in preparation for writing a short paper on your performance in this course. Don't evaluate the course—it may have been bad or good—but simply evaluate how you performed. Although you may need to mention some weakness or strength of the course, the emphasis should be on how you reacted to that weakness or strength.

Don't be afraid to be honest. This isn't an occasion for apple-polishing. If you've gained little, you'll write a better paper by saying so than by trying to make up phony gains. Someone who has gained little may write a better paper than someone who has gained much. How well the paper is organized and whether there are plenty of specific examples will determine the effectiveness of the paper.

Before starting your paper, write your thesis statement, listing your supporting points. If you've made gains, list the kinds—gain in writing skill, gain in confidence, gain in study habits. . . . Or, if you've gained little, list the reasons why—lack of time, lack of interest, getting off to a bad start. . . .

Since no one will have all gains or all losses in any course, you may want to include in your introduction or conclusion a sentence about the other side.

Answers

Answers

Words Often Confused (p. 10)

EXERCISE 1

1. are
2. our, new
3. do, feel
4. conscious
5. new

6. It's
7. are
8. hear, an
9. course
10. know, chose, our, already

EXERCISE 2

1. hear
2. It's, an
3. course, accept
4. are
5. conscious

6. do, course
7. know, our
8. hear
9. it's
10. conscience

EXERCISE 3

1. It's, your
2.
3. where
4. are
5. course

6. chose
7.
8.
9. where
10. are, their

EXERCISE 4

1. an
2. conscious
3. knew
4. chose, do
5. hear

6. effect
7. new, hear
8. advice
9. an
10. It's, an, have

EXERCISE 5

1. choose
2. already, know, it's, choose
3. are
4. already
5. do

6. compliments
7. conscious, have
8. or
9. know, an, effect
10. choose

EXERCISE 6

1. an, Here, are
2. know
3. It's
4. know
5. It's

6.
7. course, it's
8. knew
9. know
10. It's, its, it's

EXERCISE 7

1. an
2. conscious
3. choose, are
4. an
5. an, effect

6. course, already, knew, know
7. does, it's, break
8. accept, advice, conscience, do
9. or
10. have

EXERCISE 8

1. choose, choose
2. know, have
3. have, compliment
4. conscience
5. course, forth, course

6. accept
7. complement
8. know, do, course, it's
9. hear, effect, our
10. already, an

EXERCISE 9

1. knew, except
2. an
3. choose
4. feel
5. or

6. except
7. an
8. It's, or
9. course, accept, accept
10. compliment

EXERCISE 10

1. have, course
2. It's, an, effect
3. new, all ready
4. Our, advice, accept
5. do, course

6. know, it's, accept
7. hear, course, courses
8. chose, or, have
9. conscience, forth
10. already, compliment

More Words Often Confused (p. 20)

EXERCISE 1

1. knew, quite
2. accept, an
3. course, chose, clothes
4. weather, our
5. an, led
6. through
7. already, knew
8. course
9. then, advice
10. except

EXERCISE 2

1. an, new
2. It's
3. Their, are
4. do
5. are
6.
7. hear
8. There, are
9. choose
10.

EXERCISE 3

1. already
2. course
3. two
4. their, an, effect
5. hear
6. it's
7. too
8. our
9. Then, are
10. it's

EXERCISE 4

1. an
2. It's, it's
3. An, its
4. than
5. through
6. you're
7. It's, quite, an, through
8. course, through
9. Then, past, where
10. quite

EXERCISE 5

1. knew
2. know, they're, through
3. It's
4. led, an
5. an
6. passed
7. Then
8. There, than, accept
9. their
10. were, new

EXERCISE 6

1. quite, an
2. past
3. their, than
4. forth
5. course, there, no, their
6. there, where
7. Then
8. were
9. right
10. know, whose

EXERCISE 7

1. then, an
2. quite
3. two
4. weather, choose
5. It's, quite

6. do
7. effect
8. course, are
9. quite
10. do

EXERCISE 8

1. past
2. accept, advice
3. new
4. It's
5. know, do

6. does, course
7. there, are
8. where
9. Do
10. then, their

EXERCISE 9

1. conscious, their
2. it's
3. quite
4. course
5. Then

6. two, our
7.
8.
9. There
10. know, further

EXERCISE 10

1. there, peace
2. It's, its
3. It's
4. there, no, or
5. than, past

6. there
7. through
8. here, where
9. new, are
10. morale, Their

Proofreading Exercise (p. 26)

I LEARNED TO PAINT

Yesterday I learned to paint. Oh, I had painted before, and I thought I
knew
~~new~~ how. But that was before yesterday.

who's
Yesterday a friend ~~whose~~ a professional painter helped me paint my

apartment. First of all, we spent hours filling all the cracks and removing all

the hooks and nails and outlet covers. We washed the kitchen walls to get off any grease, and we lightly sanded one wall that was rough. Of ~~coarse~~ *course*

we had ~~all ready~~ *already* moved all the furniture away from the walls. We didn't

even open the paint cans until the day was half over. ~~Than~~ *Then* we used paint-

brushes to paint all the corners and edges that a roller wouldn't get to.

Finally, in the very last hour of ~~are~~ *our* long . . .

Contractions (p. 28)

EXERCISE 1

1. We're, I'm
2. shouldn't
3. isn't
4. That's
5. I'm

6. that's
7. everybody's
8. you'd
9. We're, it's
10. That's, It's

EXERCISE 2

1. I've
2. I'd
3. It's
4. I'd
5. I'd

6.
7.
8. wasn't
9. I'd
10. I'd

EXERCISE 3

1. I've
2. Won't, doesn't
3. it's, that's
4. he's
5. It's

6. That's
7. I've, I've
8. That's, haven't
9. Let's
10. I'll, can't, I'm

EXERCISE 4

1. There's, you've
2. that's, wouldn't
3. It's, it'll, won't
4. It's, I'm, wouldn't
5. It's, it's, it'll

6. I've, haven't
7. I've, it's
8. I've, I'm
9. It's (first one)
10. I've

EXERCISE 5

1. I've
2. I'm
3. didn't
4. you're, who'll, you'll
5. you're, you'll

6. you'd
7. you'd
8. you'd
9. It's
10. I'm

EXERCISE 6

1. don't
2. don't
3. they're
4. It's
5. I've, they're

6. aren't
7. I've, that's
8.
9. That's
10. doesn't

EXERCISE 7

1. We've, we've
2. It's, I'm
3. I'm, we've
4. You're, you'd
5. you'll

6. You'll, I've
7. I'm
8. It's, that's
9. It's, they're, they're
10. They're

EXERCISE 8

1. wasn't, I'd
2. I've
3. It's (first one)
4. It's
5. wasn't

6. wasn't
7. it's
8. that's
9. couldn't
10. there's, I'd

EXERCISE 9

1. I'd
2. I'd
3. I've, don't
4. don't, what's, isn't
5.

6. what's
7. what's
8. I'm
9.
10. it's

EXERCISE 10

1. I'm
2. It's, that's
3. don't
4. I'm, I've, I'm
5. It's, don't

6. don't, there's
7. you've, it's
8. I've
9. That's, I'm
10. that's, it's

Possessives (p. 36)

EXERCISE 1

1. everybody's
2. Jennifer's
3.
4. Jerome's, Connie's
5. Andy's

6. day's
7. Everybody's
8. Andy's
9. Ashley's
10. people's

EXERCISE 2

1. body's
2. body's
3. body's
4. person's
5.

6. One's
7. hand's
8.
9. surgeon's
10. hands'

EXERCISE 3

1. everyone's
2. person's, person's
3. students'
4. Sue's
5. Nick's, Sandburg's

6. Bev's, Dickens'
7. everyone's
8. students', instructor's
9. everybody's
10. instructor's, students'

EXERCISE 4

1. brother's
2. everybody's
3. mom's
4. sister's
5. dad's

6. brother's, friends'
7. everybody's
8. Dad's
9. brother's
10. anybody's

EXERCISE 5

1. Ivan's
2. daughter's
3. children's
4. Ivan's
5. afternoon's

6. monkeys'
7.
8.
9.
10.

EXERCISE 6

1. sister's
2. semester's
3. Women's
4. Dad's
5. friend's

6. girls'
7. sister's, friend's
8.
9.
10. sister's

EXERCISE 7

1. Ohio's
2.
3.
4. Greeks'
5.

6. today's
7. Rockne's
8. Ohio's
9. Namath's
10. Dempsey's

EXERCISE 8

1. brother's
2. family's
3. day's
4. beginner's
5. brother's

6. family's
7. dad's
8. sister's
9. week's
10. brother's

EXERCISE 9

1. Japan's
2. child's
3. Japan's
4. parents'
5. country's

6. People's
7. women's, men's
8. Children's
9. Women's
10. Japan's

EXERCISE 10

1. world's
2. world's
3.
4. world's
5.

6. country's
7. country's
8. world's
9. world's
10. country's

Review of Contractions and Possessives (p. 41)

EXERCISE 1

1. There'll, I'm
2. Loren's, doesn't, he's
3. He'd, he'll
4. I'm, aren't
5. We're
6. we'll, Women's

7. we'll
8. It's, Rogers', children's
9. It's
10.
11. Rogers'
12. It's, that's

EXERCISE 2

There's a little lake with steep rocky sides and crystal clear water that you can see down into forever. Some say it's bottomless, but everyone agrees it's deep.

There's one spot where a big tree grows over the lake, and someone's tied a rope to one of its branches to swing on. It's a great sensation, I discovered, to swing out over the water and then let go. I think everyone gets an urge to yell as loud as possible to enhance an awkward dive. It's a great feeling to cast off from the high rocks holding onto the rope as it swings out over the water. Just before the farthest point of the rope's travel is the best place to let go and drop into the water. Those with initiative try flips and twists as they dive, but however it's done, it's a great sensation. Some say it's for kids, but I hope I never grow too old to have fun at it.

Rule for Doubling a Final Consonant (p. 45)

EXERCISE 1

1. putting
2. controlling
3. admitting
4. mopping
5. planning
6. hopping
7. jumping
8. knitting
9. marking
10. creeping

EXERCISE 2

1. returning
2. swimming
3. singing
4. benefiting
5. loafing
6. nailing
7. omitting
8. occurring
9. shopping
10. interrupting

EXERCISE 3

1. beginning
2. spelling
3. preferring
4. interpreting
5. hunting
6. excelling
7. wrapping
8. stopping
9. wedding
10. screaming

EXERCISE 4

1. feeling
2. murmuring
3. turning
4. weeding
5. subtracting
6. streaming
7. expelling
8. missing
9. getting
10. stabbing

EXERCISE 5

1. forgetting
2. misspelling
3. fitting
4. planting
5. pinning

6. trusting
7. sipping
8. flopping
9. reaping
10. fighting

Progress Test (p. 46)

1. B	6. A	11. A
2. A	7. B	12. B
3. B	8. B	13. B
4. B	9. A	14. A
5. A	10. B	15. B

Finding Subjects and Verbs (p. 60)
EXERCISE 1

1. I visited
2. trip was
3. dunes shift
4. lake is
5. I watched

6. I walked
7. I saw
8. voices broke
9. dunes are
10. stars seem

EXERCISE 2

1. "black holes" were
2. "black hole" is
3. gravity crushed
4. gravity crushed
5. it "disappeared"

6. It became
7. sun is
8. It is
9. galaxies are
10. (You) try

EXERCISE 3

1. names have
2. Monday is
3. Tuesday is
4. Wednesday is
5. Thursday is

6. Friday is
7. Saturn gave
8. day is
9. people say
10. (You) think

EXERCISE 4

1. brother, I went
2. space is
3. buses bring
4. races are
5. outriders are
6. outriders toss
7. they jump
8. wagon starts
9. accidents are
10. It is

EXERCISE 5

1. Litter is
2. mountain has
3. camp is
4. Climbers leave
5. They leave
6. They leave
7. Nepal hopes
8. rule requires
9. job is
10. expedition plans

EXERCISE 6

1. Scientists wanted
2. It is
3. Antarctica is
4. scientists wanted
5. they brought
6. They succeeded
7. dog became
8. chicks nestle
9. chick nestled
10. scientists have

EXERCISE 7

1. nighthawks swoop
2. They become
3. (You) watch
4. nighthawk emits
5. It has
6. nighthawk opens
7. It catches
8. nighthawks nest
9. They sit
10. (You) listen

EXERCISE 8

1. sleds are
2. racing is
3. races are
4. racers call
5. dogs have
6. They love
7. dogs run
8. they stay
9. mushers prepare
10. It is

EXERCISE 9

1. libraries contain
2. exhibits include
3. Center, Library are
4. Gerald Ford is
5. One is
6. other is
7. latter offers
8. Library overlooks
9. It draws
10. people visited

EXERCISE 10

1. Library has
2. Library contains
3. Center illustrates
4. home is
5. Library is

6. reason is
7. Library celebrated
8. presidents attended
9. It is
10. (You) visit

Proofreading Exercise (p. 64)

SUGAR RAY LEONARD

People find it hard to believe that Sugar Ray Leonard, the boxing cham-

pion, grew up in poverty. They think that anyone who speaks as well as he

does must ~~of~~ *have* come from at least a middle-class home. But ~~Leonards~~ *Leonard's* par-

ents were poor. He was one of seven children and ~~didnt~~ *didn't* go beyond high

school. He was eager to succeed, however, and his ambition ~~lead~~ *led* him to

work on language skills. . . .

Subjects Not in Prepositional Phrases (p. 66)
EXERCISE 1

1. One ~~of the most interesting places on our trip~~ was the Japanese garden ~~in the East-West Center in Honolulu~~.
2. We followed a bamboo-shaded path ~~through the garden~~.
3. Clumps ~~of ferns~~ bordered the path.
4. ~~Near the path~~ flowed a little stream.
5. ~~In small pools beside the stream~~ were orange and black and white tropical fish.
6. Here and there were Japanese stone lanterns.
7. ~~At the top of the garden~~ was a small waterfall.
8. Stone slab steps ~~beside the waterfall~~ led ~~to a Japanese teahouse~~.
9. An atmosphere ~~of peace~~ enveloped the garden.
10. Some ~~of the best things in life~~ are still free.

EXERCISE 2

1. The living room ~~in my apartment~~ was dull and uninteresting.
2. It contained plenty ~~of ordinary furniture~~ but nothing exciting.
3. Not a single piece ~~of furniture~~ was worth a second look.
4. I had to do something ~~about it.~~
5. I didn't have a lot ~~of money~~ to spend however.
6. Therefore ~~from a nearby greenhouse~~ I bought a large potted palm.
7. I set that palm carefully ~~in one corner of the living room.~~
8. Then I walked ~~across the room~~ to see the effect.
9. Amazing! That one palm gave the entire room a tropical atmosphere.
10. And I've enjoyed my living room ever since.

EXERCISE 3

1. The largest island ~~in the world~~ is Greenland.
2. New Guinea ~~in the Pacific~~ is the second largest.
3. Both ~~of these islands~~ contain unexplored regions.
4. The interior ~~of Greenland~~ is ~~under an ice cap.~~
5. ~~In New Guinea~~ a rugged interior discourages travel.
6. Some ~~of the primitive people in New Guinea~~ still use stone tools.
7. Their small thatched houses often stand ~~on poles above the swampy ground.~~
8. Villages sometimes communicate ~~by the beat of drums.~~
9. Many ~~of the people~~ have little knowledge ~~of our civilization.~~
10. Some ~~of the tribes~~ never go ~~outside their own valleys.~~

EXERCISE 4

1. One ~~of the greatest magicians of all time~~ was Houdini.
2. ~~After his birth in Budapest in 1874,~~ his family moved ~~to New York City.~~
3. ~~From the age of fourteen,~~ he practiced magic tricks.
4. ~~At 17,~~ he became a professional magician.
5. One ~~of his tricks~~ was his Metamorphosis Trick.
6. The meaning ~~of metamorphosis~~ is "change."
7. ~~In this trick~~ he escaped, ~~with his hands bound, from a locked trunk.~~
8. Then Houdini's brother, ~~with hands also bound,~~ appeared ~~in the trunk.~~
9. ~~On another occasion~~ forty thousand people watched Houdini's daring handcuffed jump ~~from a Pittsburgh bridge.~~
10. ~~In about three minutes~~ he freed himself ~~under water.~~

EXERCISE 5

1. The forty-ninth <u>state</u> <u>is</u> one ~~of the most scenic places in the United States~~.
2. ~~At the beginning of last summer~~ <u>I</u> <u>flew</u> ~~to Anchorage in Alaska~~.
3. ~~From there~~ <u>I</u> <u>took</u> a number ~~of backpacking trips~~.
4. <u>Alaska</u> <u>has</u> 8,000 miles ~~of scenic highways~~.
5. ~~Within its vastness~~, <u>everything</u> <u>is</u> big.
6. ~~For example~~, the <u>Malaspina Glacier</u> <u>is</u> 1,700 square miles ~~in area~~.
7. <u>One</u> ~~of the longest navigable rivers in the world~~ <u>is</u> the Yukon.
8. The 20,320-foot <u>Mount McKinley</u> <u>is</u> the tallest peak ~~in North America~~.
9. <u>Snow</u> perpetually <u>covers</u> the upper two-thirds ~~of the mountain~~.
10. <u>Mount McKinley</u> <u>is</u> ~~in Denali National Park~~.

EXERCISE 6

1. <u>Tobagganing</u> ~~over hard packed snow~~ <u>is</u> an exciting sport.
2. The <u>Indians</u> <u>were</u> the first to use toboggans.
3. <u>They</u> probably <u>transported</u> things ~~on them~~.
4. A modern <u>toboggan</u> <u>carries</u> as many as twelve people.
5. A <u>steersman</u> ~~in the rear~~ <u>trails</u> a foot ~~in the snow~~ to guide the toboggan.
6. ~~In the Far North~~ <u>snowshoeing</u> <u>is</u> popular.
7. <u>Snowshoes</u> ~~for traveling in the woods~~ <u>are</u> only two feet long.
8. But Alaskan <u>snowshoes</u> ~~for racing~~ <u>are</u> seven feet long.
9. The <u>first</u> to use snowshoes <u>were</u> the Indians.
10. <u>They</u> probably <u>tied</u> branches ~~of a fir tree to their feet~~.

EXERCISE 7

1. road is
2. Canada completed
3. it goes
4. monument is
5. highway spans
6. road crosses
7. parks are
8. parks are
9. number are
10. highway comes

EXERCISE 8

1. I read
2. weather was
3. Shepard waited
4. weather improved
5. rocket roared
6. He hurtled
7. dangers bothered
8. He looked
9. he reached
10. flight was

EXERCISE 9

1. It's
2. terrier got
3. terrier digs
4. Companion comes
5. companion shares

6. Preposterous means
7. horse is
8. we use
9. leader scratched
10. they started

EXERCISE 10

1. organization includes
2. One is
3. organization wants
4. members outfit
5. devices enable

6. organization invented
7. children use
8. organization helps
9. It co-sponsors
10. Americans find

More about Verbs and Subjects (p. 71)

EXERCISE 1

1. I read
2. I had heard
3. tree is
4. It grows
5. Loggers considered, threw, used

6. community announced
7. Taxol is made, slows
8. it takes
9. trees are
10. research is

EXERCISE 2

1. zoos were
2. animals were kept
3. zoos have
4. animals roam
5. reason is

6. species become, prospect is
7. Zoos are promoting
8. Zoos have undertaken
9. number should increase. Many will be turned
10. Visitors enjoy

EXERCISE 3

1. (You) browse
2. you will find
3. man weighed
4. (You) do be discouraged
5. record is

6. album is
7. race was
8. speed is
9. poem is
10. It appeared, has appeared

EXERCISE 4

1. Seals spend, are descended
2. They have, breathe, bear
3. seal can close, can hold
4. It uses, uses
5. seals spend, go

6. seals travel
7. one knows
8. seals gather
9. seals were killed
10. conservationists have been

EXERCISE 5

1. Cities may look
2. skyscrapers are going
3. Building goes, is
4. floors have been excavated
5. equipment is
6. advantage is
7. climate varies, remains
8. Most is lighted
9. lenses beam
10. Occupants find

EXERCISE 6

1. Lincoln was born
2. cabin was chinked, had
3. cabin has been placed
4. Lincoln moved, spent
5. He worked, studied
6. Lincoln was elected
7. New Salem has been reconstructed
8. Visitors can ramble
9. buildings have been reproduced, furnished
10. Visitors can take

EXERCISE 7

1. I have been learning
2. tongue may be
3. Badgers can run
4. atoms are
5. span was
6. star is
7. words are
8. form was
9. Egyptians extracted, rubbed
10. jar was

EXERCISE 8

1. I have been reading
2. He is
3. Kip did
4. He burst
5. training prepared
6. he won
7. He returned, won
8. he represents
9. He, wife have taken
10. *Sports Illustrated* called

EXERCISE 9

1. Shoes have had
2. people covered, held
3. Sandals have been found
4. people wore, tied
5. persons wore
6. shoes were
7. Edward II originated
8. ladies imitated, wore
9. shoes were made
10. shoes were made

EXERCISE 10

1. I have been reading
2. products were named
3. products were named
4. names have
5. Chevrolet was named
6. coffee was served, took
7. Teddy Roosevelt asked, called
8. buses were painted
9. owner likened
10. buses got

Correcting Run-together Sentences (p. 78)

EXERCISE 1

1. It takes, development is called
2. eggs are laid, caterpillars emerge
3. caterpillars eat, caterpillars may be eaten
4. caterpillar sheds, skin is
5. caterpillar is, it sheds
6. it has turned, chrysalis is
7. chrysalis is, Changes are occurring
8. it cracks, butterfly emerges
9. wings dry, harden; monarch flies
10. It goes

EXERCISE 2

1. math.
2. up.
3. professor,
4. chance.
5. work.
6. hours.
7.
8. grades. During
9. came,
10. mark.

EXERCISE 3

1. me. She
2. busy,
3. listen;
4. career. Then
5. time,
6. years. Then
7.
8. receiving;
9. work,
10. write,

EXERCISE 4

1. Uemura. He
2. world. Every
3. Huskies. It
4. F.
5. underwear,
6. dogs,
7.
8. supply. Then
9. bag,
10. returned,

EXERCISE 5

1. world. It
2. participated,
3. them,
4.
5. crowd. In
6. athletes. They
7. success. She
8. Olympics. She
9.
10. competition. It

EXERCISE 6

1. disability. The
2. disability. Then
3. esteem. Their
4. Olympics. Her
5.
6. struggle. The
7. sports,
8.
9. free,
10. disadvantaged,

EXERCISE 7

1. decline. The
2. ponds,
3. toads,
4. organized. The
5.
6. toads,
7. help,
8.
9. countries,
10.

EXERCISE 8

1. school.
2. one,
3. stove;
4. early. She
5. them,
6. double. Two
7. bottle,
8. blackboards,
9. schoolyard,
10. out,

EXERCISE 9

1. quotations. Many
2. indicated. You
3. one. Unstring
4. know. It
5. dark. The
6. money. That . . . advice. Don't
   . . . nickel. Invest . . . yourself.
7. career. None
8. wane. When
9. duck. Keep . . . surface,
10. tree. You . . . it, or

Correcting Fragments (p. 87)

EXERCISE 1

1. <u>You</u> <u>have</u> to practice until <u>using</u> the rules of writing <u>becomes</u>

   automatic.

2. When <u>you</u> <u>know</u> a few rules, <u>writing</u> <u>becomes</u> easier.

3. The only <u>difference</u> between an independent and a dependent

   clause <u>is</u> that the dependent <u>clause</u> <u>begins</u> with a dependent

   word.

4. If <u>you</u> <u>know</u> the dependent words, <u>you'll</u> <u>have</u> no trouble.

5. If <u>you</u> <u>don't</u>, <u>you</u> <u>may</u> not <u>punctuate</u> your sentences correctly.

6. A <u>comma</u> <u>is</u> <u>required</u> when a dependent <u>clause</u> <u>comes</u> first in a

   sentence.

7. When a dependent clause comes first in a sentence, a comma often prevents misreading.

8. When you have done a few sentences, the rule becomes easy.

9. It will help you when you are punctuating your papers.

10. When you punctuate correctly, your reader can read with ease.

EXERCISE 2

1. that is working day and night
2. which amounts to about 3,000 pounds of dead plants and animals per acre every year
3. which may number ten billion in just 60 cubic inches of forest soil
4. until it can be eaten by earthworms and insects
5. As these creatures pass the debris through their digestive systems
6. which then nourish new plants and animals
7. that without earthworms all vegetation would perish
8. which involves billions of organisms
9. Although pine needles may take three or four years to be turned into soil
10. that recycles the forest floor

EXERCISE 3

1. that I never knew before
2. which is the first "surround" music hall in the country
3. Whereas most seats are within 65 feet of the stage
4. which opened in 1978 to raves from the public and from music and architecture critics
5. that have "surround" music halls
6. that the city with the most telephones per capita is Washington, D.C.
7. whereas the national average is 77 phones per 100 persons
8. that amaze me
9. that the light from one galaxy started to come to us 100 million years ago when dinosaurs were on earth
10. that one teaspoonful of it would weigh as much as 200 million elephants

EXERCISE 4

1. That's the place where we camped last year.
2. I cooked the dinner while she sat in the shade and drank lemonade.
3.
4. I'll phone her because I know she will understand.

5. After I came home and took a long shower, I was ready to practice.
6. I'm staying away from the coffee maker because most of my nervousness is caused by drinking too much coffee.
7. As I become more and more sure of myself, I'm enjoying my speech course.
8.
9. Before I took this course and learned a few rules, my writing was impossible to read.
10.

EXERCISE 5

1. Yesterday we went to the zoo because I hadn't been there for ages.
2. We went first to the sea lion tank because I wanted to feed the sea lions.
3. They ignored the fish that we threw to them because they had been fed too many fish.
4. Long ago they were named sea lions because someone thought they roared like lions.
5. They are really a type of seal and are related to fur seals, although they lack the valuable coats of the fur seals.
6. In another part of the zoo small whales performed tricks, since they can be trained just like seals.
7. Next we saw a sable antelope who had a one-day-old baby.
8. She prodded the baby with her knee because she wanted to make it walk.
9. She was persistent until finally she made it take a couple of steps.
10. Since I always learn a lot at the zoo, I should go more often.

EXERCISE 6

1. Although I've often said "busy as a beaver," I really knew nothing about beavers.
2. Now I know a little because I've read an article about them.
3. A beaver's four front teeth are constantly growing because the beaver wears them down by gnawing trees to make dams.
4. Since a beaver's teeth are sharp, a beaver can cut down a small willow in only a few minutes.
5. When the tree suddenly begins to totter, then the beaver dashes for safety.
6. When finally all is quiet again, the beaver then returns to work.
7. Because a family of beavers work hard, they can fell a thousand trees in a year.
8. A beaver has a flat tail that he uses in many ways.
9. When he stands up to gnaw a tree, his tail serves as a prop.
10. When he slaps his tail against the water, his tail sounds an alarm.

EXERCISE 7

1. One Christmas when I was about eleven, I got a new hockey stick.
2. Since I thought I could play better with a new stick, I was inspired.
3. Because we played with a tennis ball on the street, we called it street hockey.
4. The goalie wore a baseball glove on one hand while he wielded a hockey stick with the other.
5. As we hit that tennis ball hard, he tried to keep us from shooting it past him.
6. When it got really cold in the winter, then we flooded the backyard.
7. When the ice finally became solid, my brother and I put on our skates.
8. Since we played with a real puck, we pretended we were stars of the Maple Leafs.
9. Because the whole neighborhood gathered at our "rink," we felt like real pros.
10. Those were exciting games that left some great memories.

EXERCISE 8

1. When I watched a "National Geographic Special" last night, I learned about a world that I didn't know existed.
2. That world is the rain forests that form a band around the earth along the equator.
3. Since the rain forests get from 100 to 400 inches of rain a year, there is sometimes too much water.
4. When wasps need to dry out their nests, they simply drink the water and spit it out over the edge of the nest.
5. Because insects swarm over the trees, the trees have to protect themselves against the insects.
6. The acacia tree is protected by ants that live in the tree.
7. When other insects attack the acacia, the ants then attack the invaders and save the acacia.
8. One insect in the rain forest has skin that is so nutritious that it can't be wasted.
9. When the insect sheds its skin periodically, it then eats every bit of it.
10. I'd like to learn more about the rain forests because they are colorful and amazing.

More about Fragments (p. 94)

EXERCISE 1

1. Thinking we had missed the turn several miles back, we turned around.
2. She left me standing there holding the bag.
3. Not just kids my own age but younger and older people were there too.
4. Never believing anyone would come to my rescue, I tried to swim ashore.
5. The important thing was not whether we won or lost.
6. I was tired of going to meetings that served no purpose.
7.
8. He did only the things that he wanted to do.
9. Her confidence was built up after each win.
10. If she were someone whom I could sit down and talk to, it would be easier.

EXERCISE 2

1.
2. Writing a clear thesis statement and backing it up with reasons is always important.
3.
4.
5. If you do things for others without being asked, you'll be appreciated.
6. That is something that will take years of experience to learn.
7.
8.
9.
10. I'm constantly striving to improve my writing.

EXERCISE 3

1. I decided to look up all the words I don't know.
2.
3. I did something that I had always wanted to do.
4. I'm going to start now while I still have time to finish my paper.
5.
6. That is what I should have done long ago.
7. I hear that the Mounties always get their man.
8. She was making the most of every opportunity.
9. I've just learned that the Nile is the longest river in the world.
10.

EXERCISE 4

. . . That someone special will have a chance to spend two years in another country, to live and work in another culture, to learn a new language and acquire new skills.

The person we're looking for might be a farmer, a forester, a retired nurse, a teacher, a mechanic, or a recent college graduate.

We need someone . . . to help people live better lives.

We need someone special, and we ask a lot but only . . . If this sounds interesting to you, maybe you're the person we're looking for—a Peace Corps volunteer. . . .

EXERCISE 5

Come to Canada where there is endless surprise. Around the corner, down the road, just over the hill, wherever you turn, your Canadian vacation is a medley of fascinating histories and colourful cultures. Here honoured customs live on amid the modern, and old-world customs live beside the cosmopolitan. And here your pleasure and comfort is always our first concern.

EXERCISE 6

. . . Who cares about smoggy skies and polluted lakes? Who cares about empty cans and trash littering our countryside? Who cares about plants and trees and animals dying in our forests? . . .

Review of Run-together Sentences and Fragments (p. 98)

1. Robert Frost is undoubtedly the most beloved American poet. People who are indifferent to most poetry can often quote "Birches" or "Stopping by Woods on a Snowy Evening." He . . .
2. There's a place set deep in the woods of northern Minnesota that is very special to me. Every time I go there I'm surrounded with feelings of serenity. The quietness of the area is something that I don't find anywhere else. There's an occasional cry of a hawk circling up above, and sometimes I hear chipmunks scurrying around in the leaves on the ground. These noises always make me feel closer to nature. I . . .
3. I began wrestling seriously in my freshman year. The wrestling coach was walking around and talking to the kids playing football. He was looking for recruits for the upcoming wrestling season. Several of my friends had decided that they would go out for the team. I decided wrestling would be a good way to keep busy through the

winter. Looking back over my wrestling years, I feel it was good for me. I learned that through hard work I could accomplish my goals. My . . .

"I Have a Dream . . ."
Martin Luther King, Jr.

Five score years ago, a great American, in whose symbolic shadow we stand, signed the Emancipation Proclamation. This momentous decree came as a great beacon light of hope to millions of Negro slaves who had been seared in the flames of withering injustice. It came as a joyous daybreak to end the long night of captivity.

But one hundred years later, we must face the tragic fact that the Negro is still not free. One hundred years later, the life of the Negro is still sadly crippled by the manacles of segregation and the chains of discrimination. One hundred years later, the Negro lives on a lonely island of poverty in the midst of a vast ocean of material prosperity. One hundred years later, the Negro is still languished in the corners of American society and finds himself an exile in his own land. So we have come here today to dramatize an appalling condition.

In a sense we have come to our nation's Capital to cash a check. When the architects of our republic wrote the magnificent words of the Constitution and the Declaration of Independence, they were signing a promissory note to which every American was to fall heir. This note was a promise that all men would be guaranteed the unalienable rights of life, liberty, and the pursuit of happiness.

It is obvious today that America has defaulted on this promissory note insofar as her citizens of color are concerned. Instead of honoring this sacred obligation, America has given the Negro people a bad check, a check which has come back marked "insufficient funds." But we refuse to believe that the bank of justice is bankrupt. We refuse to believe that there are insufficient funds in the great vaults of opportunity of this nation. So we have come to cash this check—a check that will give us upon demand the riches of freedom and the security of justice. We have also come to this hallowed spot to remind America of the fierce urgency of *now*. This is no time to engage in the luxury of cooling off or to take the tranquilizing drug of gradualism. *Now* is the time to make real the promises of Democracy. *Now* is the time to rise from the dark and desolate valley of segregation to the sunlit path of racial justice. *Now* is the time to open the doors of opportunity to all of God's children. *Now* is the time to lift our nation from the quicksands of racial injustice to the solid rock of brotherhood.

Using Standard English Verbs (p. 104)

EXERCISE 1

1. walked, happened
2. doesn't, wants
3. dropped, returned
4. does
5. asked
6. helped
7. finished, talked
8. discussed, helped
9. said, enjoyed
10. worked, work

EXERCISE 2

1. asked
2. pleased, asked
3. walked, ordered
4. likes, ordered
5. were
6. had, needed
7. do
8. have, want
9. did, watched
10. work, am

EXERCISE 3

1. happened
2. walked, asked
3. supposed
4. learned
5. asked
6. walked
7. had
8. interested
9. am
10. learned

EXERCISE 4

1. jogged
2. were, arrived
3. like
4. wanted, was
5. is, hope
6. like
7. is
8. plan
9. intend
10. aren't, are

EXERCISE 5

1. attended
2. play, played
3. expect
4. worked, learned
5. was
6. practiced, like
7. enjoy
8. plan
9. hope
10. change, have

EXERCISE 6

1. wrote
2. learned
3. were just insects that
4. learned, destroy
5. sting, they are
6. die
7. sleep
8. lay eggs, starts
9. am
10. Are you

Using Helping Verbs and Irregular Verbs (p. 111)

EXERCISE 1

1. liked, met
2. met, builds
3. supposed
4. met, taught
5. devoted, taught
6. gives, given
7. became, designs
8. concerned
9. caught
10. supposed, surprised

EXERCISE 2

1. intends, is
2. plans, does
3. attend
4. has
5. wonder, does
6. says, does
7. intends, hopes
8. were, were
9. missed, were
10. was, have

EXERCISE 3

1. had
2. wish, had
3. knew, made
4. understood
5. offer, make
6. solve, talking
7. be
8. is
9. use
10. has, spend

EXERCISE 4

1. suprised me when my brother told me he is
2. found out it's hard to keep a job if you haven't finished
3. worked
4. got
5. is
6. will only be
7. says he doesn't
8. wants
9. hopes he will
10. hope

EXERCISE 5

1. learned, weren't
2. finished, was too embarrassed
3. come
4. should have. I'll be
5. Are you
6. am going. He has, we are
7. does
8. doesn't. Will you need
9. I am
10. I'll see

Avoiding Dialect Expressions (p. 114)

EXERCISE 1

1. I'd like to go, but I haven't time.
2. I haven't done any of my homework for tomorrow.
3. This book is hard to read, and anyway it's not interesting.

4. My friend did well on the test last week.
5. He should be proud of himself because that test was hard.
6. Did you read all those books we were supposed to read?
7. I never read any of them.
8. I watched TV last night and didn't do any reading.
9. I'm not watching any TV tonight.
10. I want to do well on that test tomorrow.

EXERCISE 2

1. My brothers and I are planning to take a trip somewhere this summer.
2. But we haven't decided yet where we'll go.
3. My brother Torrence wants to go fishing in Wisconsin.
4. I've never liked fishing.
5. My other brother doesn't want to go anywhere that we've been before.
6. I want to find an atlas that shows where the state parks are.
7. I've never been to any of them.
8. I'd like to go to one of them if it isn't too far.
9. Anyway we have lots of time to decide.
10. I'll probably let my brothers suit themselves about where we go.

Progress Test (p. 117)

1. B	6. B	11. A
2. B	7. A	12. A
3. B	8. B	13. A
4. A	9. A	14. B
5. A	10. B	15. B

Making Subjects, Verbs, and Pronouns Agree (p. 120)

EXERCISE 1

1. gets
2. are, miss
3. writes, hands
4. includes, are
5. sorts
6. gets her
7. get theirs
8. like
9. doesn't
10. gives

EXERCISE 2

1. is
2. were
3. were
4. gives
5. include

6. show
7. is
8. reveals
9. show
10. is

EXERCISE 3

1. is
2. take
3. wish
4. get
5. type

6. has
7. doesn't
8. take
9. finds his
10. wish

EXERCISE 4

1. has, her
2. is
3. drives
4. have
5. have

6. have
7. doesn't
8. helps
9. helps, is
10. is

EXERCISE 5

1. has
2. have
3. have, is
4. are
5. have, is

6. want
7. come
8. varies
9. is
10. comes

EXERCISE 6

1. wants
2. are
3. is
4. are
5. look

6. wants
7. are, grow
8. plan
9. has
10. intend

EXERCISE 7

1. are
2. lie
3. have
4. stand
5. cover

6. are
7. are
8. hope
9. suits
10. think

EXERCISE 8

1. is
2. wants
3. are
4. have
5. seems

6. has
7. doesn't
8. is
9. doesn't
10. are

Choosing the Right Pronoun (p. 125)

EXERCISE 1

1. me
2. him
3. He
4. me
5. me

6. I
7. us
8. We
9. I
10. I

EXERCISE 2

1. I
2. he, I
3. him, me
4. he, I
5. we

6. him, me
7. we
8. him, me
9. He, I
10. us

EXERCISE 3

1. I
2. her
3. I
4. me
5. I

6. me
7. me
8. me
9. Carol and I
10. We

EXERCISE 4

1. Jason and I
2. him, me
3. me
4. he and I
5. I

6. me
7. I
8. him, me
9. me
10. he, I

EXERCISE 5

1. My brother and I
2. I am
3. him and me
4. I
5. I

6. me
7. I
8. us
9. we
10. he and I

Making the Pronoun Refer to the Right Word (p. 128)

EXERCISE 1

1. When Curt showed his father the dented fender, his father . . .
2. His father said, "You will . . ."
3. She showed us a conch shell and explained how the mollusk lives in it.
4. The parents take turns supervising the park playground, where the children . . .
5. He said to his instructor, "I don't think you understand the novel."
6. His instructor said, "Maybe I haven't . . ."
7. The clerk said to his boss, "I am . . ."
8. When the professor talked with him, Roland was really worried.
9. She said to her girlfriend, "Your record collection needs . . ."
10. She said to the job applicant, "Come back after you have . . ."

EXERCISE 2

1. His motorcycle hit a parked car, but the car . . .
2. As I went up to the baby's carriage, the baby . . .
3. Rebecca said to her mother, "My wardrobe is . . ."
4. As soon as the carburetor was adjusted, I drove my car home.
5. I couldn't find the catsup bottle, and I don't like hamburger without catsup.
6. His father was going to have . . .
7. Susanne said to Cynthia, "I failed the exam."
8. Her shyness kept . . .
9. He finished typing his paper and took it to class.
10. When we couldn't find the cake plate, we decided my husband must have eaten the cake.

EXERCISE 3

1. When the dentist pulled the tooth, the child screamed.
2. I finished my exam, put down my pen, and handed my paper in.
3.
4. My parents disapproved of my decision to take a different job.
5. When I opened the dog's carrying case at the airport, the dog ran away.
6. The cars streamed by, but no one paid . . .
7. John said to Max, "Your parakeet is loose in your room."
8. It wasn't easy, but I finally made up my mind to major in math.
9. When Debbie phoned, her mother was quite ill.
10. He said to the salesperson, "Come back when I'm not so rushed."

EXERCISE 4

1. He said to his father, "Your car needs a . . ."
2. After I read about Tom Dooley's career in medicine, I decided that I wanted to be a doctor.
3. After talking to the boss, Alfredo was . . .
4. He loves to wrestle and spends most of his time wrestling.
5. The park commission established a hockey rink where people . . .
6. The doctor said to the orderly, "You've . . ."
7. She said to her sister, "Take my car."
8. My car hit a truck, but my car . . .
9. She said, "Mother, you're . . ."
10. As we approached the nest, the robin . . .

EXERCISE 5

1. She said to her daughter, "I was always too shy."
2. Erica's mother said, "You may wear my . . ."
3. He said, "Dad, I've made . . ."
4. She slammed her cup into the saucer and broke the saucer.
5. I enjoy figure skating and would like to be a figure skater . . .
6. The president said to the chief accountant, "I made an error in reporting my income."
7. Hawaii has June . . .
8. She was excited when her . . .
9. He said to his father, "You . . ."
10. His father said, "I don't . . ."

Correcting Misplaced or Dangling Modifiers (p. 132)

EXERCISE 1

1. He watched her strolling along garbed . . .
2. My brother-in-law took me to the hospital after I broke . . .
3. We watched hundreds of fireflies glowing . . .
4. After I had finished . . .
5. After I had cleaned the cage and put . . .
6. I discovered my boyfriend sound . . .
7.
8. When I was six, my mother . . .
9. I gave to a charity that blue suit I didn't . . .
10. While I was answering . . .

EXERCISE 2

1. Cruising in the glass-bottom boat, we could see hundreds . . .
2. While the baby was playing on the floor, I noticed that it . . .
3. After I was wheeled . . .
4. While Mark was watching the foofball game, his bike . . .
5. The bank will make loans of any size to . . .
6. Rounding a bend in the road, I was confronted by . . .
7. Flying at an altitude of 10,000 feet, I could see . . .
8. After I had finished mowing . . .
9.
10. Because I had broken . . .

EXERCISE 3

1. After I had done . . .
2. I spotted a monarch butterfly flitting . . .
3. After I drank . . .
4. We thought the cows looked contented standing . . .
5. The Museum of Science and Industry is the most interesting museum that I have visited in the city.
6. She was going out with a man named Harold, who . . .
7. We gave all the meat we didn't want to the cat.
8.
9. Determined to learn to write, I slowly mastered the textbook.
10. After we had a quick . . .

EXERCISE 4

1. The little town where I was born is . . .
2. From nine until five every day except Friday, you may visit . . .
3.
4. She put the clothes she had not worn back . . .
5. Although it is almost ten years old, he . . .
6. I saw that my little car was smashed beyond repair.
7. I went to see what was the matter with my puppy, who was barking . . .
8. Sitting there looking out over the water, she finally made . . .
9. Because the child was crying pitifully, I tried to find his mother.
10. Because he is a . . . .

EXERCISE 5

1. A man sold me a secondhand car with generator trouble.
2. I read in the evening paper that . . .
3. We gave the Boy Scouts all the newspapers that have been . . .
4. She left on the table the meat . . .
5. The police made a report about . . .
6. I watched the wren building its nest and twittering . . .

7. Because he was a conceited . . .
8. After my dog had smelled up the whole house, I finally
   gave it . . .
9. While I was . . .
10. Because I was unsure . . .

Using Parallel Construction (p. 138)

EXERCISE 1

1. or skiing without . . .
2. and good plays . . .
3. and even sail . . .
4. and clear thinking.
5. or law.
6. and especially camping . . .
7. but how you do it.
8.
9. to get our instruments
   tuned immediately . . .
10. I need her.

EXERCISE 2

1. whatever your obligations . . .
2. and maybe also a bit of luck.
3. how to organize my time . . .
4. but also to comprehend
   more . . .
5. and of course the balmy . . .
6.
7. and lots of . . .
8.
9. and the degree of . . .
10. and national cemeteries.

EXERCISE 3

1.
2. and then getting our
   route . . .
3. and the shoemaker.
4. and earn praise . . .
5. and in buckets.
6. but to design closed . . .
7. as to ship them.
8.
9. and has a strange . . .
10. and a place where auctions
    were held.

EXERCISE 4

1. and that the number . . .
2.
3. simply become dumping . . .
4. and that is today part . . .
5. across deserts . . .
6. areas for conservation of . . .
7. or horseback riding.
8.
9.
10. and fast gaining . . .

EXERCISE 5

. . . across deserts, mountains, streams, and fields. . . . wild horses,
cougars, and wolves . . . climbed down to a support beam beneath the

track, braced himself on the beam, hung onto his 75-pound bicycle, watched the raging river below, and heard the freight train roaring above him. . . . he had to carry, push, shove, or drag . . .

EXERCISE 6

. . . an operator would answer, listen to my request, leaf through the pages of her directories . . . and then read it to me. . . . the operator speaks to me, listens to my request, plucks my desired number from millions of listings, and has it read to me . . .

EXERCISE 7

1. Recycling cans and bottles has been worthwhile.
    1.
    2. It has prevented littering.
    3.
2. Air bags should be standard equipment on new cars.
    1.
    2.
    3. They are worth the cost.
3. My summer job on the playground for the handicapped was valuable.
    1.
    2.
    3. It gave me an opportunity to do something for society.
4. A camping trip in Estes Park gave me some new insights.
    1.
    2. I have a new interest in nature.
    3. I learned something about ecology.
5. Improving one's vocabulary is important.
    1.
    2. It will lead to a more successful career.
    3. It will give one personal satisfaction.

Correcting Shift in Time (p. 143)
EXERCISE 1

1. walked
2. decided
3. began
4. gave
5. decided
6. registered
7. came
8. learned
9. described
10. came

EXERCISE 2

1. explains
2. is told
3. says that it must be
4. couldn't get near, and they had

5. made a mad dash
6 It also says
7. can't leave the marshy water they are in

EXERCISE 3

. . . still he left . . .

EXERCISE 4

. . . Then Andrew Jackson decided . . . A fearless servant had . . .

EXERCISE 5

. . . One little girl was . . . One boy was tapping . . . One was trying to propel . . . Another was walking . . . Thus they were gaining . . .

EXERCISE 6

. . . reached for my bearskin blanket . . . I reached but couldn't find it. I checked the floor to see if it had . . . My mind woke . . . I paused and tried . . . I couldn't see . . .

I got up, groped for the light switch, and saw that my desk drawers were . . . And there was . . .

Now my mind raced as I scanned . . . my TV was . . . someone had been . . . someone had been looking . . . gave up . . .

EXERCISE 7

. . . so I grabbed . . .

. . . as we moved higher and saw . . .

. . . It seemed so easy . . . and I nervously tried . . . we weren't going to suddenly fall . . .

I learned . . . I learned . . . Then I was reminded . . . my instructor asked me if I knew where we were. It had been . . . I had no idea . . .

Correcting Shift in Person (p. 150)
EXERCISE 1

1. I feel so good when I
2. we have good weather
3. order their gowns
4. as I get older I become
5. one should get
6. we could see

7. people can find work if they are willing to take what they
8. we got tired
9. we could see
10. Beginning drivers should stay . . . until they

EXERCISE 2

1. After finishing that course in psychology, I was
2. One needs to exercise every day if one wants
3. I can be perfectly frank
4. The two days I spent in Williamsburg were not enough to see all I wanted to see.
5. To succeed in college, a good vocabulary is essential.
6. She wore a fancy costume to
7. he expects it to be finished by
8. I felt lucky
9. After watching TV for a whole evening, I realized
10. we could hear

EXERCISE 3

1.
2.
3.
4.
5. if I'm careful, I
6. But if I haven't . . . I crash
7. Then I
8. that I soar
9. Windsurfing isn't easy
10.

EXERCISE 4

. . . sensory cells in the ears. . . . one should wear ear plugs when mowing a lawn or riding . . . Everyone needs to be aware of these sounds that can damage the hearing . . .

EXERCISE 5

. . . Walking into the Grocery Hall of Fame in Vancouver, British Columbia, is like . . . In the American Museum of Fly Fishing in Manchester, Vermont, are the rods . . .

EXERCISE 6

. . . It was amazing to see fifteen handicapped people . . .

EXERCISE 7

. . . today the line marking the division between the two parts can be seen. . . . but the ascent can also be made . . .

Correcting Wordiness (p. 156)

EXERCISE 1

1. An experienced player would have known what to do.
2. My college roommate was coming to see me.
3. Electronics is a good field to go into.
4. We have two May birthdays in our family.
5. My grandfather told me this story.
6. The government should speed up the judicial process.
7. Justice should be swift and sure.
8. I grew up in a small town.
9. I was too busy to accept their invitation.
10. I didn't know she was leaving.

EXERCISE 2

1. History interests me.
2. The professor makes his subject interesting.
3. No doubt he spends a great deal of time preparing each lecture.
4. This polish will make your shoes last twice as long.
5. A friend of mine has a unique invention.
6. The taxpayers objected.
7. We started at 5 A.M. and got there at 6 P.M.
8. In August most of our employees take a vacation.
9. I have not had time to prepare an agenda for this afternoon's meeting.
10. I want to repeat my conclusion.

EXERCISE 3

1. The purple martin circled the martin house for half an hour and then disappeared.
2. He was arrested for drunken driving.
3. Modern medicine has practically wiped out polio.
4. A number of spectators couldn't get seats.
5. The grandstand should be larger.
6. A fly has suction cups on its feet, enabling it to walk on the ceiling.
7. My hardest exam last semester was psychology.
8. The exam included things I had forgotten.
9. The magpie is a large bird with a black head, a long greenish tail, and white wing patches.
10. She will always do what she promises.

EXERCISE 4

1. Although I hadn't eaten since morning, I wasn't hungry.
2. I hope I'll find a job soon.
3. Since the meeting hadn't been announced, not many people came.

4. Ten people were planning to come.
5. Within three months, six in the department have resigned.
6. I learned to identify three kinds of ivy on this morning's field trip.
7. I've gained 10 pounds since I began this diet.
8. At the opening of the new store, everyone there received a gift.
9. I use too many words in my writing.
10. Many people do the same.

EXERCISE 5

1. What has been accomplished is a result of the cooperation of the administration, faculty, students, and library staff.
2. So that they will always be available, periodicals do not circulate. Many divisions have facilities for copying articles.
3. The Information Center gives assistance in using the card catalogue and basic reference works. A library orientation program explains library procedures and the interlibrary loan service.
4. The Reserve Reading Room contains required reading for current courses.
5. The Music Division has 10 listening stations, six of which are equipped with cassette recorders.
6. Much material essential to a new library is no longer available in printed form, but the library contains over one million items on microfilm, microcards, and microfiche, as well as microprint machines for making copies.

Avoiding Clichés (p. 161)

EXERCISE 1

1. We had planned to go to the lake, and I was up early.
2. But my wife and son were still asleep.
3. I started the breakfast, but I couldn't get the orange juice can open.
4. Finally I did get the breakfast on the table and called the others. I was determined to get started on our trip.
5. When they finally came downstairs, they were hungry but complained that the toast was cold.
6. I told them they should be grateful that breakfast was ready.
7. Eventually we started, but we had gone only a mile when it began to rain.
8. Finally the skies cleared, and we got to the lake.
9. Our son immediately jumped into the lake because he's a great swimmer.
10. My wife soon followed him, but I just sat on the beach and rested.

Review of Sentence Structure (p. 162)

1. A	6. B	11. B	16. B	21. B
2. B	7. A	12. B	17. A	22. B
3. B	8. A	13. A	18. B	23. A
4. A	9. B	14. A	19. B	24. A
5. A	10. A	15. B	20. B	25. B

Punctuation (p. 168)

EXERCISE 1

1. country. It's
2. farmhouse;
3. remodeling. We'll
4.
5. these:

6. interests. Not
7. work. It
8. off. At
9. slowly. There's
10. surroundings. We

EXERCISE 2

1. snow?
2. ice?
3. children. It
4. sterile. Actually
5. snow. The

6.
7. crystals. They
8. shapes. Their
9. snowflake. The
10. alike. Most

EXERCISE 3

1. cans? The
2. them;
3.
4. preserve. Another
5. mushrooms. Others

6. me.
7. path.
8. ecology. It
9. things:
10. cleanup?

EXERCISE 4

1. pests. Now
2. following:
3. world. They're
4. design;
5. thread. It

6. ways:
7. world. Some . . . pinhead;
8. difficulty. It
9. male. Sometimes
10. nature. They

EXERCISE 5

1. winters? Some
2. round. There
3. snow;
4. grow. A
5. age:

6. ice cap;
7. icebergs. They
8. tiny;
9. above the water. Also
10. water. The

EXERCISE 6

1. road?
2. highways. One
3. 1973. They
4. too. The
5. roads. Moreover

6. past:
7. changed. Plank
8. has. Visitors
9. commercialism:
10. roads:

EXERCISE 7

1. roots. It's
2. happen. They
3. roots:
4. "to believe." About
5. believable. Anything

6. beliefs. *Credentials*
7. "study of." It
8. "earth";
9. "ancient";
10. "star." *Astrology*

EXERCISE 8

1. PATH. It
2. "together";
3. "against";
4. words:
5. sounds. A

6. afar. A
7. apart;
8.
9. roots. They
10. me.

EXERCISE 9

. . . in one day? I have. It's not easy. . . . Oh, my poor knees! After the first day I was ready to give up. By the next . . . twelve-year-old girls. We rode the 495 miles . . . at the western border of Iowa; seven days later . . . eastern border. The people in the Iowa towns . . . the reason that they welcomed us. It was just . . .

EXERCISE 10

. . . cream pies. Then . . . something more—coconut milk. . . . on palms. They either fall . . . selling them. He took a machete . . . all day. The only size . . .

Commas (Rules 1, 2, and 3) (p. 174)

EXERCISE 1

1.
2. had,
3. college,
4. college,
5. work,

6. work,
7. grade,
8. learn,
9. learning,
10. future,

EXERCISE 2

1. sky,
2. Dipper,
3.
4. Star,
5. Cassiopeia,
6. interested,
7. Boötes,
8.
9. mythology,
10. me,

EXERCISE 3

1. devastation,
2. Helens,
3. ash,
4. eruption,
5. later, tiny fir trees, pink fireweed,
6. pocket gophers, elk,
7. ladybugs, black ants,
8. back,
9. timber,
10. years,

EXERCISE 4

1. things,
2. invention,
3. milk, honey,
4. 1777,
5. ice, and . . . cream, sugar, eggs,
6. crank,
7. freezer,
8. hour, the . . . frozen,
9. rapidly,
10. melt,

EXERCISE 5

1. birds,
2. ways,
3. example,
4.
5. Guyana, South America,
6. runner, of course,
7. altitudes,
8. comparison,
9. hour,
10. record,

EXERCISE 6

1. freestanding poles,
2. Vancouver,
3. house,
4. house,
5. people,
6. legends, or . . . raven, bear, beaver, frog,
7. represented,
8. height,
9. uses,
10. trees,

EXERCISE 7

1. Galesburg, Illinois, on January 6,
2. wagon, porter in a barbershop, sceneshifter in a theater,
3. fields, washed dishes at hotels in Kansas City, Omaha, and Denver,
4. college, became a newspaper reporter,
5. "Chicago,"
6. World,"
7. things,
8. country,
9. poems,
10. poetry,

EXERCISE 8

1. Wales,
2. designed, built,
3. 22,000 pounds,
4. United States,
5. years,
6. carillons,
7. complexity,
8. carillons, for example,
9. electronically,
10. hour,

EXERCISE 9

The Guinness Book of World Records hasn't always been around. It had its beginning in 1951 when some sportsmen in Ireland disagreed about which was the fastest flying game bird. Sir Hugh Beaver, managing director of Guinness Breweries, said it was the golden plover, but he was unable to prove his point because no book contained the information. He decided to create his own book, and four years later he published *The Guinness Book of World Records*. In 1974 the book became the world's all-time best-selling copyright book and thus earned its own place in *The Guinness Book of World Records*. By mid-1990 it had a cumulative sale in 39 languages in excess of 65 million copies, and its sales are increasing by 50,000 copies a week.

Commas (Rules 4, 5, and 6) (p. 181)
EXERCISE 1

1. Yes, Gregg,
2. evening, however,
3. wait, therefore,
4.
5. it,
6. wish, Felipe,
7. Surfing, however, won't . . . degree,
8. television,
9. Well, . . . do, I guess,
10. Yes,

EXERCISE 2

1. who, I understand,
2. Maturity, the lecturer explained,
3.
4. person, on the other hand,
5. people, therefore,
6. said, furthermore,
7. disagreement, he said,
8. mature, he said,
9. unimportant, the lecturer continued,
10. relationships, it seems,

EXERCISE 3

1. cottage,
2. chess,
3. know, however,
4. games, which . . . civilization,
5.
6.
7. tug-of-war, which . . . modern,
8. Furthermore,
9. Surprisingly,
10. Hey, Sybil,

EXERCISE 4

1. Avalanches, I thought,
2. Now, however,
3.
4.
5. avalanches,
6. patrollers, who . . . jackets,
7.
8.
9.
10. Switzerland, for example, in
. . . 1950–51, which . . .
times,

EXERCISE 5

1.
2. skin, however,
3. skin, on the other hand,
4. toad, which . . . land,
5. tongue, which . . . sticky,
6.
7. song, which . . . females,
8. eggs,
9. tadpoles,
10. toads,

EXERCISE 6

1. write, some people say,
2. should, some think,
3. us, however,
4. can, in fact,
5.
6. drill, we are told,
7. test, which . . . computer,
8. necessary, it seems clear,
9. more, undoubtedly,
10.

EXERCISE 7

1. home, we must admit,
2. lay, of course,
3. picture,
4. were, as a rule,
5. were, of course,
6. homes, in comparison,
7.
8. ways, however,
9.
10. it, I fear,

EXERCISE 8

1. Leakey, widow . . . Leakey,
2. Laetoli, a remote . . .
Tanzania,
3. Gorge, 25 miles . . . north,
4. Now, however,
5.
6. footprint, according . . .
dating,
7. man,
8.
9. skeleton, which . . . song,
10.

EXERCISE 9

1. shocked, quite naturally,
2. frightening, according to the
environmentalists,
3. waste, according . . . Agency,
4. companies, of course,
5. wastes, regardless . . .
potency,
6. rest, which . . . fields,
7. are, according . . . Council,
8. these, it is estimated,
9.
10. years,

Review of the Comma (p. 186)

EXERCISE 1

1. When I have a lot of things to do,
2.
3. When I finish a job, I cross it off the list, but not until every job is crossed off,
4. Yes, my friends,
5.
6. . . . Oklahoma City, Oklahoma, on July 19,
7. Stock, the . . . Orchestra,
8. . . . recycled,
9. Some experiments have been conducted with chimpanzees,
10. A chimpanzee can . . . person can,
11. If the first few shots are unsuccessful,
12. The chimpanzee, however,
13. If the aiming tests are made too difficult,
14. . . . airplanes, Polaroid cameras, food freezers, frozen vegetables, radar, V-8 engines, electric razors, electric typewriters, drive-in movie theaters, color television, the United Nations, the atomic bomb,

Quotation Marks (p. 188)

The italicized titles below would, of course, be underlined in writing or typing.

EXERCISE 1,

1. "A college education is one of the few things a person is willing to pay for and not get,"
2. "Americans have more timesaving devices and less time than any other group of people in the world,"
3. "If all misfortunes were laid in a common heap," said Socrates, "from which everyone would have to take an equal portion, most people would be content to take their own and depart."
4.
5. "I have been brought up to believe that how I see myself is more important than how others see me,"
6. Speaking of his life of unceasing effort, the great pianist Jan Paderewski said, "Before I was a master, I was a slave."
7. "An excellent plumber is infinitely more admirable than an incompetent philosopher,"
8.
9. "The secret of happiness is not in doing what one likes," said James M. Barrie, "but in liking what one has to do."
10.

EXERCISE 2

1. In an art gallery a man said to his wife, "I know what that artist is trying to say. He's trying to say he can't paint worth a damn!"
2. "The important thing in life is not the person one loves. It is the fact that one loves," said Marcel Proust in his novel *Remembrance of Things Past.*
3. "A diplomat is someone who remembers a lady's birthday but forgets her age,"
4. "By working faithfully eight hours a day," said Robert Frost, "you may eventually get to be a boss and work twelve hours a day."
5.
6. Alexander Woollcott said, "All the things I really like to do are either immoral, illegal, or fattening."
7. "More and more I came to value charity and love of one's fellow beings above everything else,"
8. "A man who uses a great many words to express his meaning is like a bad marksman who, instead of aiming a single stone at an object, takes up a handful and throws at it in hopes he may hit,"
9. A Sioux Indian prayer says, "Great Spirit, help me never to judge another until I have walked in his moccasins for two weeks."
10. In describing the Taj Mahal, Rufus Jones said, "Only a few times in one's earthly life is one given to see absolute perfection."

EXERCISE 3

1. "What's the most important thing you've learned in this class?"
2. "Learning to write a complete thesis statement," Alex said, "because it's going to help me in my writing for other courses."
3. "I know that's important," Brenda replied, "but it's not most important for me."
4. "What's most important for you?"
5. "My biggest improvement has been learning to write concisely. My papers used to be so wordy."
6. "That never was my problem," he said. "My biggest achievement besides learning about thesis statements is that I finally decided to learn to spell."
7. "And have you improved?"
8. "Tremendously," he said. "I used to spell every word wrong. Now I just spell every other word wrong."
9. "Come on! You're not that bad. I read one of your papers, and there wasn't a single misspelled word."
10. "I'm getting there,"

EXERCISE 4

1. "Do commas and periods go inside the quotation marks?"
2. "Of course," Brenda replied. "They'd look lost on the outside."
3. "I guess they would,"

4. "Is there anything more you want to know about punctuation?"
5. "What do you do if you want to quote a whole paragraph from a book?"
6. "If the quotation is more than five lines long, then you punctuate it differently from ordinary quotations,"
7. "How?"
8. "You indent the whole quotation five spaces, single-space it, and forget about the quotation marks,"
9. "I suppose that makes it stand out clearly as quoted material."
10. "Exactly,"

EXERCISE 5

1. "And what have you been doing with yourself?"
2. "Oh, I've been doing a lot of reading for one thing,"
3. "Still learning new words?"
4. "Sure, I'm always learning new words," Natalie said. "Yesterday I learned what *energize* means."
5. "And what does it mean?"
6. "Well, the root *erg* means a unit of energy, or work, and *energize* means to give energy to. For example, some people find cold showers energizing,"
7. "I prefer to get my energy some other way," Kevin said. "I suppose that same root *erg* is in *energy* and *energetic*."
8. "Right. And it's also in *metallurgy*, which means working with metals. Another interesting word is *George*. *Geo* means earth, and *erg* means work. Therefore *George* is an earth worker or farmer."
9. "I never knew that before," Kevin said. "It really helps to know word roots."
10. "It helps me,"

EXERCISE 6

1. "I had three chairs in my house: one for solitude, two for friendship, and three for society," wrote Henry David Thoreau in his book *Walden*.
2. "Sometimes," wrote Thoreau, "as I drift idly on Walden Pond, I cease to live and begin to be."
3. "If a man does not keep pace with his companions," Thoreau said, "perhaps it is because he hears a different drummer."
4. Victor Hugo wrote, "The greatest happiness of life is the conviction that we are loved, loved for ourselves, or rather loved in spite of ourselves."
5. "No matter what happens," said Marcus Aurelius, "you can control the situation by your attitude."
6. "It's very hard to take yourself too seriously when you look at the world from outer space,"

7. "If I could choose one degree for the people I hire, it would be English," says a senior vice president of the First Atlanta Corporation. "I want people who can read and speak in the language we're dealing with."
8. "All of our people—except full-blooded Indians—are immigrants, or descendants of immigrants,"
9. "Subsidies for growing and promoting tobacco are maintained, but school health programs are slashed. Social benefits are denounced as handouts, but it is proposed to open up vast areas of public lands to developers in what may be the greatest giveaway in our history,"
10. I used to read *Newsweek*, but now I read *Time*.

EXERCISE 7

1. In an article on the way pollutants are carried by air currents throughout the world, Michael H. Brown says, "A molecule you're inhaling now could have been expelled by a man in the seventeenth century or by a woman in China two weeks ago."
2. Last year I read Steinbeck's novel *Grapes of Wrath*.
3.
4. "Falling to the chain saw at the rate of 170 acres a day," said the lecturer, "the virgin woodlands of the Pacific Northwest—with their dependent communities of plants and wildlife—have become a battleground for loggers and environmentalists."
5. "The essence of genius is to know what to overlook,"
6. "A friend is a person with whom I may be sincere," said Ralph Waldo Emerson. "Before him I may think aloud."
7. "There's a difference," said a spokesperson for the Council of the Blind, "between people who can see and people who have vision."
8.
9. For my birthday I was given a subscription to *National Wildlife*.
10. The famous book *Bartlett's Familiar Quotations* is being revised by Justin Kaplan.

Capital Letters (p. 195)
EXERCISE 1

1. City, Hall
2.
3. Victorian
4. Russia, Hall
5. Philharmonic
6. Center, City
7.
8.
9. Street
10. Hall

EXERCISE 2

1. *Civilisation*
2. History
3. English
4. Literature, Renaissance
5. Renaissance
6. Man Is an Island
7.
8. University
9. English, French
10. River

EXERCISE 3

1. Day
2. Uncle, South
3. East, Airlines
4. Junior College
5. Second Avenue
6.
7. Cousin
8. Dad's
9. Memorial Day
10. Mom

EXERCISE 4

1.
2. See
3. Good
4.
5.
6.
7. This
8.
9. Professor
10.

EXERCISE 5

1.
2. College
3. State University
4.
5. Candle Burns at Both Ends
6. Mom
7. Mom's
8.
9. Western Tool Works, Inc.
10.

EXERCISE 6

1.
2. College
3. Motor Company
4. Institute of Technology, College
5. College
6. Landscaping Company
7. State University
8.
9. Day
10.

EXERCISE 7

1. City
2. *Book of World Records*
3.
4. Spanish
5. Siberian, Arabian
6. *Looking Glass*
7.
8. Dad
9. Shopping Center
10. North America, Antarctica

EXERCISE 8

1. Day
2. South, Northwest
3. *World Atlas*
4. River
5.

6. Duck Lake
7. Fourth
8. Senator, Elks Hall
9.
10. River

Review of Punctuation and Capital Letters (p. 199)

EXERCISE 1

1.
2. When a dependent clause comes first in a sentence,
3. The proper use of commas, I've found,
4. Stop! I'll go with you. Can you wait until 5 P.M.?
5. . . . Texas, Franklin Pollard says, "We had three rooms and a path."
6. . . . Community College
7. . . . "The Lake Isle of Innisfree."
8. . . . University of Wisconsin in Madison,
9. Heiden, an eighteen-year-old,
10. I think, Dad,

EXERCISE 2

1. . . . walkers. An adult roadrunner, which is only 9 inches tall,
2. "Life lived at its best is full of daily forgivin' and forgettin',"
3. children:
4. . . . says: "I had no shoes and complained until I met a man who had no feet."
5. pain:
6. America. A big . . . Canada, and . . . Mexico, and
7. . . . Union,
8. . . . developed. Much
9. . . . cook. He
10. Commas are like pounds. You either have too many or too few,

EXERCISE 3

1. A study has shown that children whose TV viewing was cut back to no more than one hour a day improved their grades in school and seemed happier. They played more with other children and increased their concentration in school. One child changed from a passive loner into a friendly playmate. Then when the study was concluded, . . .
2. A hundred years ago when Edison was working on his first tin

horn phonograph, he wasn't even thinking about music. He just wanted to make a dictating machine. In fact it took almost a whole generation for musicians to get interested in recordings. Fortunately . . .

3. An Assyrian stone tablet of about 2800 B.C. makes the following statements: "Our earth is degenerate in these latter days; bribery and corruption are common; children no longer obey their parents; the end of the world is evidently approaching."

EXERCISE 4

1. Yesterday I had my first solo flight at the Flying Club. It's an amazing feeling when your instructor tells you to go flying alone. Then after you take off, you look around and find you really are alone. At that point it's too late to change your mind. You've got to land by yourself sooner or later. It's a great sensation. It's . . .
2. The federal budget speaks in terms of billions, but how much *is* a billion dollars? If a man stood over a big hole in the ground and dropped in a $20 bill every minute day and night, it . . .
3. There have been six basic changes in the tools people write with since the cave dwellers used sharp stones to scratch pictures on their stone walls. First came the quill pen. Then came the lead pencil. Next came the fountain pen. In about 1870 came the first typewriter. By 1960 the electric typewriter was taking over, and . . .

Proofreading Exercise 1 (p. 202)

THE BIG GRIN ON MY FACE

One afternoon I was driving my car when I ~~notice~~ *noticed* a pinging noise in my engine. In a few days the pinging grew to a thumping and then to a loud clunking that couldn't be ignored.

My knowledgeable friends broke the news to me that it was undoubtedly my main engine bearings **,** and in the same breath they mentioned sums like four or five hundred dollars. Being a poor student, I had only two alternatives—walk or fix it myself.

forced   *choose*

Necessity ~~force~~ me to ~~chose~~ the latter alternative, and I found myself up to my elbows in grease and grime for the next few days. With the help of a lot of free advice from friends, who claimed to be undiscovered mechanical geniuses, and the guidance of a library book on engines, I removed and disassembled the whole thing.

An engine is something I take for granted as long as it goes, and only
There
when it fails, do I really appreciate how intricate and complicated it is. ~~Their~~ are all kinds of odd-shaped, highly polished parts, each one for some function. My taking the engine apart was like a little boy fixing an alarm clock.
Each
~~each~~ new piece was so interesting and so completely unfathomable.

Then when it was all in pieces, the reassembly with new parts began, along with the job of trying to remember where each nut and bolt belonged. This work was a lot slower and required more help, but it was encouraging to watch the motor grow with each new piece.

Finally if was all connected in the car and ready to be tested. It had taken weeks of late evenings of work, but now it was ready at last. My friends stood around offering final advice and checking to make sure I had remembered everything. I held my breath and turned the key—the engine started and turned, a little rough at first, but soon it ran smoothly.

"Eureka! I've done it!" I shouted.
overwhelmed
I was ~~overwhelm~~ with a great feeling of accomplishment, and . . .

Comprehensive Test on Entire Text (p. 206)

1. We girls made the ~~deserts~~ *desserts* for the party **.** ~~everyone like~~ *Everyone liked* them.

2. The altos carried the melody **.** ~~the~~ *The* sopranos ~~sung~~ *sang* the accompaniment.

3. Joe Namath was a talented quarterback in high school **.** ~~his~~ *His* team won lots of championships.

4. When we got to the end of the detour **,** we ~~turn~~ *turned* south and then ~~West~~ *west*.

5. ~~Which~~ *It* turned out to be the wrong thing to do.

6. Each of her trophies ~~are~~ *is* displayed in ~~it's~~ *its* proper place on the shelf.

7. Working hard that semester **,** ~~my grades improved~~ *I improved my grades.*

8. I enjoy math **,** social studies **,** and gym **,** but I find chemistry and ~~english~~ *English* difficult.

9. Making the most of every opportunity that came her way **,** *she succeeded.*

10. He spends most of his time **,** however **,** reading comic books **,** and ~~you cant~~ *one can't* do that and get satisfactory grades.

11. I ~~eant~~ *can't* decide whether to get a job **,** take a trip **,** or ~~whether I should~~ just loaf this summer.

12. Yes **,** ~~personally~~ I think ~~Amys~~ *Amy's* costume is more striking than ~~Beverlys~~ *Beverly's*.

13. She took ~~to~~ *too* many ~~cloths~~ *clothes* along on her trip **:** party dresses **,** beachwear **,** and half a dozen other outfits.

14. Her mother and father are sending her to ~~a~~ *an* exclusive school, but
she ~~dont~~ *doesn't* appreciate it.

15. Leroy ~~told~~ *said to* his father, ~~he was~~ *"I am* embarrassed by ~~his~~ *my* old car.*"*

16. ~~Their quiet~~ *They're quite* pleased with ~~there~~ *their* new car although it was ~~to~~ *too*

    expensive.

17. Joan, you ~~was~~ *were* driving ~~to~~ *too* fast when we ~~past~~ *passed* that cop.

18. We ~~didnt~~ *didn't* like the amendment**;** furthermore we ~~refuse~~ *refused* to vote for

    it.

19. ~~James~~ *James'* invitation to my girlfriend and me came as a surprise.

20. Each of the leaves ~~are quite~~ *is* unique in ~~their~~ *its* vein patterns.

21. ~~Ive~~ *I've* been wondering about you and hoping for a letter.

22. She memorized Masefield's poem ''Sea Fever'' from his book

    Salt Water Ballads.

23. John Masefield, who became poet laureate of England, was born

    on June 1, 1878, in Ledbury, Herefordshire, England.

24. ''Life's always a struggle**.** ~~if~~ *If* anything's easy, it's not likely to be

    worthwhile,'' said Hubert Humphrey.

25. ''When you get to the end of your rope,'' said Franklin D. Roo-

    sevelt, ''tie a knot and hang on.''

26. If I had known you ~~was~~ *were* coming, I would ~~of~~ *have* prepared a special

    meal.

27. Last week they ~~develop~~ *developed* a plan, and then they ~~proceed~~ *proceeded* to carry it

    out.

28. He decided to join Fritz and me on the golf course.

29. *Their* ~~There~~ house is in a better location than ~~our's~~ *ours*.

30. When you wind up a clock**,** you start it**;** when you wind up a

speech**,** you end it.

Writing
EXERCISE 1 (p. 212)

2. Looking for a job
   Writing a good résumé
   Preparing for an interview

3. Camping out
   Equipment for camping out
   Buying the right sleeping bag

4. My trip to Washington, D.C.
   The National Air and Space Museum
   The Wright brothers' first plane

EXERCISE 2 (p. 218)

I've decided to change my major to computer science.
   1. There will probably be more jobs available in computer science.
   2. A knowledge of computers is required in almost every field.
   3. I'll be able to use my math skills.
Acid rain is harming the country in many ways.
   1. It's killing evergreen trees in many areas.
   2. It's killing the fish and amphibians in lakes.
   3. It's hurting farm crops.
   4. It's eroding buildings and monuments.
I'm doing three things to improve my study habits.
   1. I'm listing each day the things I must do.
   2. I'm studying in the library where it's quiet.
   3. I'm not quitting until my work is finished each night.

EXERCISE 3 (p. 225)

First of all,
Also, *or* Then too,
Also, *or* Then too,
Furthermore
As for me,
Finally,

Summary of "The Jeaning of America— and the World" (p. 233)

An American symbol of equality now spreading throughout the world is a simple pair of pants called blue jeans. In 1850 Levi Strauss, a Bavarian-born Jew, made the first pair for a miner in San Francisco. Their popularity grew, but one miner complained that the pockets tore. As a joke, his pockets were riveted by a blacksmith, and jeans have had rivets ever since. Thirty years later Levi Strauss & Co. was selling not only to working people but to all classes in 35 countries. With a sales force of 22,000 the company now sells 83,000,000 blue jeans each year.

Index

a, an, 7
abbreviations, 166
accept, except, 7
addresses, commas in, 174
advise, advice, 7
affect, effect, 7
agreement
   of subject and pronoun, 119
   of subject and verb, 118
all ready, already, 8
application letter, 248
are, or, our, 8

brake, break, 8
breaking words into parts, 43

capital letters, 194
choose, chose, 8
clauses
   dependent, 85
   essential and nonessential, 180
   independent, 76–77
cliché, 160
clothes, cloths, 8
coarse, course, 8
colon, 167
comma, 173–80
comma splice (*see* run-together
   sentences)
complement, compliment, 8
conscious, conscience, 9
contractions, 27

dash, 167
dates, commas in, 174
dependent words, 85
dessert, desert, 9
dialect expressions, 114
dictionary, use of, 49–55
do, due, 9
does, dose, 9
doubling a final consonant, 44

evaluation, writing an, 250
exclamation point, 166

feel, fill, 9
fourth, forth, 9
fragment, sentence, 85, 93
free writing, 211

have, of, 9
hear, here, 10

interrupter, commas around, 179
introductory expression, comma after,
   174
it's, its, 10

knew, new, 10
know, no, 10

lead, led, 17
letter of application, 248
limiting the topic, 212
loose, lose, 17

modifier
   dangling or misplaced, 131
moral, morale, 17

organizing a paper, 221

paragraph writing, 223
parallel construction, 136–37
   in thesis statement, 137
passed, past, 17
passive voice, 107
past participle, 107
period, 166
personal, personnel, 17
piece, peace, 17
possessives, 33–35
prefixes, 43
prepositional phrases, 65

principal, principle, 18
principal parts of verbs, 109–10
progress tests, 46, 117
pronouns
    agreement of, 118–19
    possessive form, 34
    reference of, 127
    subject and nonsubject forms, 119
proofreading aloud, 230
proofreading exercises, 25, 39, 60, 95,
    111, 129, 158
punctuation marks, 166–67

question mark, 166
quiet, quite, 18
quotation marks, 187

résumé, 249
rewriting, 228
right, write, 18
run-together sentences, 76–77

semicolon, 76, 166
shift
    in person, 149
    in time, 143
specific details, 213
spelling
    doubling a final consonant, 44
    list of frequently misspelled words,
      47
    words broken into parts, 43
    words often confused, 7–10, 17–19
standard English verbs, 101–3

subjects and verbs, 59–60
summary writing, 233

tests
    comprehensive, 206–7
    progress, 46, 117
than, then, 18
their, there, they're, 18
thesis statement, 217
threw, through, 18
title
    capitalization of, 215
    for a paper, 215
topic, 212
transition words, 225
two, too, to, 19

usage (*see* words often confused)

verbs
    helping, 107
    principal parts, 109–10
    regular and irregular, 107–10

weather, whether, 19
were, where, 19
who's, whose, 19
woman, women, 19
wordiness, 155
words often confused, 7–10, 17–19
writing
    eight steps to better, 210

you're, your, 18